CHEWY COOKIES

CHEWY COOKIES

The Ultimate Comfort Food

Eileen Talanian

PRIMA PUBLISHING

Prima Publishing and its colophon are trademarks of Prima Communications, Inc.

Library of Congress Cataloging-in-Publication Data
Talanian, Eileen.
Chewy cookies : over 125 fabulous recipes / Eileen Talanian.
p.   cm.
Includes index.
ISBN 0-7615-0004-9 (paperback)
1. Cookies.   I. Title.
TX772.T35   1995
641.8'654—dc20
[347.30652]   95-1516
CIP

96 97 98 99 AA 10 9 8 7 6 5 4 3 2

Printed in the United States of America

How to Order:
Single copies may be ordered from Prima Publishing, P.O. Box 1260BK, Rocklin, CA 95677; telephone (916) 632-4400. Quantity discounts are also available. On your letterhead, include information concerning the intended use of the books and the number of books you wish to purchase.

To Benjamin and Emily Mae,
the sweetest cookies of all,

and to Michael,
with all my love

Contents

Acknowledgments

I would like to thank Jennifer Basye Sander, Senior Editor at Prima Publishing, for having faith in me for this project. Also, Corinne Johnson, Donna Faggi, Ellen Magee, Mary D'Amore Roche, and all of my neighbors who have been so supportive of my efforts. And Sue Dyson, my very good friend, who was kind enough to let me use Mary's recipe for sugar cookies.

Of course, I would like to thank all of the people without whom this book would not have been possible. The many tasters who diligently ate all of the test cookies (mountains of them), and who were so discerning in all of their comments: The staff and faculty at both Chestnut Hill Academy and The Springside School, in Philadelphia; the staff at Weaver's Way Co-operative in Mount Airy, Philadelphia; the kindergarten and 4-G classes at Springside; grade 3-S at Chestnut Hill Academy; Ann Dimond (when the diet police weren't around); Janet Giovanazzo; Joanne Machella; Anne Galbally and her wonderful family; all the helpful tasters at Bloomingdale's in King of Prussia; and Lisa Okoniewski. A special thank you to Marti Bowditch for solving my honey–oatmeal dilemma. Much appreciation to Leslie Yarborough, my editor. And, of course, Ben and Emily Mae, my dear children, and my husband, Michael, who has patiently tolerated so much through all of this.

Introduction

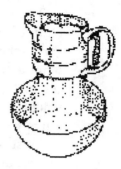

Chewy cookies . . . just the thought of them evokes a feeling of comfort and security. In a time when our lives seem to move at warp speed, chewy cookies provide an escape to a calmer, less stressful era. The aroma of freshly baked cookies wafting through the house nourishes the body and replenishes the spirit. Chewy cookies hold a special place in the American home. They conjure up memories of grandmothers and mothers proffering warm trayfuls of tempting goodies as a symbol of their devotion, and cookie jars full of the proof of their love.

For as long as I can remember, I have been baking cookies. I give them as gifts of welcome, thank you, solace, and love. They have traveled to the other side of the world and across the street. There is a great deal of satisfaction to be gleaned from mixing a few ingredients which, when combined, have such a magical effect on the lucky recipient. And besides, where else can you get such delightful instant gratification? I have yet to encounter the person who is not pleased with this tempting bounty. Cookies are, indeed, as much a pleasure to give as to receive.

Cookies are a centuries-old confection. Macaroons have been made in Italy and France for over four hundred years. The word *cookie* is believed to have come from the Dutch word *koekje* meaning "little cake." Before the age of automatic oven thermostats, a small portion of cake batter was baked first to be sure the oven was hot enough to avoid ruining the entire cake. These test cakes became known as *koekjes*. We no longer need to test the batter for oven temperature, but those "little cakes" became so popular that they have developed into the favorite pastry form today.

The recipes that follow will take you through the entire spectrum of chewy textures, from soft-chewy through dense-chewy, gooey-chewy, and crunchy-chewy. There are as many opinions of what a "chewy" cookie is as there are people who enjoy eating them. Try all of the different types, and decide for yourself which you prefer. If you have never before made dream bars or macaroons, I urge you to try them. They are chewy, moist, and irresistible.

Most of the recipes in this book are easy to make, a few are difficult, but all are chewy. This book offers something for every occasion, from snacks for your kids after school to sophisticated delicacies for presentation at a fine dinner. Cookies are a versatile medium. You can choose from dropped, bar, or hand-molded shapes. You will find here cookies containing fruits, nuts, and vegetables. And thanks to my friend Joanne Frentrop who has made me aware of lactose intolerance, you will also find a listing of dairy-free recipes in the index of this book.

Making cookies is an easy endeavor. Cookies are fairly forgiving, and even if they do not come out exactly as you have planned, everyone else will still think they are delicious. My best advice is to relax and enjoy yourself. Making cookies is a great way to share a rainy afternoon with your kids. It's a wonderful way to spend time with your friends.

So bake some cookies, relax, and enjoy the delicious fruits of your efforts.

Eileen Talanian

Notes on Baking Chewy Cookies

What makes a cookie chewy? Some people believe you can make chewy cookies by simply reducing the amount of time you bake any cookie. Not true. Those people simply don't understand chewy cookies. Underbaked cookies don't have the character and depth of flavor found in a properly baked cookie. Flavor is developed when the combined ingredients meld together to a point of baked perfection. This doesn't happen if a cookie is underbaked. I believe the confusion arises because many potentially chewy cookies are, in fact, *overbaked,* so that all of the moisture is baked out of them. This results in a dry, uninteresting cookie. In order for commercial cookies to have extended shelf life, they must have an extremely low moisture content and/or chemical preservatives. Because of this, I feel that consumers have been conditioned to believe cookies aren't completely cooked unless they are dry and crunchy.

The true secret to making chewy cookies is a combination of timing and ingredients. You must take care that your cookies are not overbaked, and you need to use those ingredients that will lend a chewy character to the dough. Oats, whole wheat flour, dried fruit, honey, molasses, brown sugar, chocolate, coconut, caramel, and marshmallows are some of the ingredients you can add to increase the chewiness of a cookie. But the real key is making sure you have the right ratio of sugar, butter, and eggs. If your recipe has a very high butter content, like shortbread dough, your cookie will have a "short" consistency. It will not be chewy. That is a chewy cookie bonus: many chewy cookies are lower in fat than other types of cookies. Sugar and eggs are the key players here. Butter takes a backseat. You'll even find in this book an entire chapter about macaroons, those wonderfully chewy, butter-free delights.

SOME COMMON-SENSE POINTERS

Of all the categories baking encompasses, cookies are the most forgiving. If you are new to baking "from scratch," this is the easiest place to start. There are few rules, and those there are simply involve exercising common sense. But, they *are* important, so I'll list them here for you:

- Use an oven thermometer to be sure you are baking at the correct temperature.
- Invest in the proper equipment, it

will make your baking experience much more pleasant.

- *Read the recipe thoroughly before you begin* to make sure you understand the procedures and that you have all of the ingredients.
- Use the best quality ingredients you can afford, because your cookies will only be as good as what you put in them.
- Measure accurately.
- Follow the directions given in the recipe.

Be sure all ingredients are at room temperature, unless otherwise stated.

EQUIPMENT

Ovens

There are two basic ovens for home use: conventional and convection. Conventional ovens are the ones most often used. Their heat source is located in the bottom of the oven. The heat rises up through the oven chamber more or less evenly, depending on how the pans are arranged in the oven. It is not advised to bake more than two sheets of cookies at a time in a conventional oven. In contrast, the heat source in convection ovens is located *behind* the oven wall. A fan circulates the warm air fairly evenly throughout the oven chamber. Convection baking produces a more evenly baked product and is especially suited to certain types of cookies. Because the warm air is circulated all around the oven, the cookies will usually bake at a lower temperature and quite often for a shorter period of time. They will be more uniformly baked. The bottoms of the cookies will not brown too quickly, leaving an incompletely baked top. In addition, you are able to put three cookie sheets in at a time. The exception to this is bar cookies. Conventional baking seems to suit bar cookies best. All of the cookie recipes in this book were tested in both a convection and a conventional oven. Where there was a perceptible benefit to convection baking, you will find temperatures given for *both* types of ovens. If I have listed only a time and temperature for a conventional oven, that indicates conventional is the preferred type of oven for that recipe. Your cookies will be fine, no matter which type of oven you have. (But if you are buying a new oven, and have the option, you would be well served to buy a combination convection/conventional oven. They work magic on many types of foods.)

Oven Thermometers

I have never encountered an oven that is precise in its temperature. You should be aware that oven temperature can vary by anywhere from a few degrees to seventy-five or more degrees from the temperature setting. The effective way to deal with this dilemma is to purchase and use an accurate mercury oven thermometer. They are available through most kitchen catalogs and at all kitchen supply stores. You can purchase one for well under ten dollars. Consider it a worthwhile investment. Any baked product can easily be ruined by an oven that is too hot or too cool. It would truly be a misfortune to spend your precious time and money baking, only to have the end result spoiled by an inaccurate oven.

Electric Mixer

A mixer is recommended, and I have written these recipes assuming you will be using one. The recipes in this book were tested on a stand mixer, which is more powerful than most hand mixers. If you are using a hand mixer, you will probably have to stir in the dry ingredients by hand, because the dough may be too stiff for your mixer. You can mix any of the recipes in this book by hand.

Utensils

In addition to a mixer, you will need the following equipment:

- dry measuring cups in graduated sizes ¼, ⅓, ½, and 1 cup
- liquid measuring cup
- measuring spoons in graduated sizes ¼, ½, and 1 teaspoon, as well as 1 tablespoon
- rubber spatula (the kind that is shaped like a spoon works efficiently)

- metal spatula for removing cookies from sheets
- racks for cooling the cookies
- oven mitts
- kitchen timer
- boar bristle pastry brush
- rolling pin
- wooden spoon
- wire whisk
- chef's knife.

Baking Pans

I have always used the kind of baking sheets with sides. They are sometimes referred to as jelly-roll pans, or cookie sheets. I like to rotate the sheets and turn them around halfway through the baking time, and I find this very difficult to do while wearing oven mitts if there are no sides on the pans. I have never noticed any irregularity in the browning of the cookies when baked on sheets with sides, nor any compromise in the quality of the baked cookies. Many cookbooks advise to use *only* flat sheets with no sides. So I did a test with my taste-testers (and there are many). They were unable to perceive any difference between cookies baked on flat sheets and those baked on sheets with sides. Baking sheets with sides can also be used for some bar cookie recipes and for many kinds of cakes. I can't think of a reason for buying flat sheets to bake cookies.

Another argument arises concerning insulated or noninsulated sheets. I do not use insulated sheets. Instead, if I'm using a conventional oven for baking cookies, I put one baking sheet inside another of the same size, which gives the same effect as using an insulated sheet. I also tested this procedure on my tasters to be sure of its validity. Using double sheets is far less expensive than purchasing insulated baking sheets. It is not necessary, however, to use double sheets or insulated sheets when using a convection oven.

Recommended Baking Pan Sizes

Invest in the following baking pans, and you will be able to bake any cookies in this book: two or more baking sheets, 10 × 15 inch, preferably nonstick, in a light color, *with sides*; 9 × 13-inch baking pan (2 inches deep); 11 × 7-inch baking pan (1½ inches deep); 8 × 8-inch and 9 × 9-inch baking pans, two or more 12-cup mini muffin pans, preferably nonstick.

Foil

You will notice in some recipes that I've called for lining the pans with foil. This is usually with bar cookies, so they will be easy to remove from the pan and cut. When lining the pans with foil, use the shiny side of the foil against the baking pan. This will help to keep the crust from browning too quickly. Be careful to gently push the foil into the corners of the pan with your knuckles, so you won't end up with rounded bottoms at the corners. Also be sure to allow for the foil to come up and over the sides of the pan. When buttering the foil, it is easiest to melt a small amount of butter and brush it on with a pastry brush. You can also use a nonstick spray for this purpose.

Parchment Paper

Cookies that you have baked on parchment do not stick to the pan, and the parchment protects the cookie bottoms from getting too brown too quickly. Your baking sheets will look newer and last longer when you use parchment. You can also wipe it off and reuse it, so it is a little less expensive than it may seem. Some of the recipes in this book specify using parchment. If that is the case, it means the cookies will stick very badly if parchment is not used. I prefer parchment to buttering a baking sheet for cookies, because I find that buttering the pan often causes the cookies to spread more than may be desired. Parchment paper is available in kitchen supply stores and in most kitchen catalogs.

"Nice-to-Have" Equipment

Cookie Scoops

In addition to the items listed above, there are the nice-to-have-but-not-necessary items, such as a spring-release cookie dough scoop similar to the kind used for ice cream, only smaller (available in most kitchen supply stores and in many kitchen catalogs). This type of scoop allows you to make your cookies all the same size so they will bake evenly. Restaurant supply stores carry them in various sizes. They are called "dishers."

Food Processor

You don't need a lot of special equipment to bake these cookies. I have not specified the use of a food processor for mixing dough, although you may find one handy for chopping nuts or fresh zest.

Mini–Food Processor

A mini–food processor is a convenience that pays for itself by saving you time in preparation of ingredients. It's not necessary, but is like having an extra pair of hands in the kitchen. A mini processor will finely chop a small amount of nuts or zest more evenly than a large processor.

Kitchen Scale

If you have a dependable kitchen scale on hand, you will not have to use measuring cups for most of your moist or dry ingredients. This is a big convenience. It's much easier to weigh eight ounces of brown sugar than it is to firmly pack it into a one-cup measure.

Zester

If you are planning to use zest on a regular basis, it's a good idea to purchase a zester, a small handheld utensil that removes just the zest from the fruit. It's a handy little tool. You can find zesters in kitchen supply stores and through most kitchen catalogs.

INGREDIENTS

It is not worth your valuable time to bake anything, unless you use quality ingredients. The quality of your cookies is only as good as the quality of the ingredients you use to make them. Use only pure extracts, real chocolate chips, fresh nuts and dried fruits, fresh flours and spices, moist coconut, and good-quality chocolate. *Unless otherwise stated, all ingredients used in making the recipes in this book should be at room temperature.*

Flour

Unbleached flour is the preferred all-purpose flour for use in these recipes. It has not been subjected to harsh bleaching chemicals and has a cleaner flavor. The recipes will also work with bleached all-purpose flour. When a recipe calls for whole wheat flour, you will get the best flavor and texture if you use stone-ground. No matter which type of flour you use, be sure it is fresh. Flour, especially whole wheat flour, which contains small amounts of natural oils, becomes rancid when it is old and will leave an unpleasant aftertaste. *Do not substitute cake flour or self-rising flour when all-purpose is called for in a recipe.*

Leavening Agents

Baking powder and baking soda are the chemical leavening agents used most often in cookie baking. When you are mixing a dough that contains high-acid ingredients (such as cocoa, chocolate, molasses, honey, buttermilk, vinegar, sour cream, brown sugar, or high-acid fruits), a simple alkaline leavening agent, baking soda, will chemically react with the acid to produce carbon dioxide, which is a gas that will form tiny bubbles within the dough as it is baking. These bubbles of gas are what causes the dough to rise. If your dough does not contain an acid to react with the baking soda, then baking powder is necessary for proper leavening. Baking powder is merely an alkaline leavening agent (such as baking soda) that is combined with an acid (such as cream of tartar) so that the necessary chemical reaction will take place to leaven your dough. Use double-acting baking powder. (It's the kind sold in the baking section of your supermarket.) Be sure you check the expiration dates on both the baking soda and baking powder you use to be sure of freshness. If it's not fresh, it will leave your cookies flat.

Zest

Citrus zest imparts a wonderful, fresh flavor to baked goods. The zest of a citrus fruit is the thin, colored part of the fruit's skin. Use a sharp vegetable peeler or knife to peel only the colored part of the peel from the fruit. The white part of the peel, called pith, is bitter, and you should take care that you do not use any of it when your recipe calls for zest. After you remove the zest from the fruit, chop it finely and then measure it. If you use a processor to chop zest, be sure to put in a couple of tablespoons of sugar from the recipe while processing, to avoid a gooey mess. Sometimes you may find yourself in need of only the juice of a citrus fruit. You can remove the zest before juicing the fruit and freeze it in a small resealable plastic bag for up to six weeks. Take it from the freezer fifteen minutes or so before you need it so it will be thawed enough to chop.

Nuts

Unless otherwise stated, all nuts used in these recipes are raw and unsalted. Buy your nuts from a source that sells a lot of them, so you will be assured of a fresh supply. Nuts that are not fresh have an unpleasant rancid flavor and odor and will render your cookies inedible. The best way to store nuts is in the freezer, either in double plastic bags or in an airtight container. Take out just what you need for a recipe and return the balance to the freezer.

Chopping Nuts

Coarsely and medium chopped nuts are best chopped by hand with a chef's knife, or in a wooden bowl with a curved chopper designed for this use. You can make finely chopped and ground nuts in a food processor or a rotary grinder. Be sure to add two tablespoons of sugar from the recipe to the nuts if you are grinding them in a processor. It will help to keep them from getting too oily, which will cause them to clump together. Be careful not to overprocess nuts, or you will end up with nut butter.

Dried Fruits

You will find many recipes in this book that call for dried fruits. Fresh dried fruits are soft and pliable and can be used right from the package. They should be stored in airtight containers at room temperature.

Extracts

Only pure extracts taste like the genuine article. I use two kinds of extract: pure vanilla and pure almond. Most other flavors can be obtained by the use of zest, liqueurs, fruits, or natural oils. Imitation flavorings taste like imitation and have an unpleasant chemical taste that will be obvious in your baked goods.

Oats

Unless otherwise specified, you can use either old-fashioned or quick oats when oats are called for in the recipes in this book. Old-fashioned oats will lend greater chewiness to the baked cookies. *Never use instant oats in the recipes in this book.* They will alter the texture of the baked cookies considerably.

Eggs

You should use fresh eggs graded *large* for all of these recipes. To bring eggs to room temperature for use in a recipe, simply place them in a bowl of very warm water while you assemble the rest of the ingredients. If you cannot use egg yolks for health reasons, you can use egg substitutes for the whole eggs called for in a recipe. There will be varying results with this substitution, depending on the recipe. Do not use egg substitutes in place of egg yolks, because they will produce disappointing results. One way to deal with this entire problem is to stick to the many recipes in this book that contain only egg whites.

Cocoa

Use unsweetened American-style (*not Dutch process*) baking cocoa in these recipes. The brands readily found in your supermarket, Hershey and Nestlé, are fine. Dutch process cocoa has been treated with an alkalizing agent, is not as deep in color, and is not as intense in flavor as American-style, nonalkalized cocoa. *Never use hot cocoa mix or chocolate milk mix.* They are made with sugar, milk solids, and various fillers and chemicals. They contain very little cocoa and will diminish the quality of your cookies.

Butter

I use only unsalted butter in my recipes. Unsalted butter has a cleaner flavor and less moisture than salted butter. The amount of water in salted butter varies from one manufacturer to the next. In addition, butter manufacturers are not consistent in the amount of salt they add to salted butter, making it difficult to determine the amount of salt you are putting in your cookies. Butter can be frozen, so if you usually use salted butter for other things, you can keep some unsalted in the freezer to use just for baking. Be sure to wrap it tightly in plastic wrap and then in a resealable plastic bag, so it doesn't pick up any unwanted flavors from the freezer. If you cannot use butter for health reasons, you may use margarine, but there will be some variation in the finished product, depending on the recipe. There is more moisture in margarine than in butter. If you use margarine, it is a good idea to chill the dough before baking the cookies, because the margarine may make the cookies spread more than usual. Do not use soft tub margarine. The recipes may be seriously affected by its high moisture content.

Softening Butter

Butter needs to be soft to blend properly with the other ingredients in the recipe. If it is too hard, it will form tiny clumps in the dough and will affect the results of the cookies. If you have forgotten to take out the butter from the refrigerator or freezer to soften, don't despair. There are two methods you can use to soften it. If you have a microwave oven, break up the butter into one-inch chunks and put it into a microwavable bowl large enough to hold it. Cover the bowl with a paper towel and microwave for about fifteen to twenty seconds for cold butter or thirty to forty-five seconds for frozen butter. Check to see if it has softened, and if not, return it to the microwave oven for ten more seconds, repeating this last step until it is soft enough. If you have no microwave oven, break the butter into half-inch pieces and put it into a small covered saucepan over very low heat. When the butter just starts to melt, remove it from the heat and stir until it is smooth, using the back of a spoon to mash any lumps out of it. Be careful not to melt the butter completely, no matter which method you use, unless the recipe specifically calls for melted butter.

Melting Butter

If you have a microwave oven, you can easily melt butter in it. Cut it into one-inch pieces and place them in a glass measuring cup covered with a paper towel. The amount of time you need to microwave the butter will depend on how cold the butter is when you start, how much butter you are melting, and how powerful your microwave oven is. Microwave for thirty seconds and check to see if it is melted. Repeat this step until it has melted completely.

Shortening

I don't use shortening in cookies, because I feel it is flavorless and leaves an unpleasant coating in the mouth. (The reason it does this is because its melting point is higher than normal body temperature. So, it doesn't melt in your mouth. Butter, on the other hand, melts below body temperature, and that is why it gives you that wonderful melt-in-your-mouth sensation.) If you choose to use shortening for some or all of the butter in these recipes, be aware that it may change the texture and will significantly affect the flavor of the finished product.

Chocolate

Accept no substitute for the real thing. Nothing else has the flavor, texture, or aroma of real chocolate. Going to the extra expense of purchasing the best-quality chocolate you can find will make the difference between a cookie that is good and a cookie that is knock-you-down delicious.

Unsweetened Chocolate

Unsweetened chocolate is just that. It is the refined, plain chocolate liquor (nonalcoholic) which is obtained by roasting cocoa beans and grinding them. It contains no added sugar and has a bitter taste. *Do not substitute any other kind of chocolate if a recipe calls for unsweetened chocolate.* Do not use the premelted packets sold as a convenience in the baking section of your store. They are not really chocolate. They are made from cocoa and vegetable oil.

Bittersweet and Semisweet Chocolate

Bittersweet and semisweet chocolate have added sugar and therefore less of the actual chocolate liquor than unsweetened chocolate. You can use semisweet and bittersweet chocolate interchangeably in these recipes. In a pinch, good-quality, real semisweet chocolate chips may be substituted for semisweet or bittersweet chocolate. Don't compromise the quality of your product with imitation flavored chips.

White Chocolate

White chocolate is not really chocolate. It does not contain any of the chocolate liquor from the cocoa beans. Most American-made white chocolate is a combination of vegetable fats, sugar, natural or artificial flavorings, and milk solids. European white chocolate is made with cocoa butter, sugar, milk solids, and flavorings (usually natural). Buy the European white chocolate if you have a choice, because it is immeasurably better in texture and flavor. You can substitute a good-quality white chocolate chip for chopped or melted white chocolate in the recipes in this book. Ghirardelli makes an excellent white chocolate chip, and you will find it in many grocery stores. It is the only white chocolate chip readily available that is worth buying.

Melting Chocolate

There are three methods you can use to melt chocolate. No matter which method you use, cool the chocolate for at least five minutes before you add it to the dough you are mixing, unless otherwise stated in the recipe. Water may condense on the inside of the lid of the container you are using to melt the chocolate. Be very careful not to drip any water into the chocolate during the course of melting it, because it could cause the chocolate to "seize," in which case it will become hard and grainy. Do not let even a drop of moisture fall into the melting chocolate. When melting white chocolate, be careful to use low temperatures and watch that it doesn't scorch. White chocolate is more fragile and reacts to heat much more quickly than regular chocolate.

Microwave Method

If you have a microwave oven, put the chopped chocolate into a covered microwavable dish and microwave for one to two minutes. Check the chocolate. If it is mostly melted, remove it and stir until it is completely smooth. If it is not mostly melted, repeat the process until it is. Chocolate melted in the microwave will still hold its shape when it begins to melt, so don't be fooled. Take care that you don't burn the chocolate by microwaving too long.

Double Boiler Method

Another way to melt chocolate is in a double boiler over very hot, *not boiling,* water. If you don't have a double boiler, you can place a heat-proof bowl over a pot of hot water. Be sure the bowl does not touch the water. Place the chopped chocolate into the top part of the double boiler, cover, and check it after a few minutes. When it is mostly melted, remove the pan from over the water and stir the chocolate until it is completely smooth.

Direct Heat Method

You can also place the chopped chocolate into a small, heavy saucepan and stir *constantly* over very low heat until most of the chocolate is melted. (This method requires constant stirring to be sure the chocolate doesn't scorch.) Remove from the heat and continue stirring until the chocolate is completely smooth. Because it is very easy to scorch the chocolate using this method, it is generally safer to use either the microwave or double boiler method.

Chopping Chocolate

Some of the recipes in this book call for chopped chocolate. To chop chocolate, you should put the block of chocolate on a clean, dry, odor-free chopping board and use a long, sharp chef's knife to chop. Place the knife on the chocolate about half an inch from the edge of the chocolate. Hold the knife handle in one hand, and place your other hand on the back of the blade end. Rock the knife firmly back and forth until you have chopped completely through the chocolate. Any chunks of chocolate that are too large should be cut into smaller pieces.

Graham Cracker Crumbs

When a recipe calls for graham cracker crumbs, you need to finely crush them either by hand or in a food processor. A food processor will do a superb job. Break the crackers into small pieces and place them into the container of a food processor. Pulse on and off several times to further break up the crackers and then turn the machine on and process for about ten to fifteen seconds or until the crackers have been crushed to a fine powder. If you don't have a food processor, a good way to crush graham crackers is to put them into a resealable plastic bag and roll them firmly with a rolling pin until they

are finely crushed. With either method, the crumbs should be as uniform in size as possible.

ACCURATE MEASURING

Measuring your ingredients accurately is just as important as using good-quality ingredients.

How to Measure Dry Ingredients for Recipes in This Book

When measuring a dry ingredient such as flour, spices, salt, a leavening agent, or sugar, spoon it into the appropriate-sized dry measuring cup or measuring spoon, heaping it up over the top. Then take a straight-edged utensil, such as the back of a knife or an icing spatula, and scrape off the extra. Do not pack down or shake what you are measuring, because if you do, you will end up with more of that ingredient than you want.

How to Measure Liquid Ingredients

Liquids need to be measured in a clear liquid measuring cup that is placed on a level surface. The cup should be at eye-level so you can be sure of an accurate measure. When you measure small amounts of liquid, such as vanilla, hold the measuring spoon over a small cup or bowl. Then empty the measuring spoon into the dough mixture. This way you will avoid the risk of accidentally overpouring the ingredient directly into the dough.

How to Measure
Moist Ingredients

Some ingredients, such as brown sugar, dried fruits, and coconut, must be firmly packed into the measuring cup to get an accurate measure. Use a dry measure for these items. Fill the measuring cup so the ingredient is heaping and press down very firmly with your hand. Add more of the ingredient and repeat until the cup is packed full and even with the top of the measure. You will not be able to get an accurate measure if you use a liquid measuring cup for dry ingredients.

STARTING TO BAKE COOKIES

Before you start to make any recipe, you should *always* read it through completely to be certain you understand it. Next, take out all of the ingredients you will need, to be sure you have everything. It is very distressing to be at a critical point in the mixing process and find you are missing a key ingredient. Warm any ingredients to room temperature as required. Then take out all of the equipment you will need to complete the recipe. Prepare the pans, if necessary. Use the size pan that is called for in the recipe. If you change the size of the pan for bar cookies, it will affect their outcome. When all of these things are assembled, you should chop, plump, melt, or otherwise prepare any ingredients as indicated in the ingredients list of your recipe. You will feel less stress and enjoy baking more if you have followed these steps before you start mixing. Now you are ready to begin.

How to Freeze Cookies
and Bar Cookies

One of the advantages of baking a batch of cookies is that you can wrap some of them up and freeze them to have later. For the best results, freeze the cookies as soon as possible after they are completely cooled. When you freeze cookies or bar cookies the most important thing to remember is that you want them airtight, with as little air as possible inside the package and freeze them unfrosted. The best way to do this is to wrap the cookies individually with plastic wrap and then put all of the wrapped cookies into a plastic container or a resealable plastic freezer bag. Cookies can be frozen for up to two months. Be sure to write the date on the bag so you know how long they have been in the freezer. When you are ready to use them, remove only what you need from the bag or container and place them, still in their plastic wrap, on a wire rack for at least thirty minutes, until they come to room temperature. When you are ready to serve them, remove the plastic wrap. Add any frosting at this time.

A Chip off the Old Block

There is no other cookie that is so loved and revered in America as the chocolate chip. It is the rare individual who doesn't salivate at the mere thought of sinking his or her teeth into a freshly baked cookie packed with soft chunks of chocolate. The recipes that follow are rich with chocolate chunks or chips. You can use less chocolate than I call for in these recipes, but then, what's the point?

Chewy Chocolate-Chunk Cookies

Dense, chewy, and loaded with chocolate, this is a cookie few can resist. A rich brown-sugar dough is completely surrounded by chunks of deep, dark chocolate.

Makes about 3½ dozen 2-inch cookies.

- 1   **cup all-purpose flour, preferably unbleached**
- ½   **cup whole wheat flour, preferably stone-ground**
- ½   **cup old-fashioned or quick rolled oats, uncooked (not instant)**
- ½   **teaspoon baking soda**
- ½   **cup unsalted butter**
- ½   **cup brown sugar, firmly packed**
- ⅓   **cup granulated sugar**
- 1   **large egg**
- 1½   **teaspoons pure vanilla extract**
- ¼   **teaspoon salt**
- ⅔   **cup walnuts, ground**
- 18   **ounces semisweet chocolate chunks or real semisweet chocolate chips**

Preheat convection ovens to 310 degrees Fahrenheit or conventional ovens to 325 degrees Fahrenheit. Set the racks in the conventional oven so they divide the oven into thirds. You will *not* need to line the cookie sheets with parchment paper for this recipe. If you are baking in a conventional oven, put one baking sheet inside another of the same size to make a double pan, or use insulated pans to protect the bottoms of the cookies.

Stir together the flours, oats, and baking soda in a small bowl and set aside.

In an electric mixer on medium speed, combine the butter, sugars, egg, vanilla, and salt. Beat until thoroughly mixed on low speed, then increase to medium-high, and beat for 2 minutes. The mixture will become fluffy and light in color. Scrape the bowl with a rubber spatula. Add the flour mixture and beat on low to combine, about 1 minute. Mix in the nuts and chocolate chips, beating on low speed until evenly combined. Using a wooden spoon or rubber spatula, stir the mixture, scraping down to the bottom of the bowl, to be sure it is evenly mixed.

Drop the dough by heaping teaspoonfuls onto baking sheets, flattening them slightly with the heel of your hand. Do not make them too thin—they should be about ½ inch thick. Place the pans in the preheated oven and bake approximately 13 to 15 minutes, reversing the cookie sheets and switching them top to bottom halfway through the baking time. The cookies are done when they are set but not firm. The cookies will be very light brown, and your finger will leave an imprint if you touch them gently. They will become firmer as they cool, so be careful not to overbake them. When they are done, cool them on the baking sheets for a few minutes, and then move them to cooling racks to finish cooling.

Store the cooled cookies in an airtight container for up to 1 week, or freeze them for up to 2 months. (See freezing instructions on page 12.)

Chewy Chocolate-Chunk Cookies go perfectly with milk or coffee.

Chewy Oatmeal Chunk Cookies

Chewy, thick, and satisfying, this is a cookie that will please young and old alike. Don't overbake it, or it will become hard and crunchy.

Makes about 3½ dozen 2½-inch cookies.

1¾ cups brown sugar, firmly packed
1   teaspoon baking soda
½   teaspoon salt
1½ teaspoons baking powder
¾   cup unsalted butter
2   large eggs
2   teaspoons pure vanilla extract
3   tablespoons milk
2   cups quick or old-fashioned
      rolled oats, uncooked
      (not instant)
1¾ cups all-purpose flour, preferably
      unbleached
1½ cups coarsely chopped pecans
1   cup sweetened coconut, flaked or
      shredded, firmly packed
15 ounces chopped semisweet
      chocolate or real semisweet
      chocolate chips

Preheat convection ovens to 310 degrees Fahrenheit or conventional ovens to 325 degrees Fahrenheit. Set the racks in the conventional oven so they divide the oven into thirds. You will *not* need to line the pans with parchment for this recipe. If you are baking in a conventional oven, put one baking sheet inside another of the same size to make a double pan, or use insulated pans to protect the bottoms of the cookies.

Using an electric mixer on medium speed, combine the brown sugar, baking soda, salt, and baking powder for about 20 to 30 seconds or until thoroughly mixed. Add the butter and beat on medium speed for about 2 minutes, or until light in color and fluffy. Scrape the bowl with a rubber spatula. Add the eggs, vanilla, and milk and beat on low speed for about 20 seconds to combine, then increase speed to medium and beat for about 2 minutes, until smooth. Pour in the oats and flour all at once, and beat on low speed for about 20 seconds, just until the mixture is blended evenly. Scrape the bowl again and add the pecans, coconut, and chocolate. Beat on low just until combined, about 20 to 30 seconds.

Drop by heaping tablespoonfuls onto the baking sheets and bake in the preheated oven for about 12 to 14 minutes, reversing the baking sheets and switching them top to bottom halfway through the baking time. The cookies will still feel soft, but will become firm as they cool, so it is important that they not be overcooked. When they are done, let them cool on the baking sheets for 5 minutes, then move them to wire racks to finish cooling.

Store the cooled cookies in an airtight container for up to 6 days, or wrap tightly and freeze for up to 2 months. (See freezing instructions on page 12.)

Chewy Oatmeal Chunk Cookies make a great after-school snack and are sturdy enough to be shipped.

Macadamia and White Chocolate-Chunk Drops

The combination of white chocolate and macadamia nuts is irresistible. A hint of orange is added here, which gives the cookies a delightfully fresh flavor. This is a soft-chewy cookie.

Makes about 5 dozen 2-inch cookies.

- 2¾ **cups all-purpose flour, preferably unbleached**
- ½ **teaspoon baking powder**
- ½ **teaspoon baking soda**
- ½ **cup unsalted butter**
- ½ **cup brown sugar, firmly packed**
- ½ **cup granulated sugar**
- 2 **large eggs**
- ¼ **teaspoon salt**
- 2 **tablespoons orange juice, preferably fresh squeezed**
- 1 **tablespoon orange zest**
- 9 **ounces white chocolate, cut into ½-inch chunks, *or* good-quality white chocolate chips, such as Ghirardelli**
- 1 **cup macadamia nuts, coarsely chopped**

Preheat convection ovens to 310 degrees Fahrenheit or conventional ovens to 325 degrees Fahrenheit. Set the racks in the conventional oven so they divide the oven into thirds. You will *not* need to line the pans with parchment for this recipe. If you are baking in a conventional oven, put one baking sheet inside another of the same size to make a double pan, or use insulated pans to protect the bottoms of the cookies.

With an electric mixer set on medium speed, beat the sugars, baking soda, and baking powder for 20 seconds. Add the butter, eggs, salt, juice, and zest and beat on medium speed for about 3 minutes. The mixture will become fluffy and light in color. It may look curdled, but that is all right. Scrape the bowl with a rubber spatula, and add the flour mixture. Beat on low speed for about 1 minute or until the flour is blended in. Scrape the bowl again with a rubber spatula. Mix in the chocolate and nuts on low just until thoroughly combined. Using a wooden spoon or rubber spatula, stir the dough briefly to be sure it is evenly mixed, especially at the bottom of the bowl.

Drop by rounded teaspoonfuls onto baking sheets, and bake in a preheated oven approximately 11 to 13 minutes, reversing the baking sheets and switching them top to bottom halfway through the baking time. The cookies will be set but not firm and will just start to become light brown. Do not overbake them. They will become firmer as they cool. When the cookies are finished baking, remove the pans from the oven and let the cookies cool on the pans for a few minutes. Then move the cookies to cooling racks until completely cooled.

Store the baked cookies in an airtight container for up to 5 days, or freeze them for up to 2 months. (See freezing instructions on page 12.)

Macadamia and White Chocolate-Chunk Drops pair perfectly with coffee or milk and are especially nice with cappuccino.

Orange-Pecan
Chocolate-Chip Cookies

Chunky, sweet, and intense with fresh orange flavor, you will not want to miss this cookie if you enjoy the flavor of orange.

Makes 3 dozen 2½-inch cookies

½	**cup brown sugar, firmly packed**
⅓	**cup granulated sugar**
½	**teaspoon baking soda**
1	**teaspoon baking powder**
½	**cup unsalted butter**
1	**large egg**
1	**teaspoon pure vanilla extract**
1	**tablespoon orange juice**
1½	**tablespoons fresh grated orange zest**
1½	**cups all-purpose flour, preferably unbleached**
½	**cup coarsely chopped macadamia nuts**
½	**cup ground pecans**
12	**ounces real semisweet chocolate chips**

Preheat convection ovens to 310 degrees Fahrenheit or conventional ovens to 325 degrees Fahrenheit. Set the racks in the conventional oven so they divide the oven into thirds. You will *not* need to line the pans with parchment for this recipe. If you are baking in a conventional oven, put one baking sheet inside another of the same size to make a double pan, or use insulated pans to protect the bottoms of the cookies.

Using an electric mixer on medium speed, mix the brown sugar, sugar, baking soda, and baking powder for about 20 to 30 seconds, or until thoroughly combined. Add the butter, egg, vanilla, juice, and zest and beat on medium speed until mixed, about 2 minutes. Scrape the bowl with a rubber spatula and add the flour all at once, beating on low for about 30 seconds, or until blended evenly. Scrape the bowl again and add the nuts and chips. Beat on low speed for 15 to 20 seconds, or until thoroughly combined. Using a rubber spatula, scrape the sides of the bowl and stir the dough to be sure it is evenly mixed.

Drop by heaping teaspoonfuls onto the baking sheets and bake in the preheated oven for 13 to 15 minutes, reversing the cookie sheets and switching them top to bottom halfway through the baking time. The cookies are done when they are just turning brown and barely firm to the touch. When they are done, cool them on the baking sheets for about five minutes, then move them to wire racks to finish cooling.

Store the completely cooled cookies in an airtight container for up to 6 days, or freeze them, wrapped tightly, for up to 2 months. (See freezing instructions on page 12.)

Orange-Pecan Chocolate-Chip Cookies make a great picnic dessert with iced tea or cider.

Black and Whites

Dark and dense and loaded with white chocolate chunks, this is the reverse of the standard chocolate-chip cookie. Serve it to adults or kids, pack it in lunch boxes, or have it for dessert after a nice meal. They are versatile and delicious.

Makes 3½ dozen 3-inch cookies.

1¾   cups granulated sugar
1   teaspoon baking soda
¾   cup unsalted butter
2   large eggs
2   teaspoons pure vanilla extract
1   cup unsweetened cocoa powder
2½   cups all-purpose flour, preferably unbleached
12   ounces chopped white chocolate or good quality white chocolate chips, such as Ghirardelli

Preheat convection ovens to 310 degrees Fahrenheit or conventional ovens to 325 degrees Fahrenheit. Set the racks in the conventional oven so they divide the oven into thirds. You will *not* need to line the pans with parchment for this recipe. If you are baking in a conventional oven, put one baking sheet inside another of the same size to make a double pan, or use insulated pans to protect the bottoms of the cookies.

Using an electric mixer on medium speed, mix the sugar and baking soda for about 20 seconds, or until thoroughly combined. Add the butter, eggs, and vanilla and beat on medium speed for 2 minutes, until fluffy and light in color. Scrape the bowl with a rubber spatula and add the cocoa, beating on low speed for 30 seconds. Scrape the bowl again and add the flour, beating on low speed for about 20 seconds, just until the flour is mixed in. Add the white chocolate and beat on low for 10 seconds, just to mix evenly. Using a rubber spatula or wooden spoon, scrape the bottom and sides of the bowl and stir the dough to be sure it is evenly mixed.

Drop by heaping teaspoonfuls onto the baking sheets and bake in the pre-heated oven for 13 to 15 minutes, reversing the cookie sheets and switching them top to bottom halfway through the baking time, reversing the baking sheets and switching them top to bottom halfway through the baking time. The cookies will be just turning brown and barely firm to the touch. When they are done, cool them on the baking sheets for about 5 minutes, then move them to wire racks to finish cooling.

Store the completely cooled cookies in an airtight container for up to 5 days, or wrap tightly and freeze for up to 2 months. (See freezing instructions on page 12.)

Black and Whites are chocolate milk cookies.

Chocolate-Chunk Banana Chewies

For those of you who love the combination of bananas and chocolate, here is a cookie just for you. A rich banana dough is interspersed with chocolate chunks and walnuts to produce a large, flavorful, moist cookie that is soft-chewy.

Makes 4 dozen 3-inch cookies.

- ¾ cup brown sugar, firmly packed
- ¼ cup granulated sugar
- 1 teaspoon baking powder
- ½ teaspoon baking soda
- 1 teaspoon ground nutmeg
- ½ cup unsalted butter
- 2 large eggs
- 1 teaspoon pure vanilla extract
- 1 cup whole wheat flour, preferably stone-ground
- 1 cup mashed ripe banana (1 large and 1 medium banana)
- 1¼ cups all-purpose flour, preferably unbleached
- 1 cup coarsely chopped walnuts
- 12 ounces chopped semisweet chocolate or real semisweet chocolate chips

Preheat convection ovens to 325 degrees Fahrenheit or conventional ovens to 350 degrees Fahrenheit. Set the racks in the conventional oven so they divide the oven into thirds. You will *not* need to line the pans with parchment for this recipe. If you are baking in a conventional oven, put one baking sheet inside another of the same size to make a double pan, or use insulated pans to protect the bottoms of the cookies.

Using an electric mixer set on medium speed, combine the brown sugar, sugar, baking powder, and baking soda for 20 seconds. Add the butter, eggs, and vanilla and beat on medium speed for 2 minutes, until light in color and fluffy. Scrape the bowl with a rubber spatula and add the whole wheat flour. Beat on low speed for 30 seconds to mix evenly and add the banana. Beat on low speed for 30 seconds and scrape the bowl with a rubber spatula. Add the all-purpose flour, walnuts, and chocolate chips. Beat again on low speed for 30 seconds, to blend in the flour.

Drop by rounded tablespoonfuls onto the baking sheets and bake in the preheated oven for 12 to 14 minutes, reversing the baking sheets and switching them top to bottom halfway through the baking time. Do not overbake. The cookies will barely feel firm to the touch when they are done, and they will be lightly browned. They will firm up as they cool. Remove the pans from the oven and set on wire racks to cool for 5 minutes. Using a metal spatula, remove the cookies from the baking sheets and place them on the wire racks to finish cooling.

Store the cooled cookies in an airtight container for up to 5 days, or wrap tightly and freeze for up to 2 months. (See freezing instructions on page 12.)

Chocolate-Chunk Banana Chewies are a delight with cold milk.

White Chocolate and Almond Chocolate-Chip Cookies

A rich white-chocolate dough is the background for toasted almonds and dark chocolate. These are tantalizing treats. The white chocolate in the dough lends a chewiness to the cookies that is well complemented by the almonds.

Makes 4 dozen 3-inch cookies.

- 8 ounces chopped white chocolate or good-quality white chocolate chips, such as Ghirardelli
- 2 cups raw (skins on) almonds
- 1 cup granulated sugar
- 1 cup brown sugar, firmly packed
- 1 teaspoon baking powder
- ½ teaspoon baking soda
- ½ cup unsalted butter
- 2 large eggs
- 2 teaspoons pure vanilla extract
- 3 cups all-purpose flour, preferably unbleached
- 12 ounces chopped semisweet chocolate or real chocolate chips

Preheat convection ovens to 310 degrees Fahrenheit or conventional ovens to 325 degrees Fahrenheit. Set the racks in the conventional oven so they divide the oven into thirds. You will *not* need to line the pans with parchment for this recipe. If you are baking in a conventional oven, put one baking sheet inside another of the same size to make a double pan, or use insulated pans to protect the bottoms of the cookies.

Melt the white chocolate in a covered microwavable dish for 2 minutes in the microwave oven, or place in a heavy pan on the stove top over low heat, until the chocolate is almost melted. Stir with a wire whisk until smooth and all of the chocolate is melted. Add the vanilla and stir to blend thoroughly. Set aside.

Spread the almonds in a single layer in a baking pan and bake in the preheated oven for about 8 minutes. Remove the pan from the oven and set on a wire rack to cool. When cool, chop coarsely and set aside.

Using an electric mixer set on medium speed, combine the brown sugar, sugar, baking powder, and baking soda for 20 seconds. Add the eggs, butter, and vanilla and beat on medium speed for 2 minutes, until light in color and fluffy. Scrape the bowl with a rubber spatula and add the melted chocolate. Beat on low speed for 30 seconds to mix evenly and add the flour and chocolate chips. Beat again on low speed for 30 seconds, to blend in the flour.

Drop by rounded tablespoonfuls onto the baking sheets and bake in the pre-heated oven for 12 to 14 minutes, revers-ing the baking sheets and switching them top to bottom halfway through the baking time. The cookies will barely feel firm to the touch when they are done, and they will be lightly browned. Re-move the pans from the oven and set on wire racks to cool for 5 minutes. Using a metal spatula, remove the cookies from the baking sheets and place them on the wire racks to finish cooling.

Store the cooled cookies in an airtight container for up to 5 days or wrap tightly and freeze for up to 2 months. (See freez-ing instructions on page 12.)

White Chocolate and Almond Chocolate-Chip Cookies are wonderful with espresso or as a lunchtime snack.

Triple Chocolate Sour Cream Treats

Three kinds of chocolate are matched with a rich chocolate dough to produce a moist, dark, and seductive cookie that will linger in your memory like an old love. The sour cream in this recipe enhances the keeping properties of these pleasing treats.

Makes 4 dozen 3-inch cookies.

½   **cup unsalted butter**
3   **ounces unsweetened chocolate**
¾   **cup granulated sugar**
½   **cup brown sugar, firmly packed**
½   **teaspoon baking powder**
½   **teaspoon baking soda**
1   **large egg**
1   **teaspoon pure vanilla extract**
1¼ **cups all-purpose flour, preferably unbleached**
½   **cup sour cream (not low fat)**
6   **ounces real semisweet chocolate chips**
6   **ounces real milk chocolate chips**
6   **ounces good-quality white chocolate chips, such as Ghirardelli**

Preheat convection ovens to 325 degrees Fahrenheit or conventional ovens to 350 degrees Fahrenheit. Set the racks in the conventional oven so they divide the oven into thirds. You will *not* need to line the cookie sheets with parchment paper for this recipe. If you are baking in a conventional oven, put one baking sheet inside another of the same size to make a double pan, or use insulated pans to protect the bottoms of the cookies.

Melt the butter and the chocolate together in a covered microwavable dish for 2 minutes in the microwave oven, or place in a heavy pan on the stove top over low heat, until the chocolate is almost melted. Remove the mixture from the heat and stir with a whisk until smooth. Let the chocolate mixture cool for about 5 minutes.

Using an electric mixer on medium speed, combine the sugar, brown sugar, baking powder, and baking soda for 20 seconds. Add the egg and vanilla and beat on medium speed for 2 minutes, until fluffy and light in color. Scrape the bowl with a rubber spatula and add ¾ cup of the flour, beating on low speed for 20 seconds, just until it is blended in. Scrape the bowl again and add the sour cream, beating on low speed for about 20 seconds. Again scrape the bowl and add the remaining ½ cup of the flour and all of the chocolate chips. Mix on low speed just until the flour is blended in. Using a wooden spoon or rubber spatula, stir the mixture, scraping down to the bottom of the bowl, to be sure it is evenly mixed.

Drop the dough by rounded tablespoonfuls onto the baking sheets and bake in the preheated oven for 13 to 15 minutes, reversing the baking sheets and switching them top to bottom halfway through the baking time. The cookies will just start to feel firm to the touch. Do not overbake. Remove the pans from the oven and set on a wire rack to cool.

When completely cool, store in an airtight container for up to 1 week, or wrap tightly and freeze for up to 2 months. (See freezing instructions on page 12.)

Triple Chocolate Sour Cream Treats are quadruply delicious with chocolate milk.

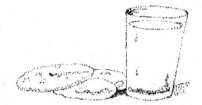

For Chocolate Lovers Only

Americans are in the throes of an intense love affair with chocolate. For those of us who are self-confessed chocoholics, there is no such thing as too much chocolate. This chapter offers several intense chocolate cookies that are sure to satisfy the most passionate chocophiles. Be forewarned—your chocolate cookies will only be as good as the quality of the chocolate you use in them.

Dark, Fudgy Orange-Pecan Drops

Moist, chewy, and resplendent with chocolate, the combination of chocolate and orange in these cookies will titillate your senses, while the pecans offer the perfect foil to the chewy texture. These are best eaten within one or two days.

Makes about 4 dozen 2½ inch cookies.

- **8** ounces bittersweet or semisweet chocolate, coarsely chopped
- **4** ounces unsweetened chocolate, coarsely chopped
- **10** tablespoons unsalted butter, softened
- **½** cup unsweetened cocoa powder
- **1½** cups all-purpose flour, preferably unbleached
- **1** teaspoon baking soda
- **½** teaspoon salt
- **1** cup brown sugar, firmly packed
- **½** cup granulated sugar
- **3** large eggs
- **2** tablespoons finely chopped orange zest
- **1½** teaspoons pure vanilla extract
- **1½** cups pecans, coarsely chopped

Preheat convection ovens to 310 degrees Fahrenheit or conventional ovens to 325 degrees Fahrenheit. Set the racks in the conventional oven so they divide the oven into thirds. You will *not* need to line the cookie sheets with parchment paper for this recipe. If you are baking in a conventional oven, put one baking sheet inside another of the same size to make a double pan, or use insulated pans to protect the bottoms of the cookies.

In a heavy saucepan over low heat, or in a glass measuring cup in the microwave oven, melt the chocolates and butter. Stir until smooth, using a wire whisk. Set aside to cool.

In a small bowl, stir together the cocoa, flour, baking soda, and salt. Set aside.

Beat the sugars, eggs, vanilla, and zest on medium speed in a mixer for 3 minutes. The mixture will become fluffy and light in color. Scrape the bowl with a rubber spatula. With the mixer on low speed, add the melted chocolate and butter and beat until thoroughly mixed, about 1 minute. Scrape the bowl once again. Sprinkle the flour mixture over the dough and mix on low speed until evenly blended, about 1 minute. Stir in the nuts. Using a wooden spoon or rubber spatula, stir the mixture, scraping down to the bottom of the bowl, to be sure it is evenly mixed. Let the dough rest for 5 minutes. Drop by rounded tablespoonfuls onto the baking sheets. Bake in a preheated oven for about 11 to 13 minutes, reversing the baking sheets and switching them top to bottom halfway through the bak-

ing time. The cookies will feel barely firm to the touch. When the cookies are done, remove the pans from the oven and *let the cookies cool completely on the baking sheets*. The cookies will be crumbly while warm, but will firm up as they set.

Store the cooled cookies in an airtight container for up to 2 days, or freeze them for up to 2 months. (See freezing instructions on page 12.)

Dark, Fudgy Orange-Pecan Drops mate perfectly with a tall glass of cold milk or a mug of hot coffee.

Chocolate Peppermint Patties

I love the combination of chocolate and peppermint. The allure of the dark chocolate in this cookie is perfectly complemented by the heady sensation of the peppermint. This is a chewy, flavorful cookie that makes your mouth yearn for more.

Makes 3 dozen 2-inch cookies.

8	ounces semisweet or bittersweet chocolate, coarsely chopped
2	tablespoons unsalted butter
6	ounces chocolate-covered peppermint patties, chopped
1⅓	cups all-purpose flour, preferably unbleached
½	teaspoon baking soda
¼	teaspoon baking powder
2	large eggs
½	cup granulated sugar
1	teaspoon pure vanilla extract
¼	teaspoon salt

Preheat convection ovens to 330 degrees Fahrenheit or conventional ovens to 350 degrees Fahrenheit. Set the racks in the conventional oven so they divide the oven into thirds. You *will* need to line the cookie sheets with parchment paper for this recipe. If you are baking in a conventional oven, put one baking sheet inside another of the same size to make a double pan, or use insulated pans to protect the bottoms of the cookies.

In a heavy saucepan over low heat, or in a glass measuring cup in the microwave oven, melt the chocolate and butter. Remove from the heat, and add the chopped peppermint patties. Stir until smooth, using a wire whisk. Set aside to cool.

In a small bowl, stir together the flour, baking soda, and baking powder. Set aside.

With a mixer on medium speed, beat the eggs, sugar, vanilla, and salt about 3 minutes, until the mixture is fluffy and light in color. Scrape the bowl with a rubber spatula. Add the chocolate mixture and beat on low for 1 minute. Scrape the bowl again, and add the dry ingredients. Beat on low until evenly mixed, about 1 minute. Using a wooden spoon or rubber spatula, stir the mixture, scraping down to the bottom of the bowl, to be sure it is evenly mixed. Let the dough rest for 5 minutes at room temperature.

Drop by rounded teaspoonfuls onto the prepared baking sheets. Bake for 10 to 12 minutes, reversing the baking sheets and switching them top to bottom halfway through the baking time. The cookies will just start to feel firm. Do not overbake them. When they are done, remove the sheets from the oven and let the cookies cool on the sheets for 5 minutes. Using a metal spatula, move the cookies to cooling racks until completely cool.

Store the cooled cookies in an airtight container for up to 1 week, or freeze for up to 2 months. (See freezing instructions on page 12.)

Chocolate Peppermint Patties and milk make a perfect match.

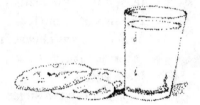

Rich Cocoa and Nut Cookies

While some of us are attracted to the rich and intense, others find their comfort with a more subtle companion. A milk chocolate rather than dark chocolate flavor embraces you here. The soft chewiness of the cookie is a nice counterpoint to the crunch of the walnuts. They are better the second day.

Makes about 3½ dozen 2-inch cookies.

- 1½ **cups unsweetened cocoa powder**
- 2½ **cups all-purpose flour, preferably unbleached**
- 2 **cups walnuts (about 8 ounces) coarsely chopped**
- 1 **teaspoon baking soda**
- 1 **cup unsalted butter**
- 8 **ounces cream cheese, room temperature**
- 5 **large eggs**
- 2 **cups granulated sugar**
- 2 **teaspoons pure vanilla extract**

Preheat convection ovens to 325 degrees Fahrenheit or conventional ovens to 350 degrees Fahrenheit. Set the racks in the conventional oven so they divide the oven into thirds. You *will* need to line the cookie sheets with parchment paper for this recipe. If you are baking in a conventional oven, put one baking sheet inside another of the same size to make a double pan, or use insulated pans to protect the bottoms of the cookies.

In a small bowl, stir together the cocoa, flour, walnuts, and baking soda. Set aside.

With a mixer set on medium speed, beat the butter, cream cheese, eggs, sugar, and vanilla for 3 minutes, until fluffy and light in color. Scrape the bowl with a rubber spatula and add the dry ingredients. Beat on low until thoroughly combined, about 1 minute. Using a wooden spoon or rubber spatula, stir the mixture, scraping down to the bottom of the bowl, to be sure it is evenly mixed.

Drop the dough by heaping tablespoonfuls onto the prepared pans. Bake for 11 to 13 minutes, or until the cookie springs back when gently touched. Halfway through the baking time, reverse the sheets and switch them top to bottom. When the cookies are done, remove from the oven and cool on the baking sheets for 5 minutes. Slide the parchment, with the cookies still on it, off the sheets and onto racks to cool.

Store the completely cooled cookies in an airtight container for up to 5 days, or freeze for up to 2 months. (See freezing instructions on page 12.)

Rich Cocoa and Nut Cookies pair nicely with milk.

Chocolate Oatmeal Spice Cookies

If you shy away from dark chocolate because you feel it is too bitter, this cookie offers a chocolate taste that is sweeter and more like milk chocolate. The spices are mild and not overpowering. This is a homey, pleasant cookie that is soft-chewy. Try it with a mug of hot chocolate while you cuddle by the fireplace.

Makes about 4 dozen 1¾-inch cookies.

- 1½ **cups all-purpose flour, preferably unbleached**
- 1½ **cups quick-cooking rolled oats (uncooked)**
- ½ **cup unsweetened cocoa powder**
- 1 **teaspoon baking soda**
- ¼ **teaspoon baking powder**
- 2 **teaspoons ground cinnamon**
- ¼ **teaspoon ground cloves**
- ½ **cup unsalted butter**
- ¾ **cup brown sugar, firmly packed**
- ½ **cup granulated sugar**
- 2 **large eggs**
- 1½ **teaspoons pure vanilla extract**

Preheat convection ovens to 325 degrees Fahrenheit or conventional ovens to 350 degrees Fahrenheit. Set the racks in the conventional oven so they divide the oven into thirds. You will *not* need to line the cookie sheets with parchment paper for this recipe. If you are baking in a conventional oven, put one baking sheet inside another of the same size to make a double pan, or use insulated pans to protect the bottoms of the cookies.

In a medium-size bowl using a wire whisk, stir the flour, oats, cocoa, baking soda, baking powder, cinnamon, and cloves. Set aside.

With an electric mixer on medium speed, beat the butter, brown sugar, sugar, eggs, and vanilla until the mixture is fluffy and light in color, about 2 minutes. Scrape the bowl with a rubber spatula and add the dry ingredients, blending on low speed until the dough is evenly mixed, about 30 to 40 seconds. Using a wooden spoon or rubber spatula, stir the mixture, scraping down to the bottom of the bowl, to be sure it is evenly mixed.

Drop the dough by rounded teaspoonfuls onto the baking sheets and bake in the preheated oven for about 12 minutes, reversing the baking sheets and switching them top to bottom halfway through the baking time. The cookies will just start to feel firm. Do not overbake them. Cool the cookies for 5 minutes on the cookie sheets, and then carefully remove them to wire racks to finish cooling.

Store the completely cooled cookies in an airtight container for up to 4 days, or freeze for up to 2 months. (See freezing instructions on page 12.)

The flavors in Chocolate Oatmeal Spice Cookies are perfectly complemented by a glass of milk.

Chocolate Caramel Fantasies

A truly great flavor combination is that of chocolate, caramel, and nuts. This cookie has a dark chocolate batter with veins of rich caramel and pecans running through it. Because the caramel is not mixed into the dough and is marbled through it, you get the marvelous taste of caramel in every bite. If you don't like nuts, you can omit the pecans and use white chocolate chips instead. Either way, the cookies are outstanding.

Makes 3 dozen 2½-inch cookies.

2	ounces chopped semisweet chocolate
2	ounces unsweetened chocolate
24	vanilla caramels, unwrapped
2	tablespoons heavy cream
1	cup brown sugar, firmly packed
½	teaspoon baking soda
½	cup unsalted butter
2	large eggs
2	teaspoons pure vanilla extract
1	cup unsweetened cocoa powder
¼	cup milk
1½	cups all-purpose flour, preferably unbleached
1½	cups coarsely chopped pecans or good-quality white chocolate chips such as Ghirardelli

Preheat convection ovens to 310 degrees Fahrenheit or conventional ovens to 325 degrees Fahrenheit. Set the racks in the conventional oven so they divide the oven into thirds. Line the cookie sheets with parchment paper for this recipe. If you are baking in a conventional oven, put one baking sheet inside another of the same size to make a double pan, or use insulated pans to protect the bottoms of the cookies.

Melt the chocolate in a covered microwavable dish for 2 minutes in the microwave oven, or place in a heavy pan on the stove top over low heat, until the chocolate is almost melted. Remove from the heat and stir with a whisk until smooth. Let the chocolate cool for about 5 minutes.

Place the caramels and cream in a heavy saucepan over medium-low heat, stirring, until the caramels melt. Remove from the heat and continue stirring until smooth. The mixture should be thick. Let it cool slightly while you mix the dough.

Using an electric mixer on medium speed, combine the brown sugar and baking soda for 20 seconds. Add the butter, eggs, and vanilla and beat on medium speed for 2 minutes, until fluffy and light in color. Scrape the bowl with a rubber spatula and add the cocoa, beating on low speed for 20 minutes, just until it is blended in. Scrape the bowl again and add the chocolate and then the milk, beating on low speed for about 20 seconds after each addition. Again scrape the bowl and add the flour and pecans or chocolate chips. Mix on low speed just until the flour is blended in. Using a wooden spoon or rubber spatula, stir the mixture, scraping down to the bottom of the bowl, to be sure it is evenly mixed. Pour the melted caramels and cream onto the dough in the bowl and stir a few times with a wooden spoon. You do not want to mix the caramel into the dough, just swirl it through the dough.

Drop the dough by rounded tablespoonfuls onto the prepared baking sheets and bake in the preheated oven for 13 to 15 minutes, reversing the baking sheets and switching them top to bottom halfway through the baking time. The cookies will just start to feel firm to the touch. Do not overbake. Remove the pans from the oven and set on a wire rack to cool.

When completely cool, store in an airtight container for up to 1 week, or wrap tightly and freeze for up to 2 months. (See freezing instructions on page 12.)

Milk, chocolate or plain, is a compatible companion to Chocolate Caramel Fantasies.

The Best Bars in Town

When you're in the mood for something chewy and sweet but don't want a lot of fuss, bar cookies are just the ticket. No dropping or shaping of dough is required, and you only have to prepare one pan for baking. Bar cookies fill the spectrum from simple and homey to rich and elegant. Take them to a school bake sale, or offer them for dessert at a special dinner. This section contains two types of bar cookies: brownies, which are bars that are made with chocolate batter; and blondies, which in some cases contain chocolate chips, but are made with a light-brown batter.

Chewy "Chunky Bar" Brownies

Remember those wonderful, chubby Chunky Bars we all ate as kids? Dense and chewy, rich and filled with nuts, chocolate chunks, and raisins, this brownie appeals to the inner child in all of us.

Makes about 32 2¼ × 2½-inch bar cookies.

1   cup unsalted butter
10 ounces bittersweet chocolate, coarsely chopped
2   cups all-purpose flour, preferably unbleached
⅔   cup unsweetened cocoa powder
1   teaspoon baking soda
1   cup granulated sugar
1   cup brown sugar, firmly packed
4   large eggs
1   tablespoon pure vanilla extract
½   teaspoon salt
6   ounces coarsely chopped bittersweet chocolate
1   cup raisins, cut in half, *or* 1 cup dried currants
2   cups coarsely chopped *unsalted* roasted mixed nuts (no peanuts), about ½ pound

Place rack in the center and preheat a conventional oven to 350 degrees Fahrenheit. Line a 9 × 13-inch baking pan with foil.

Melt the butter and the chocolate together in a covered microwavable dish for 2 minutes in the microwave oven, or place in a heavy pan over low heat on the stove top, until the chocolate is almost melted. Remove the mixture from the heat and stir with a whisk until smooth. Let the chocolate mixture cool for about 5 minutes.

In a small bowl, stir together the flour, cocoa, and baking soda with a wire whisk. Set aside.

Put the sugars, eggs, vanilla, and salt into the mixer bowl, and beat on medium speed for about 2 minutes. The mixture will lighten in color and become thick and smooth. Scrape the bowl with a rubber spatula and add the melted chocolate mixture. Beat on medium speed about 1 minute, until evenly combined. Scrape the bowl with a rubber spatula and add the flour mixture. Beat on low about 30 seconds, or just until thoroughly combined. Scrape the bowl again and add the chocolate, raisins or currants, and the nuts. Beat on low just until combined. Using a wooden spoon or rubber spatula, stir the mixture, scraping down to the bottom of the bowl, to be sure it is evenly mixed.

Spread evenly into the prepared pan and bake for 30 to 35 minutes, reversing the baking sheets and switching them top to bottom halfway through the baking time. When done, the surface will feel slightly firm in the center. Remove from the oven and cool in the pan on a wire rack. Cut into bars when completely cooled.

Store the cooled bars in an airtight container for up to 4 days, or wrap tightly and freeze for up to 2 months. (See freezing instructions on page 12.)

Chewy "Chunky Bar" Brownies taste wonderful with hot coffee or cold milk.

White Chocolate and Almond Bars

Gooey-chewy and incredibly rich, a melted white-chocolate dough is enhanced by toasted almond chunks. This is an adult bar. No kids allowed.

Makes about 32 1 × 3¼-inch bar cookies.

1   **cup whole natural (skins on) almonds, about 4 ounces**
5⅓   **ounces (⅔ cup) unsalted butter**
10   **ounces white chocolate, coarsely chopped, or 10 ounces good-quality white chocolate chips, such as Ghirardelli**
2   **cups all-purpose flour, preferably unbleached**
¾   **teaspoon baking powder**
3   **large eggs**
½   **cup granulated sugar**
1¼   **cups brown sugar, firmly packed**
3   **tablespoons almond liqueur**

Frosting:

6   **ounces white chocolate, coarsely chopped**
2   **tablespoons unsalted butter**

Preheat a conventional oven to 350 degrees Fahrenheit. Line a 9 × 13-inch baking pan with foil.

Toast the almonds on a baking sheet in a single layer in the preheated oven for about 7 or 8 minutes. Remove the baking sheet from the oven and let the nuts cool. When they are cool, coarsely chop them, and set them aside.

Melt the butter and the chocolate together in a covered microwavable dish for 2 minutes in the microwave oven, or place in a heavy pan on the stove top over low heat, until the chocolate is almost melted. Remove the mixture from the heat and stir with a whisk until smooth. Let the chocolate mixture cool for about 5 minutes.

In a small bowl, stir together the flour and baking powder with a wire whisk. With a mixer on medium speed, beat the eggs, sugars, and liqueur for 2½ minutes until the mixture becomes light in color and thick. Scrape the bowl with a rubber spatula. Add the melted chocolate and butter and beat on low for 1 minute. Scrape the bowl again and add the flour mixture. Beat on low speed for about 30 seconds, just until thoroughly blended. Scrape the bowl again and add the chopped almonds, stirring to mix. Using a wooden spoon or rubber spatula, stir the mixture, scraping down to the bottom of the bowl, to be sure it is evenly mixed.

Scrape the dough into the prepared pan, smoothing the top with a rubber spatula. Bake in the preheated oven for about 30 minutes, reversing the baking pan halfway through the baking time. The bars are done when they are lightly browned. Remove from the oven and let cool in the pan on a wire rack.

Make the frosting. Melt the butter and the chocolate together in a covered microwavable dish for 1 minute in the microwave oven, or place in a heavy pan on the stove top over low heat, until the chocolate is almost melted. Remove the mixture from the heat and stir with a whisk until smooth. Let the chocolate mixture cool for about 5 minutes.

When completely cool, frost, and cut the bars.

Store the completely cooled bar cookies in an airtight container for up to 4 days, or wrap tightly and freeze for up to 2 months. (See freezing instructions on page 12.)

White Chocolate and Almond Bars pair well with liqueurs, coffee, or milk.

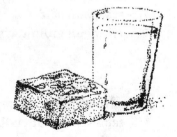

Hazelnut-Cinnamon Bars

The blend of spice and coffee flavors in this bar go nicely with the toasted hazelnuts. The texture is soft-chewy, with a little crunch from the nuts.

Makes 3 dozen 1 × 3¼-inch bars.

1½ cups hazelnuts (filberts)
2   tablespoons instant espresso powder *or* 3 tablespoons instant coffee powder
½   cup light cream
1½ cups all-purpose flour, preferably unbleached
½   teaspoon baking soda
1   teaspoon baking powder
¼   cup melted butter
½   cup brown sugar
½   cup granulated sugar
2   tablespoons corn syrup
¼   teaspoon salt
1   teaspoon ground cinnamon

Glaze:
¼   cup confectioners' sugar, stirred to eliminate lumps
1   tablespoon coffee-flavored liqueur
1   tablespoon unsalted butter, melted

Preheat a conventional oven to 325 degrees Fahrenheit. Line a 9 × 13-inch baking pan with foil and brush it with softened butter.

Toast the hazelnuts in the preheated oven for about 9 minutes or until the skins are cracked and the nuts start to brown slightly. Let the nuts cool for about 5 minutes and then rub them vigorously inside a kitchen towel with the palms of your hands, to remove most of the skins. Chop the skinned nuts fine and set aside.

In a glass measuring cup using the microwave oven, or in a small saucepan on the stove top, heat the espresso powder with the cream until completely dissolved. Remove from the heat and stir to mix.

In a small bowl with a wire whisk, stir together the flour, baking soda, and baking powder. Set aside.

Using an electric mixer on medium speed, beat the melted butter, brown sugar, sugar, and corn syrup until light colored and smooth. Scrape the bowl with a rubber spatula and add the espresso-cream mixture, the salt, and the cinnamon. Beat on medium speed just until evenly mixed. Scrape the bowl again and beat in the flour mixture and the finely chopped nuts on low speed, just until thoroughly blended, about 20 to 30 seconds. Using a wooden spoon or rubber spatula, stir the mixture, scraping down to the bottom of the bowl, to be sure it is evenly mixed.

Pour into the prepared pan and bake in the preheated oven for 25 to 30 minutes, turning the pan around halfway through the baking time so it will bake evenly.

While the bars are baking, make the glaze. Stir the confectioners' sugar with a wire whisk or a fork to remove any lumps and add the melted butter and liqueur. Stir with the whisk until smooth.

When the bars are done, remove them from the oven and let them cool in the pan for about 5 minutes. Then spread the glaze over the warm bars, using a rubber spatula. Let the bars cool completely in the pan before cutting.

Store the completely cooled bars in an airtight container for up to 6 days or freeze them, wrapped tightly, for up to 2 months. (See freezing instructions on page 12.)

Hazelnut-Cinnamon Bars are a perfect match for a cup of coffee or cappuccino and taste great with orange juice or milk.

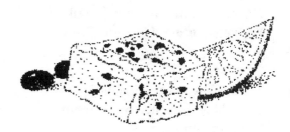

Rocky Roads

What list of bar cookie recipes would be complete without one for Rocky Roads? This is a popular cookie with both adults and children. They are chocolaty and delicious, with a soft, chewy texture enhanced by the crunch of the nuts.

Makes 2 dozen bars.

3   **ounces unsweetened chocolate, coarsely chopped**
¾   **cup unsalted butter**
1   **teaspoon pure vanilla extract**
1½   **cups granulated sugar**
¾   **teaspoon baking powder**
3   **large eggs**
1   **cup all-purpose flour, preferably unbleached**
1⅓   **cups miniature marshmallows**
1⅓   **cups unsalted peanuts (no skins)**

Frosting:
4   **ounces sweet chocolate**
2   **tablespoons heavy (whipping) cream**

Preheat a conventional oven to 325 degrees Fahrenheit. Line an 8 × 8-inch baking pan with foil and brush it with softened butter.

Melt the butter and the chocolate together in a covered microwavable dish for 2 minutes in the microwave oven, or place in a heavy pan on the stove top over low heat, until the chocolate is almost melted. Stir with a wire whisk until the mixture is smooth and all of the chocolate is melted. Add the vanilla and stir to blend thoroughly. Set aside.

Using an electric mixer on medium speed, blend the sugar and baking powder for about 20 seconds, or until evenly combined. Add the eggs and beat 2 minutes on medium speed. The mixture will be light yellow and thick. Add the chocolate mixture and beat on medium speed for 30 to 40 seconds, or until well blended. Scrape the bowl with a rubber spatula and add the flour, beating on low for 20 to 30 seconds, or until thoroughly mixed. Scrape the bowl again and add the marshmallows and nuts on low speed, blending for 15 to 20 seconds. Using a wooden spoon or rubber spatula, stir the mixture, scraping down to the bottom of the bowl, to be sure it is evenly mixed.

Pour into the prepared pan, and spread the dough evenly with a rubber spatula. Bake in the preheated oven for 25 minutes, reversing the baking pan halfway through the baking time. The crust will be dull and cracked. Cool in the pan.

Make the frosting while the bars are cooling. Melt the cream and the chocolate together in a covered microwavable dish for 2 minutes in the microwave oven, or place in a heavy pan on the stove top over low heat, until the chocolate is almost melted. Stir with a wire whisk until the mixture is smooth and all of the chocolate is melted. Set aside to cool. When completely cool, frost and cut into bars.

Store the completely cooled bars in an airtight container for up to 5 days, or wrap tightly and freeze for up to 2 months. (See freezing instructions on page 12.)

Rocky Roads are a natural companion to a cold glass of milk.

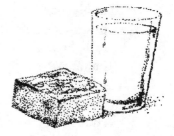

Chocolate-Chip Oatmeal Bars

As bars go, these are sweet, chewy, and chocolaty. They get their chewy texture from the oats. (You can vary the chewiness by using quick or old-fashioned oats. The old-fashioned oats will give you a chewier texture.) This is a great weeknight dinner-at-home treat, or a nice surprise in a lunch box.

Makes 16 1¾ × 2¾-inch bars.

- ¾   **cup brown sugar, firmly packed**
- 2   **teaspoons baking powder**
- ¼   **teaspoon salt**
- ½   **cup unsalted butter**
- 2   **large eggs**
- ½   **cup milk**
- 2   **teaspoons pure vanilla extract**
- 1   **cup all-purpose flour, preferably unbleached**
- 1½ **cups quick or old-fashioned rolled oats, uncooked (not instant)**
- 9   **ounces real semisweet chocolate chips, or chopped semisweet chocolate**
- 1   **cup coarsely chopped walnuts (optional)**

Preheat a conventional oven to 350 degrees Fahrenheit. Line a 7 × 11-inch baking pan with foil and brush it with softened butter.

Using a mixer on medium speed, beat the brown sugar, baking powder, and salt for 20 seconds to combine. Add the butter and beat on medium speed for 2 minutes. The mixture will be light in color and fluffy. Add the eggs, milk, and vanilla and beat on low speed for 20 seconds to combine, then increase speed to medium and beat for 2 minutes. The mixture should be smooth. Beat in the flour and oats on low speed for 20 to 30 seconds, until blended, then stir in the chocolate and walnuts. Using a wooden spoon or rubber spatula, stir the mixture, scraping down to the bottom of the bowl, to be sure it is evenly mixed.

Spread evenly in the prepared pan and bake in the preheated oven for 25 minutes, reversing the baking pan halfway through the baking time. The surface will be slightly firm to the touch and light brown. Remove from the oven and cool on a wire rack. Cut into bars when cool.

Store the cooled bars in an airtight container for up to 1 week, or wrap tightly and freeze for up to 2 months. (See freezing instructions on page 12.)

Chocolate-Chip Oatmeal Bars are a sweet welcome-home treat after school, served with milk or hot chocolate.

Maple Walnut Bars

The familiar, pleasant flavor of pure maple syrup adds a homespun touch to these bars. Freeze them, wrapped individually, to have on hand for take-along snacks or brown-bag desserts. They are dense-chewy and delicious.

Makes 16 1¾ × 2¾-inch bars.

- ¾ **cup brown sugar, firmly packed**
- ½ **teaspoon baking powder**
- ½ **teaspoon ground nutmeg**
- ½ **cup unsalted butter, melted**
- 3 **large egg yolks**
- 1 **teaspoon pure vanilla extract**
- ½ **cup pure maple syrup**
- 1½ **cups all-purpose flour, preferably unbleached**
- 1 **cup chopped walnuts**

Preheat a conventional oven to 350 degrees Fahrenheit. Line a 7 × 11-inch baking pan with foil and brush it with softened butter.

Using an electric mixer on medium speed, blend the brown sugar, baking powder, and nutmeg for 20 seconds. Add the melted butter and yolks and beat on medium speed for 2 minutes, until the mixture is smooth. Scrape the bowl with a rubber spatula and add the vanilla and maple syrup and beat on medium speed for 20 seconds. Add the flour and nuts all at once and beat on low speed for 30 seconds until blended. Scrape the bottom and sides of the bowl with a rubber spatula to be sure the dough is mixed evenly.

Scrape the dough into the prepared pan, using the rubber spatula to smooth the surface. Bake in the preheated oven for 30 to 35 minutes, reversing the baking pan halfway through the baking time. The surface will feel just firm to the touch. Remove from the oven and set on a wire rack. Cut into bars when completely cool.

Store the cooled bars in an airtight container for up to 6 days, or wrap tightly and freeze for up to 2 months. (See freezing instructions on page 12.)

Serve Maple Walnut Bars with milk or juice for an enjoyable afternoon snack.

Oatmeal Brickle Bars

To satisfy an intense sweet tooth, try one of these bars. It is dense and chewy with a crunch from the brickle chips. Lest you feel guilty, they have the healthful addition of raisins and oats.

Makes 32 1½ × 2¼-bars.

- 1¼ **cup brown sugar, firmly packed**
- ¾ **cup granulated sugar**
- ½ **teaspoon baking powder**
- ½ **teaspoon baking soda**
- ¾ **cup unsalted butter**
- 2 **large eggs**
- 1 **teaspoon pure vanilla extract**
- 2 **tablespoons milk**
- 1½ **cups all-purpose flour, preferably unbleached**
- 3 **cups old-fashioned or quick rolled oats, uncooked (not instant)**
- 2 **cups golden raisins**
- 2 **packages (6 ounces each) almond brickle chips**

Preheat a conventional oven to 350 degrees Fahrenheit. Line a 9 × 13-inch baking pan with foil and brush it with softened butter.

Using a mixer on medium speed, blend the brown sugar, sugar, baking powder, and soda for 20 seconds. Add the butter and beat on medium speed for 2 minutes, until fluffy and light in color. Add the eggs, vanilla, and milk and beat on medium speed for 2 minutes, until smooth. Scrape the bowl with a rubber spatula and add the flour, oats, raisins, and brickle chips, beating on low speed for 30 to 40 seconds, until evenly blended. Scrape the bottom and sides of the bowl with a rubber spatula to be sure the dough is mixed evenly.

Scrape the dough into the prepared pan and smooth with the rubber spatula. Bake in the preheated oven for 30 minutes, reversing the baking pan halfway through the baking time. The top will be lightly brown and feel just firm to the touch.

Remove from the oven and set on a wire rack to cool. Cut into bars when cool.

Store the bars in an airtight container for up to 1 week, or wrap tightly and freeze for up to 2 months. (See freezing instructions on page 12.)

Oatmeal Brickle Bars are a great midnight snack with milk.

Chocolate Fudgies

Reminiscent of a flourless torte, these bars have a light, chewy texture with a deep chocolate flavor. If you prefer, you can replace the walnuts with toasted hazelnuts. Either way, they won't last long.

Makes 32 1 × 3¼-inch bars.

4   ounces chopped unsweetened
        chocolate
4   large egg whites
2   cups confectioners' sugar,
        stirred with a fork to
        eliminate lumps
1   tablespoon pure vanilla extract
1⅓ cups finely ground walnuts, or
        ground toasted hazelnuts
        (filberts)

Preheat a conventional oven to 350 degrees Fahrenheit. Line a 9 × 13-inch baking pan with foil and brush it with softened butter.

Melt the chocolate in a covered microwavable dish for 2 minutes in the microwave oven, or place in a heavy pan on the stove top over low heat, until the chocolate is almost melted. Stir with a wire whisk until smooth and all of the chocolate is melted. Stir to blend thoroughly. Set aside to cool.

Using an electric mixer on medium speed with a wire whisk attachment if available, beat the egg whites until soft peaks form. Add the confectioners' sugar slowly, continuing to beat on medium speed, until the whites are stiff. The whites will hold a peak when you remove the beater. Beat in the vanilla. With a rubber spatula or wire whisk gently fold in the melted chocolate and ⅔ cup of the walnuts, being careful not to stir hard, or the egg whites will become deflated. Spread into the prepared pan and sprinkle the remaining walnuts over the top.

Bake in the preheated oven about 20 minutes, reversing the baking pan halfway through the baking time. Bars will be just firm. Remove the pan from the oven and set it on a wire rack to cool. Cut into bars.

Store the cooled bars in an airtight container for up to 3 days, or wrap tightly and freeze for up to 2 months. (See freezing instructions on page 12.)

Nothing goes better with Chocolate Fudgies than a tall glass of cold milk, but you might want to serve this special bar with coffee for an after-dinner dessert.

Black-and-White Brownies

Dense, chewy, and intensely delicious, this will be a recipe you will make again and again. The classic combination of dark and white chocolate is rich and satisfying. The clean chocolate flavors in the frosting are a refreshing change from the usual sugary types. Two different chocolates are swirled together over the brownie to create a beautiful bar, indeed.

Makes 20 1¾ × 2¼-inch bars.

5	ounces unsweetened chocolate, chopped
⅔	cup unsalted butter
1½	teaspoons pure vanilla extract
1½	cups granulated sugar
2	large eggs
1	large egg yolk
¼	teaspoon salt
⅔	cup all-purpose flour, preferably unbleached
9	ounces good-quality white chocolate chips, such as Ghirardelli, or 9 ounces of white chocolate, chopped

Frosting:

3	ounces semisweet or bittersweet chocolate
3	ounces white chocolate, chopped, or good-quality white chocolate chips
2	tablespoons heavy cream, divided

Preheat a conventional oven to 350 degrees Fahrenheit. Line a 9 × 9-inch or a 7 × 11-inch baking pan with foil and brush it with softened butter.

In a heavy saucepan over medium heat, melt together the unsweetened chocolate and the butter, stirring constantly. Remove from the heat and add the vanilla and sugar, stirring with a wooden spoon to blend well. Alternatively, melt the unsweetened chocolate and the butter in a microwave oven for 2 or 3 minutes in a 6- or 8-cup glass measure. Add the eggs, 1 at a time, stirring with the spoon after each egg is added, until the mixture is well blended. Add the yolk and salt and stir again until blended evenly. Then stir in the flour and chips, being sure the flour is mixed in thoroughly. Scrape the bottom and sides of the bowl with a rubber spatula or wooden spoon to be sure the dough is mixed evenly.

Pour the batter into the prepared pan and smooth with the wooden spoon. Bake in the preheated oven for 30 to 35 minutes, reversing the baking pan halfway through the baking time. The top should appear dull. Remove the pan from the oven and set on a wire rack to cool.

Meanwhile, make the frosting. Melt each of the chocolates separately in covered microwavable dishes for 2 minutes in the microwave oven, or place in heavy pans on the stove top over low heat, until the chocolate is almost melted. Stir with a wire whisk until smooth and all of the chocolate is melted. Add 1 tablespoon of heavy cream to each chocolate and stir with a wire whisk until smooth. Pour the two frostings on the brownies, forming alternating stripes, 2 stripes of each chocolate. Using a butter knife or the edge of a rubber spatula, swirl through the chocolate frostings to form an attractive design. Let the brownies cool completely before cutting into bars.

Store the cooled bars in an airtight container with wax paper between layers for up to 6 days, or wrap tightly and freeze for up to 2 months. (See freezing instructions on page 12.)

Black-and-White Brownies are definitely a milk treat.

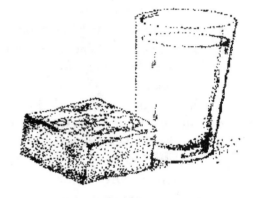

Chocolate Coconut Chews

One of nature's perfect marriages is coconut and dark chocolate. Rich, sweet without being too sweet, it is a mouth-watering combination, enhanced here by the dense chewiness of the texture. This bar cookie gives you a one-two punch of dark chocolate taste with a sweet, chewy ending of coconut. Offer these as a rich finale to a simple dinner.

Makes 3 dozen 1 × 2-inch bars

1   cup all-purpose flour, preferably unbleached
1½ cups unsweetened cocoa powder
2   cups sweetened flaked coconut, about 10 ounces, firmly packed
3   large eggs
6   ounces (¾ cup) unsalted butter
2   cups granulated sugar
⅛   teaspoon salt
2   teaspoons pure vanilla extract *or* pure almond extract

Preheat a conventional oven to 350 degrees Fahrenheit. Line a 9 × 13-inch baking pan with foil.

In a medium-size bowl stir together the flour, cocoa, and coconut until evenly combined. With a mixer on medium speed, beat together the eggs, butter, sugar, salt, and vanilla or almond extract for 3 minutes, until the mixture is light colored and fluffy. It may look curdled, but that is all right. Scrape the bowl and add the cocoa mixture. Beat at medium speed just until thoroughly combined, about 30 seconds. Using a wooden spoon or rubber spatula, stir the mixture, scraping down to the bottom of the bowl, to be sure it is evenly mixed.

Spread the mixture into the prepared pan and bake in a preheated oven for about 30 minutes, just until the surface of the cake feels firm at the center of the pan. Reverse the baking pan halfway through the baking time. Remove the pan from the oven and cool the pan on a wire rack. When completely cool, cut into bars.

Store the cooled bars in an airtight container for up to 5 days, or wrap tightly and freeze for up to 2 months. (See freezing instructions on page 12.)

Chocolate Coconut Chews are delicious when served with coffee or milk and are perfectly complemented by good-quality vanilla ice cream.

Chocolate Honey Nut Chews

When you crave chocolate but don't want something too sweet, these little bars will do the trick. The honey supplies a chewy moistness that is tantalizing, contrasting enjoyably with the crunchiness of the nuts. The honey also extends the keeping quality of the bars.

Makes 32 1 × 3¼-inch bars.

- ½ **cup unsalted butter**
- ½ **cup mild-flavored honey such as orange blossom**
- 2 **ounces unsweetened chocolate**
- ¾ **cup firmly packed brown sugar**
- 1 **cup all-purpose flour, preferably unbleached**
- ½ **teaspoon baking soda**
- 2 **cups coarsely chopped walnuts**
- 2 **large eggs**

Melt the butter, honey, chocolate, and brown sugar in a medium-size covered microwavable dish for 2 minutes in the microwave oven, or place in a medium size heavy pan on the stove top over low heat, until the chocolate is almost melted. Stir with a wire whisk until smooth and all of the chocolate is melted. Set aside to cool for 10 minutes.

Preheat a conventional oven to 350 degrees Fahrenheit. Line a 9 × 13-inch baking pan with foil and brush it with softened butter.

In a small bowl, stir the flour, baking soda, and walnuts with a fork. Set aside.

Add the eggs to the melted chocolate mixture and stir briskly with a wooden spoon until well mixed. Add the flour, baking soda, and nuts and stir again until the flour is blended in completely. Scrape the bottom and sides of the bowl with a rubber spatula or wooden spoon to be sure the dough is mixed evenly.

Spread the batter into the prepared pan and bake in the preheated oven for 25 to 30 minutes reversing the baking pan halfway through the baking time. The bar will just begin to feel firm when touched lightly with your fingertip. Remove the pan from the oven and set on a wire rack to cool. When cool, lift from the pan with the foil, carefully remove the foil, and cut into bars.

Store the cooled bars in an airtight container for up to 5 days or wrap tightly and freeze for up to 2 months. (See freezing instructions on page 12.)

Chocolate Honey Nut Chews and a warm cup of tea are a pleasant afternoon treat.

Bittersweet Double-Mocha Walnut Brownies

If wake-up calls in hotels were this chocolaty and gratifying, we would request them even if we didn't need to get up. Dense and dark with chocolate flavored with coffee, and laced with coffee flavored chocolate, such as Lindt Moccao, these bars are real eye-openers. They are perfect afternoon pick-me-ups, but don't eat them just before bedtime.

Makes 32 1 × 3¼-inch bars.

3	ounces unsweetened chocolate
¾	cup unsalted butter
1½	cups all-purpose flour, preferably unbleached
½	cup unsweetened cocoa
1	cup brown sugar, firmly packed
½	cup granulated sugar
¼	teaspoon salt
1	teaspoon baking soda
3	tablespoons instant espresso powder
2	large eggs
1	tablespoon pure vanilla extract
⅓	cup sour cream
½	cup coffee flavored chocolate chunks
1	cup coarsely chopped walnuts
6	ounces semisweet chocolate chunks or real chocolate chips

Preheat a conventional oven to 350 degrees Fahrenheit. Line a 9 × 13-inch baking pan with foil and brush it with softened butter.

Melt the chocolate and butter in a covered microwavable dish for 2 minutes in the microwave oven, or place in a heavy pan on the stove top over low heat, until the chocolate is almost melted. Stir with a wire whisk until smooth and all of the chocolate is melted. Set aside to cool.

In a medium bowl stir the flour and cocoa with a wire whisk until evenly blended. Set aside.

Using an electric mixer on medium speed, mix the brown sugar, sugar, salt, baking soda, and espresso powder for about 20 seconds, until evenly combined. Add the eggs and vanilla and beat for about 2 minutes, until the mixture is light in color and smooth. With the mixer running on low speed, add the melted chocolate mixture, beating for about 45 seconds, until blended in. Scrape the bowl with a rubber spatula and add half of the flour and cocoa mixture. Beat on low speed for about 20 seconds, scrape the bowl and add the sour cream. Beat again on low speed for 20 seconds, and scrape the bowl. Add the remaining flour and cocoa, the espresso beans, the walnuts, and the chocolate and beat on low speed just until all are blended in. Scrape the bottom and sides of the bowl with a rubber spatula or wooden spoon to be sure the dough is mixed evenly.

Scrape the dough into the prepared pan, using the rubber spatula to smooth the surface. Bake in the preheated oven for 30 to 35 minutes, reversing the baking pan halfway through the baking time. A toothpick inserted in the center of the pan will come out clean. The bars will firm up as they cool, so do not overbake them. Remove the pan

from the oven and set on a wire rack to cool. When completely cool, cut into bars.

Store the cooled bars in an airtight container for up to 4 days, or wrap tightly and freeze for up to 2 months. (See freezing instructions on page 12.)

While they are great with milk, Bittersweet Double-Mocha Walnut Brownies are extraordinary with a cup of hot coffee.

Butterscotch Bars

This is the type of bar that gave birth to the term *blondies*. It is dense and chewy with a delightful crunch of nuts and a spattering of chocolate chips. An unpretentious bar with a buttery rich brown-sugar flavor, it may be unsophisticated, but it's sincere.

Makes 20 2¼ × 2½-inch bars.

1¾ cups brown sugar, firmly packed
1½ teaspoons baking soda
½   cup unsalted butter
3   large eggs
2   teaspoons pure vanilla extract
1½ cups all-purpose flour, preferably unbleached
2   cups coarsely chopped walnuts
2   ounces real semisweet chocolate chips

Preheat a conventional oven to 350 degrees Fahrenheit. Line a 9 × 13-inch baking pan with foil and brush it with softened butter.

Using an electric mixer on medium speed, mix the brown sugar and baking soda for about 20 seconds, until evenly combined. Add the butter, eggs, and vanilla and beat for about 2 minutes, until the mixture is light in color and smooth. Scrape the bowl with a rubber spatula and add the flour, walnuts, and chips. Beat on low speed for 20 seconds, until the mixture is evenly blended. Scrape the bottom and sides of the bowl with a rubber spatula or wooden spoon to be sure the dough is evenly mixed.

Spread into the prepared pan and bake in the preheated oven for 20 to 25 minutes, reversing the baking pan halfway through the baking time. The top will be lightly browned. Remove the pan from the oven and set it on a wire rack to cool.

When completely cool, cut into bars and store in an airtight container for up to 6 days. Or, you can freeze the bars, wrapped tightly, for up to 2 months. (See freezing instructions on page 12.)

A tall glass of milk and Butterscotch Bars are a delight.

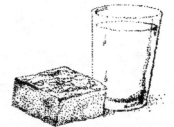

Chocolate Chocolate-Chunk Banana Bars

If you like chocolate banana sundaes, this is the bar for you. A moist, dark chocolate batter enriched with pureed banana is filled with chocolate chunks and walnuts. It is dense and chewy with the pleasant crunch of walnuts. Dust with confectioners' sugar for a pretty contrast.

Makes 32 2¼ × 1½-inch bars.

1	cup granulated sugar
1	teaspoon baking powder
½	teaspoon baking soda
⅓	cup flavorless vegetable oil
2	large eggs
¾	cup unsweetened cocoa powder
1	cup mashed ripe banana (1 large and 1 medium banana)
1	cup all-purpose flour, preferably unbleached
9	ounces chopped semisweet chocolate or real semisweet chocolate chips
1½	cups coarsely chopped walnuts confectioners' sugar for dusting

Preheat a conventional oven to 350 degrees Fahrenheit. Line a 9 × 13-inch baking pan with foil and brush it with softened butter.

Using an electric mixer on medium speed, mix the sugar, baking powder, and baking soda for about 20 seconds, until evenly combined. Add the oil and eggs and beat for about 2 minutes, until the mixture is light in color and smooth. Scrape the bowl with a rubber spatula and add the cocoa, mixing on low speed for 30 seconds. Scrape the bowl again and add the banana, beating on low speed for about 20 seconds. Add the flour, walnuts, and chocolate. Beat on low speed for 30 seconds, until the mixture is evenly blended. Scrape the bottom and sides of the bowl with a rubber spatula or wooden spoon, stirring to be sure the dough is evenly mixed.

Spread into the prepared pan and bake in the preheated oven for 25 to 30 minutes, reversing the baking pan halfway through the baking time. The top will feel firm when lightly touched with your fingertip. Remove the pan from the oven and set it on a wire rack to cool.

When completely cool, cut into bars, and store in an airtight container for up to 4 days. Or, you can freeze the bars, wrapped tightly, for up to 2 months. (See freezing instructions on page 12.)

Coffee or milk are great pairings for Chocolate Chocolate-Chunk Banana Bars.

Layered Bars

There are many layered bar cookies that are easy to make, chewy, and delicious. Some contain fruit or jam, some chocolate, and some a myriad of other ingredients. They can be made quickly and do not require shaping or dropping the dough. Because of the layers, they look like they take longer to make than they actually do. Layered bars are nice additions to a potluck dinner or special luncheon. When you are making them, make two pans at once and freeze one pan so you will have a delicious treat to take when someone else is doing the cooking.

Lemon-Filled Chews

Lemon is one of my favorite flavors, and I couldn't pass up including a lemon version of layer bars. Ground almonds in the crust offer a chewy texture and add to the overall appeal of this bar. The lemon filling creates a soft, gooey center that contrasts nicely with the chewiness of the crust.

Makes 32 2¼ × 1½-inch bars.

Crust:

½ cup unsalted butter
⅔ cup granulated sugar
1 cup all-purpose flour, preferably unbleached
1¼ cups quick-cooking rolled oats, uncooked (not instant)
½ cup finely ground almonds
1 tablespoon freshly grated lemon zest

Filling:

¼ cup water
2 large eggs
2 large egg yolks
½ cup granulated sugar
⅓ cup strained fresh lemon juice
1 tablespoon freshly grated lemon zest
4 tablespoons unsalted butter

Topping:

½ cup sliced raw almonds (skins on)

Preheat a conventional oven to 350 degrees Fahrenheit. Line a 9 × 13-inch baking pan with foil and brush it with softened butter.

Using an electric mixer on medium speed, beat together the ½ cup butter and ⅔ cup sugar for about 2 minutes, until light in color and fluffy. Add the flour and oats, mixing on low speed until evenly blended. Scrape the bowl with a rubber spatula and add the ground almonds and 1 tablespoon zest, beating on low speed for about 20 seconds. Measure 1 cup of this mixture and set it aside for the topping. Pat the rest of the mixture evenly in the bottom of the prepared pan.

Make the filling. In a heavy medium-size saucepan over medium-low heat, combine the water, eggs, egg yolks, ½ cup sugar, lemon juice, and 1 tablespoon zest, beating lightly to break up the eggs. Cook, stirring constantly so the eggs do not curdle, for about 5 to 7 minutes, until the filling is thick. Remove the pan from the heat. Add the butter, stirring until it is completely melted. Pour the hot filling over the crust in the pan.

Combine the sliced almonds with the reserved crumb mixture and sprinkle it evenly over the lemon filling. Gently pat it down.

Bake in the preheated oven for about 20 minutes, reversing the pan halfway through. The top will start to brown lightly. Remove the pan from the oven and set it on a wire rack to cool. When completely cool, cut into bars.

Store the cooled bars in an airtight container with wax paper between the layers, in the refrigerator for up to 1 week, or wrap tightly and freeze for up to 2 months. (See freezing instructions on page 12.)

Lemon-Filled Chews are a wonderful partner for hot tea.

Chocolate Oat Bars

This is a chewy, sweet, chocolaty bar that is rich and scrumptious. Use good-quality chocolate and you will be rewarded with an outstanding taste treat.

Makes 2 dozen 1½ × 3¼-inch bars

Filling:

12	ounces chopped semisweet chocolate
1	cup heavy (whipping) cream
2	tablespoons unsalted butter
⅓	cup granulated sugar
1	cup chopped walnuts (optional)
½	teaspoon pure vanilla extract (optional)

Crust and Crumb Topping:

1½	cups brown sugar, firmly packed
1	teaspoon baking soda
1	cup unsalted butter
1	teaspoon pure vanilla extract
2	cups all-purpose unbleached flour
3	cups quick-cooking rolled oats, uncooked (not instant)

Preheat a conventional oven to 350 degrees Fahrenheit. Line a 9 × 13-inch baking pan with foil and brush it with softened butter.

In a large, heavy saucepan, combine the chocolate, cream, the 2 tablespoons butter, and the sugar over medium heat, stirring constantly, until the chocolate melts and the mixture is smooth. Bring the mixture to a boil, immediately remove from the heat, and stir in the vanilla and nuts, if you are using them.

Using an electric mixer on medium speed, blend the brown sugar and baking soda for 20 seconds. Add the 1 cup butter and beat on medium speed for 2 minutes, until light in color and fluffy. Blend in the vanilla on low speed for 15 seconds. Add the flour and oats and beat on low speed for 20 to 30 seconds, until the mixture is evenly blended. It will be crumbly. Measure 3 cups of crumbs and set aside in a cool place. Pat the remaining crumb mixture firmly into the prepared pan to make a smooth, even crust. Pour the filling over the crust in the pan, and spread with a rubber spatula. Sprinkle the reserved crumb mixture over the filling as evenly as possible.

Bake in the preheated oven for 25 to 30 minutes, reversing the pan halfway through the cooking time. The bars will be nicely browned. Remove from the oven and set on a wire rack to cool. When completely cool, cut into bars.

Store the cooled bars in an airtight container with wax paper between the layers for up to 6 days, or wrap tightly and freeze for up to 2 months. (See freezing instructions on page 12.)

Chocolate Oat Bars are a delicious after-school treat served with milk.

White Chocolate-Chip Coconut Cheese Bars

Easy and delicious, this bar is an interesting alternative to cheesecake. It is a creamy, chewy combination of ingredients that will enrapture your guests at a dinner party. This bar freezes well, so make two pans and freeze one for a special occasion.

Makes 2 dozen 1½ × 3¼-inch bars.

Crust:

1½ cups chocolate wafer crumbs
2   tablespoons granulated sugar
⅓   cup unsalted butter, melted

Filling:

8   ounces cream cheese, softened
1   large egg
1   teaspoon pure vanilla extract
½   cup granulated sugar
¼   cup unsweetened cocoa powder
⅔   cup sweetened coconut, flaked or shredded, lightly packed

Topping:

6   ounces good-quality chocolate chips, such as Ghirardelli
1   cup chopped walnuts

Preheat a conventional oven to 350 degrees Fahrenheit. Line a 9 × 13-inch baking pan with foil and brush it with softened butter.

Using an electric mixer on low speed, combine the crust mixture for 1 minute. Pat into the prepared pan and bake in the preheated oven for 7 or 8 minutes. Remove from the oven and set aside on a wire rack. Do not turn the oven off.

Combine the cream cheese, the egg, and the vanilla in a mixer and beat on medium speed for 3 minutes. The mixture should be smooth. Add the sugar and beat on medium speed for 1 minute, until thoroughly blended. Add the cocoa and beat on low for 30 seconds, until evenly combined, and stir in the coconut, using a rubber spatula and scraping the sides and bottom of the bowl to be sure the filling is completely mixed.

Pour the filling over the baked crust and smooth with a rubber spatula. Sprinkle the chopped nuts and white chocolate chips over the filling and bake in the oven for about 30 minutes, reversing the pan halfway through. The bars will be lightly browned. Remove from the oven and set on a wire rack to cool. Do not cut until completely cool.

Store the bars in an airtight container with wax paper between layers in the refrigerator for up to 1 week, or freeze, wrapped tightly, for up to 2 months. (See freezing instructions on page 12.)

Enchant your dinner guests by serving White Chocolate-Chip Coconut Cream Cheese Bars with espresso or strong coffee.

Chocolate Caramel Macadamia Bars

A buttery shortbread crust and a chewy, gooey caramel topping merge to become a taste delight. If you prefer, use pecans instead of macadamias for a classic flavor combination.

Makes 20 1¾ × 2¼-inch bars.

Crust:

⅓   cup unsalted butter
3½ tablespoons granulated sugar
1   large egg white
1   tablespoon cornstarch
1   cup all-purpose flour, preferably
      unbleached
9   ounces real semisweet chocolate
      chips

Topping:

½   cup unsalted butter
½   cup brown sugar, firmly packed
⅓   cup pure maple syrup
2   cups chopped macadamias or
      other nuts
2   tablespoons heavy cream

Preheat a conventional oven to 350 degrees Fahrenheit. Line a 9 × 9-inch pan or an 11 × 7-inch baking pan with foil and brush it with softened butter.

Using an electric mixer on medium speed, beat together the butter and sugar for about 2 minutes, until light in color and fluffy. Add the egg white and beat again on medium speed for about 1 minute. The mixture will be fluffy and smooth. Scrape the bowl with a rubber spatula and add the cornstarch, beating on low speed for about 20 seconds, until blended in. Then add the flour and mix on low speed just until it is blended in. Scrape the bottom and sides of the bowl with a rubber spatula to be sure the dough is mixed evenly, and then scrape the dough into the prepared pan and smooth with the rubber spatula, forming a ½-inch rim at the edges of the pan.

Bake about 15 to 20 minutes reversing the pan halfway through. The dough will be light brown. Remove the pan from the oven and sprinkle the chips evenly over the hot crust.

Set the crust aside and make the topping. Combine the butter, sugar, and maple syrup in a small heavy saucepan over medium-high heat. Bring the mixture to a boil and boil 1 minute. Stir in the nuts. Turn off the heat and stir in the cream. The chocolate chips will have melted while you made the topping. Spread the chips over the dough and pour the topping over the crust.

Return to the hot oven for about 15 to 20 minutes. The topping will be bubbly when done. Remove the pan from the oven and set it on a wire rack to cool. When cool, cut into bars.

Store the cooled bars in an airtight container for up to 6 days, or wrap tightly and freeze for up to 2 months. (See freezing instructions on page 12.)

Chocolate Caramel Macadamia Bars are a wonderful midnight snack with warm milk.

Caramel Apple Bars

When I first started writing this book, my eight-year-old son, Benjamin, came up with the idea of making a cookie that tasted like a caramel apple. This is the result of that endeavor. Chewy with grated apples and coated with caramel and peanuts, it is delicious. I have to say Ben was right. Use a firm, tart apple like a Granny Smith that won't get mushy.

Makes 32 2¼ × 1½-inch bars.

- ¾ **cup brown sugar, firmly packed**
- ½ **teaspoon baking soda**
- 1½ **teaspoons ground cinnamon**
- ⅔ **cup unsalted butter**
- 2 **teaspoons pure vanilla extract**
- 1½ **cups all-purpose flour, preferably unbleached**
- 1¾ **cups quick-cooking rolled oats, uncooked (not instant)**
- 1½ **cups grated peeled apples**
- ½ **cup caramel ice-cream topping**
- ¾ **cup chopped roasted peanuts (skins off)**

Preheat a conventional oven to 350 degrees Fahrenheit. Line a 9 × 13-inch baking pan with foil and brush it with softened butter.

Using an electric mixer on medium speed, beat together the brown sugar, baking soda, and cinnamon. Add the butter and vanilla and beat on medium speed for 2 minutes, until smooth and light in color. Scrape the bowl with a rubber spatula and add the flour and oats, mixing on low speed for about 30 seconds to blend evenly. The mixture will be crumbly. Measure 1½ cups of the mixture and set it aside for the topping. Pat the remaining crumb mixture evenly into the prepared pan to form the bottom crust. Sprinkle the grated apples over the crust and then spread the reserved crumb mixture over the apples. Drizzle the caramel topping over the crumbs and sprinkle the peanuts on the top.

Bake in the preheated oven for 25 minutes, reversing the pan halfway through. The top will be lightly browned when done. Remove the pan from the oven and set it on a wire rack to cool. When completely cool, cut into bars.

Store the cooled bars in an airtight container for up to 5 days, or wrap tightly and freeze for up to 2 months. (See freezing instructions on page 12.)

Apple cider is a wonderful accompaniment to Caramel Apple Bars.

Caramel Nut Bars

A fantasy of chocolate, caramel, and nuts awaits you with this scrumptious bar. The base is a rich and chewy chocolate brownie, coated with caramel and pecans and drizzled with a white-chocolate glaze. Try substituting other nuts for the pecans as a variation, or using dark chocolate for the glaze.

Makes 32 2¼ × 1½-inch bars.

- ¾ cup unsalted butter
- 1½ cups granulated sugar
- 1½ teaspoons pure vanilla extract
- 3 large eggs
- ¾ cup unsweetened cocoa powder
- 1 cup all-purpose flour, preferably unbleached
- 1 cup coarsely chopped pecans

Topping:
- 30 vanilla caramels, unwrapped
- ⅓ cup heavy (whipping) cream

Glaze:
- 3 ounces good-quality white chocolate, coarsely chopped
- 1 tablespoon heavy cream

Preheat a conventional oven to 350 degrees Fahrenheit. Line a 9 × 13-inch baking pan with foil and brush it with softened butter.

Using an electric mixer on medium speed, beat together the butter, sugar, vanilla, and eggs for 2 minutes. The mixture will be light in color and fluffy. Scrape the bowl with a rubber spatula and add the cocoa, beating on low speed for 30 seconds. Scrape the bowl again and add the flour on low speed, mixing for about 20 seconds, just until it is evenly combined. Spread the batter into the prepared pan and smooth the top. Sprinkle the pecans evenly over the batter.

In a heavy saucepan over medium heat melt the caramels with ⅓ cup heavy cream, stirring constantly. Stir until smooth and pour over the pecans on the crust.

Bake in the preheated oven for 25 minutes, reversing the pan halfway through. Remove the pan from the oven and set on a wire rack to cool.

While it is cooling, make the glaze. Melt the chocolate and 1 tablespoon cream together in a covered microwavable dish for 2 minutes in the microwave oven, or place in a heavy pan on the stove top over low heat, until the chocolate is almost melted. Remove the mixture from the heat and stir with a whisk until smooth. Let the chocolate mixture cool for about 5 minutes, and drizzle it over the partially cooled bars. When completely cool, cut into bars.

Store the cooled bars in an airtight container with wax paper between the layers for up to 5 days, or wrap tightly and freeze for up to 2 months. (See freezing instructions on page 12.)

Caramel Nut Bars are terrific with any beverage, but especially with milk.

Cream Cheese–Pecan Squares

For an easy get-together, make these bars two or three days ahead and refrigerate them. They are gooey-chewy and rich, with an irresistible pecan flavor. It's like having a cheesecake in cookie form.

Makes 32 2¼ × 1½-inch bars.

Crust:

¾	**cup brown sugar, firmly packed**
¼	**teaspoon salt**
⅔	**cup unsalted butter**
1⅔	**cups all-purpose flour, preferably unbleached**
½	**cup quick-cooking rolled oats, uncooked (not instant)**
½	**cup finely chopped pecans**

Filling:

8	**ounces cream cheese, softened**
2	**large eggs**
½	**cup brown sugar, firmly packed**
½	**teaspoon pure vanilla extract**
2	**teaspoons freshly grated lemon zest**
2	**tablespoons all-purpose flour, preferably unbleached**

Topping:

1	**cup finely chopped pecans**

Preheat a conventional oven to 350 degrees Fahrenheit. Line a 9 × 13-inch baking pan with foil and brush it with softened butter.

Using an electric mixer on medium speed, beat together the butter, sugar, and salt for 2 minutes. The mixture will be light in color and fluffy. Scrape the bowl with a rubber spatula and add the flour and oats, beating for 20 seconds, just until the flour is blended in. Add the pecans and beat on low speed just to mix, about 10 seconds.

Pat the mixture into the prepared pan and bake in the preheated oven for 15 minutes. Remove the pan from the oven and set it on a wire rack.

While the crust is baking, make the filling. Using the same bowl that you mixed the crust in, beat the cream cheese, eggs, vanilla, and zest on medium speed for about 2 minutes. The mixture should be smooth. Scrape the bowl with a rubber spatula and add the flour, beating on low speed for 10 seconds.

Pour the filling over the baked crust, spreading it evenly with a rubber spatula. Sprinkle 1 cup of pecans over the filling. Bake for about 20 minutes, reversing the pan halfway through, until firm to the touch. Remove the pan from the oven and set it on a wire rack to cool.

When completely cool cut into bars. Store the cooled bars in an airtight container in the refrigerator for up to 4 days or wrap tightly and freeze for up to 2 months. (See freezing instructions on page 12.)

Cream Cheese–Pecan Squares go well with just about any beverage, but are especially enjoyable with coffee.

Easy Layered Jam Bars

As great-tasting as they are easy to make, these jam bars are sure to become a favorite for potluck dinners and weekend snacks. They are gooey-chewy and delicious. You can use any seedless jam or preserves you like. Just remember that the quality of the jam will directly impact the quality of the bars. Tart cherry preserves are especially delicious in this bar cookie. Clearbrook Farms makes the best tart cherry preserves I have ever tasted, and they can be found in many gourmet shops or better grocery stores. You can call them at 1-800-222-9966 in Fairfax, Ohio to find a store that carries their jams near you.

Makes 32 2¼ × 1½-inch bars.

Pastry:

¾   cup unsalted butter
1½ cups brown sugar, firmly packed
1½ teaspoons ground cinnamon
1   teaspoon freshly grated lemon
      zest
1½ cups quick-cooking, rolled oats,
      uncooked (not instant)
1½ cups all-purpose flour, preferably
      unbleached

Filling:

1½ cups seedless fruit preserves or
      jam, or apple butter

Preheat a conventional oven to 350 degrees Fahrenheit. Line a 9 × 13-inch baking pan with foil and brush it with softened butter.

Using an electric mixer on medium speed, beat together the butter, sugar, cinnamon, and zest for 2 minutes. The mixture will be light in color and fluffy. Scrape the bowl with a rubber spatula and add the flour and oats, beating for 20 seconds, just until the flour is blended in. Pat half of the mixture into the prepared pan. Spread the fruit filling over the bottom crust and crumble the remaining pastry mixture evenly over the filling. Bake in the preheated oven for 35 to 40 minutes, reversing the pan halfway through. The top will be lightly browned. Remove from the oven and set on a wire rack to cool. When completely cool, cut into squares.

Store the cooled squares in an airtight container with wax paper between the layers for up to 4 days or wrap tightly and freeze for up to 2 months. (See freezing instructions on page 12.)

Easy Layered Jam Bars are great with any beverage.

Cooked Fruit Bars

Akin to Easy Layered Jam Bars, but requiring a little bit more preparation, these bars are dense and gooey. You can use any combination of *dried* fruits, just be sure they are not candied. Dates, raisins, prunes, apricots, currants, and cranberries all work well. Combine several different fruits to get an interesting flavor.

Makes 32 2¼ × 1½-inch bars.

Filling:

1 **cup unsweetened apple juice or cider**
2 **cups chopped dried fruits**
¾ **cup brown sugar, firmly packed**

Crust and Crumb Mixture:

¾ **cup unsalted butter**
½ **cup granulated sugar**
1 **teaspoon ground cinnamon**
½ **teaspoon ground nutmeg**
1 **cup all-purpose flour, preferably unbleached**
2 **cups quick or old-fashioned rolled oats, uncooked (not instant)**
½ **cup sweetened coconut, flaked or shredded, firmly packed**

Line a 9 × 13-inch baking pan with foil and brush it with softened butter.

Make the filling. In a heavy saucepan over medium heat combine the juice, fruits, and brown sugar. Bring the mixture to a boil, reduce the heat and simmer the mixture until it thickens, about 10 minutes. Set aside to cool while you make the crust.

Preheat a conventional oven to 350 degrees Fahrenheit. Using an electric mixer on medium speed, beat together the butter, sugar, cinnamon, and nutmeg for 2 minutes. The mixture will be light in color and fluffy. Scrape the bowl with a rubber spatula and add the flour, oats, and coconut, beating for 20 seconds, just until the flour is blended in. Pat half of the mixture into the prepared pan. Spread the fruit filling over the bottom crust in the pan and crumble the remaining crust mixture evenly over the filling, patting down firmly with your fingertips.

Bake in the preheated oven for 35 to 40 minutes, reversing the pan halfway through. The top will be lightly browned. Remove from the oven and set on a wire rack to cool. When completely cool, cut into squares.

Store the cooled squares in an airtight container with wax paper between the layers for up to 4 days, or wrap tightly and freeze for up to 2 months. (See freezing instructions on page 12.)

You will enjoy Cooked Fruit Bars with tea or coffee for an afternoon pick-me-up.

Dream Bars

There aren't many experiences in life that can compare to the pleasure of eating a gooey, sweet dream bar. They are at once sensuous and innocent. Dream bars are a rich filling on a pastrylike crust. Their texture is similar to that of a pecan pie. Serve them at a birthday party or keep some around for those secret midnight snacks.

Sweet and Easy Dream Bars

Being the cookie snob that I am, I usually eschew the use of sweetened condensed milk in baking. But this cookie proved me wrong. It is rich, sweet, gooey, and incredibly delicious. It is also extremely easy to make.

Makes 32 2¼ × 1½-inch bar cookies.

Crust:

⅓ **cup very soft (not melted) unsalted butter**

1 **cup all-purpose flour, preferably unbleached**

⅓ **cup granulated sugar**

Filling:

1 **cup finely crushed graham cracker crumbs, about 13 squares (See page 11.)**

4 **ounces real semisweet chocolate chips, or 4 ounces of chopped semisweet chocolate**

⅔ **cup coarsely chopped walnuts, about 2¾ ounces**

⅛ **teaspoon salt**

1 **can (14 ounces) sweetened condensed milk**

Frosting:

2 **tablespoons unsalted butter**

6 **ounces white chocolate, coarsely chopped, or 6 ounces good-quality white chocolate chips, such as Ghirardelli**

Preheat a conventional oven to 350 degrees Fahrenheit. Line a 9 × 13-inch baking pan with foil and brush it with melted butter. Set the oven racks so the oven is divided in half.

Make the pastry crust. With a mixer on low speed combine the butter, flour, and sugar until the mixture starts to become crumbly. Then, with a rubber spatula, stir the pastry dough gently until the flour is mixed in. Press the mixture into the prepared pan and bake in the preheated oven for about 10 minutes. The edges will start to brown. Remove the pan from the oven and let the pastry cool while you make the filling.

Combine the graham cracker crumbs, chocolate chips or chunks, walnuts, salt, and sweetened condensed milk. Beat on medium speed until thoroughly combined, about 1 minute. Drop the filling by spoonfuls over the pastry and spread *gently* with a rubber spatula or icing knife, being careful not to pull up the delicate crust. If you take your time, you will have no problem with this step.

Bake on the middle rack of the oven for 20 minutes, reversing the pan halfway through. The bars will be lightly browned. Remove the pan from the oven and cool the bars in the pan on a wire rack.

While the bars are cooling, make the frosting. Melt the butter and the chocolate together in a covered microwavable dish for 1 minute in the microwave oven, or place in a heavy pan on the stove top over low heat, until the chocolate is almost melted. Remove the mixture from the heat and stir with a whisk until smooth. Let the chocolate mixture cool for about 5 minutes.

When the bars are completely cool, frost them. Use the foil to pull the entire cake from the pan and set it on a cutting board. Gently peel the foil from the sides of the cake and cut it into bars, carefully lifting them from the foil with a metal spatula.

Store the cooled bars in an airtight container for up to 5 days, or wrap tightly and freeze for up to 2 months. (See freezing instructions on page 12.)

Sweet and Easy Dream Bars are great with a glass of milk or a cup of hot coffee.

Peanut Butter Dreams

When I devised the recipe for these bar cookies, I thought they would be for kids only. But the adults who tasted these bars liked them even more than the kids did. They are gooey in the traditional fashion of dream bars and sweet.

Makes 30 1½ × 2½-inch bars.

Crust:

1   **cup all-purpose flour, preferably unbleached**
⅓   **cup brown sugar, firmly packed**
½   **cup unsalted butter, very soft**

Filling:

½   **cup granulated sugar**
⅓   **cup smooth or crunchy peanut butter (not natural style)**
½   **cup light corn syrup**
2   **large eggs**
¼   **teaspoon salt**
½   **teaspoon pure vanilla extract**
1   **tablespoon all purpose flour, preferably unbleached**
½   **cup sweetened flaked coconut, firmly packed (about 2½ ounces)**
4   **ounces real semisweet chocolate chips or real milk chocolate chips**

Preheat a conventional oven to 350 degrees Fahrenheit. Line a 9 × 13-inch baking pan with foil and brush with melted butter. Set the oven racks so the oven is divided in half.

Make the pastry crust. With a mixer on low speed combine the butter, flour, and brown sugar until the mixture starts to become crumbly. Then, with a rubber spatula, stir the pastry dough gently until the flour is mixed in. Press the mixture into the prepared pan and bake in the preheated oven for about 10 minutes. The edges will start to brown. Remove the pan from the oven and let the pastry cool while you make the filling.

With a mixer on medium speed, combine the granulated sugar, peanut butter, corn syrup, eggs, salt, vanilla, flour, coconut, and chips for about 1 minute, or until thoroughly mixed. Pour over the baked crust and spread evenly, using a rubber spatula or wooden spoon. Return the pan to the middle of the oven and bake for 30 to 35 minutes, or until lightly browned. Reverse the pan halfway through the baking time. Remove the pan from the oven and cool the bars in the pan on a wire rack.

When completely cool, use the foil to pull the entire cake from the pan and set it on a cutting board. Gently peel the foil from the sides of the cake and cut it into bars, carefully lifting them from the foil with a metal spatula.

Store the cooled bars in an airtight container for up to 5 days, or wrap tightly and freeze for up to 2 months. (See freezing instructions on page 12.)

Peanut Butter Dreams and milk are a great combination for kids. Adults, however, might like the blending of flavors produced with a cup of coffee.

Cherry-Walnut Dream Bars

When I was in college, our dining room served a wonderful cherry-walnut bar. I tried many times to duplicate it. Finally I came up with this version, which is very close to the original. You can use maraschino cherries in place of the dried sweetened tart cherries. It will have a different, but still delightful, flavor. The coupling of walnuts and cherries is a delicious one in this chewy, gooey bar.

Makes 2 dozen 2 × 2¼-inch bars.

Crust:

½   **cup unsalted butter, softened**
½   **cup granulated sugar**
1½ **cups all-purpose flour, preferably unbleached**

Filling:

1   **cup brown sugar, firmly packed**
½   **teaspoon baking powder**
2   **large eggs**
¼   **cup all-purpose flour, preferably unbleached**
¾   **cup dried, sweetened tart cherries, chopped**
2   **cups chopped walnuts confectioners' sugar for dusting**

Preheat a conventional oven to 350 degrees Fahrenheit. Line a 9 × 13-inch baking pan with foil and brush it with softened butter. Set the oven racks so the oven is divided in half.

Using an electric mixer on medium speed, beat the butter and sugar until fluffy and light in color, about 2 minutes. Add the 1½ cups flour and beat on low speed for about 20 to 30 seconds, just until combined. Press into the prepared pan as evenly as possible. Bake 15 minutes. Remove the pan from the oven and set it on a wire rack. Do not turn the oven off.

Using the mixer again on low speed, combine the brown sugar and baking powder, about 20 seconds. Add the eggs and beat on medium speed about 2 minutes. The mixture should be smooth. Scrape the bowl and sprinkle the flour over, blending on low speed for about 20 seconds, until thoroughly mixed. Add the cherries and walnuts and blend on low speed for 15 seconds. Pour the filling over the crust and spread evenly. Bake on the middle rack in the oven for 25 minutes, reversing the pan halfway through. The cake will be browned and firm. Remove from the oven and cool on a wire rack.

When completely cool, use the foil to pull the entire cake from the pan and set it on a cutting board. Gently peel the foil from the sides of the cake and cut the bars, carefully lifting them from the foil with a metal spatula.

Store the completely cooled bars in an airtight container for up to 5 days, or wrap tightly and freeze for up to 2 months. If desired, dust with confectioners' sugar just before serving. (See freezing instructions on page 12.)

Savor Cherry-Walnut Dream Bars with tea or coffee.

Orange-Walnut Dream Bars

Grown-up and sophisticated, this is an uptown bar. The combination of walnuts and orange catapults this crunchy, gooey-chewy bar into the realm of adulthood. It's extremely rich, so cut it into small bars. If you really wanted to be decadent you could drizzle it with melted chocolate.

Makes 4 dozen 1½ × 1½-inch bars.

Crust:
- **1 cup all-purpose flour, preferably unbleached**
- **¾ cup brown sugar, firmly packed**
- **½ cup unsalted butter, very soft**

Filling:
- **1 cup brown sugar**
- **½ teaspoon baking powder**
- **2 large eggs**
- **1½ tablespoon finely chopped orange zest**
- **1 teaspoon pure vanilla extract**
- **¼ cup all-purpose flour, preferably unbleached**
- **1½ cups (6 ounces) coarsely chopped walnuts**
- **1 cup (5 ounces) sweetened flaked coconut, firmly packed**

Preheat a conventional oven to 375 degrees Fahrenheit. Line a 9 × 13-inch baking pan with foil and brush with melted butter. Set the oven racks so the oven is divided in half.

Make the crust. With a mixer on medium speed beat together 1 cup flour, ¾ cup brown sugar, and the butter until fluffy, about 1 minute. Using your hands, pat the crust into the prepared pan. Bake for 12 minutes. The edges will start to brown. Remove from the oven and set side.

While the crust is baking, make the filling. Mix 1 cup brown sugar with the baking powder with a mixer on low speed for about 15 seconds, or until evenly combined. Add the eggs, zest, and vanilla, and beat on medium speed about 1 minute, or until smooth. Using a rubber spatula, scrape the bowl. Add the flour and beat on low speed until the flour is mixed in, about 20 to 30 seconds. Scrape the bowl again and add the walnuts and coconut on low speed. Mix for 10 to 15 seconds. Pour over the baked crust, spreading evenly with a rubber spatula. Return to the middle rack in the oven and bake for about 30 minutes, reversing the pan halfway through. The top will be lightly browned. Remove the pan from the oven and cool the bars in the pan on a wire rack.

When completely cool, use the foil to pull the entire cake from the pan and set it on a cutting board. Gently peel the foil from the sides of the cake and cut the bars, carefully lifting them from the foil with a metal spatula.

Store the cooled bars in an airtight container for up to 5 days, or wrap tightly and freeze for up to 2 months. (See freezing instructions on page 12.)

Orange-Walnut Dream Bars are a perfect match to a cup of coffee or rich hot chocolate.

Mixed Nut Dream Bars

The maple syrup in these bars lends a homey flavor that is enhanced by the combination of nuts in the filling. It is rich with brown sugar, gooey, and crunchy. Using both sliced and chopped nuts adds interest to the texture. Don't substitute pancake syrup, which has little or no maple syrup or flavor.

Makes 4 dozen 1½-inch bars.

Crust:

½ **cup unsalted butter**
½ **cup brown sugar, firmly packed**
1½ **cups all-purpose flour, preferably unbleached**

Filling:

1 **cup brown sugar, firmly packed**
½ **teaspoon baking powder**
¼ **cup pure maple syrup**
3 **large eggs**
1 **teaspoon pure vanilla extract**
2 **tablespoons unsalted butter, melted**
4 **tablespoons all-purpose flour, preferably unbleached**
¾ **cup chopped walnuts**
¾ **cup chopped pecans**
¾ **cup sliced almonds (with skins on)**

Preheat a conventional oven to 350 degrees Fahrenheit. Line a 9 × 13-inch baking pan with foil and brush it with softened butter. Set the oven racks so they divide the oven in half.

Beat the ½ cup butter and the ½ cup brown sugar until fluffy and light in color, about 2 minutes. Add the 1½ cups flour and beat on low speed until mixed well, about 30 seconds. Press into the prepared pan, spreading as evenly as possible. Bake for 15 minutes in the preheated oven, until the crust is lightly browned. Remove from the oven and set aside on a wire rack. Do not turn the oven off.

Combine the 1 cup brown sugar and baking powder on low speed for 15 seconds, to mix evenly. Add the maple syrup, eggs, vanilla, and the 2 tablespoons melted butter and mix on medium speed for about 1 minute, until smooth. Sprinkle the flour in and mix on low speed for about 15 seconds, until well combined. Add the nuts and beat on low speed just until evenly mixed, about 15 to 20 seconds. Pour over the baked crust, spreading with a rubber spatula to make an even layer. Bake on the middle rack in the oven for about 30 minutes, reversing the pan halfway through. The bars will be firm to the touch. Remove from the oven and cool in the pan on a wire rack.

When completely cool, use the foil to pull the entire cake from the pan and set it on a cutting board. Gently peel the foil from the sides of the cake and cut the bars, carefully lifting them from the foil with a metal spatula.

Store the cooled bars in an airtight container for up to 6 days, or wrap tightly and freeze for up to 2 months. (See freezing instructions on page 12.)

Mixed Nut Dream Bars taste scrumptious with coffee or milk.

Cinnamon-Coconut Dream Bars

Inside these cinnamon-scented coconut bars hides a thin layer of semisweet chocolate. It's a nice surprise flavor that marries well with the coconut and cinnamon. These bars are chewy, gooey, and delicious.

Makes 2 dozen 1½ × 3¼-inch bars.

Crust:

½   **cup unsalted butter, softened**
½   **cup confectioners' sugar, stirred with a fork to eliminate any lumps**
1¼   **cups all-purpose flour, preferably unbleached**
6   **ounces chopped semisweet chocolate *or* 1 cup real semisweet chocolate chips**

Filling:

1   **cup brown sugar, firmly packed**
½   **teaspoon baking powder**
1   **teaspoon ground cinnamon**
3   **large eggs**
1   **teaspoon pure vanilla extract**
3   **tablespoons all-purpose flour, preferably unbleached**
2   **cups sweetened coconut, flaked or shredded, lightly packed**

Preheat a conventional oven to 350 degrees Fahrenheit. Line a 9 × 13-inch baking pan with foil and brush it with softened butter. Set the racks in the oven so it is divided in half.

Using an electric mixer on medium speed, beat the butter and confectioners' sugar for about 2 minutes, or until fluffy and light in color. Add the 1¼ cups flour and beat on low speed until evenly mixed, about 30 seconds. Pat the dough into the prepared pan and bake in the preheated oven for 10 to 12 minutes. Remove the pan from the oven and sprinkle the chopped chocolate over the crust evenly. Set the pan on a wire rack and make the filling. The chocolate will melt while the filling is being made. Do not turn off the oven.

Using an electric mixer on low speed, mix the brown sugar with the baking powder and cinnamon until well combined, about 20 seconds. Add the eggs and vanilla and mix on medium speed for about 2 or 3 minutes, until smooth. Sprinkle the flour over and beat in on low speed for about 15 seconds. Scrape the bowl with a rubber spatula and add the coconut, blending on low speed for about 15 seconds.

Scrape the filling into the pan, evenly distributing over the melted chocolate. Bake on the middle rack in the oven for about 20 minutes, reversing the pan halfway through. The top will be slightly brown. Remove from the oven and cool on wire racks.

When completely cool, use the foil to pull the entire cake from the pan and set it on a cutting board. Gently peel the foil from the sides of the cake and cut it into bars, carefully lifting them from the foil with a metal spatula.

Store the cooled bars in an airtight container for up to 1 week, or wrap tightly and freeze for up to 2 months. (See freezing instructions on page 12.)

Cinnamon-Coconut Dream Bars are a great addition to a tea table, or nice to have with hot coffee.

Apricot-Pecan Dreams

The medley of pecans, apricots, and coconut creates a rich, chewy, not-too-sweet bar that is a great lunch box or picnic treat. The subtle flavor of pure maple syrup leaves a lingering, homey taste in your mouth.

Makes 2 dozen 2¼ × 2-inch bars

Crust:

½ cup unsalted butter, softened
½ cup brown sugar, firmly packed
1½ cups all-purpose flour, preferably unbleached

Filling:

¾ cup brown sugar, firmly packed
½ teaspoon baking powder
3 large eggs
¼ cup pure maple syrup (do not use maple-flavored pancake syrup)
1 teaspoon pure vanilla extract
3 tablespoons all-purpose flour, preferably unbleached
1½ cups coarsely chopped pecans
1 cup finely chopped apricots
½ cup sweetened coconut, shredded or flaked, lightly packed

Preheat a conventional oven to 350 degrees Fahrenheit. Line a 9 × 13-inch baking pan with foil and brush it with softened butter.

Using an electric mixer on medium speed, beat the butter and the ½ cup brown sugar for about 2 minutes, until fluffy and light in color. Add the 1½ cups flour and beat on low speed for 20 to 30 seconds, until well combined. Pat the dough into the prepared pan, spreading evenly. Bake in the preheated oven for 15 minutes. Remove the pan from the oven and set it aside on a wire rack. Do not turn the oven off.

On medium speed, beat the ¾ cup brown sugar and the baking powder for 20 seconds. Add the eggs, maple syrup, and vanilla and beat on medium speed for 2 minutes. Mixture will be smooth. Sprinkle the flour over and beat on low speed for about 20 to 30 seconds. Add the pecans, apricots, and coconut and stir to combine. Pour the filling over the crust and spread gently with a rubber spatula in an even layer. Bake for 35 minutes, reversing the pan halfway through. The top will be firm and slightly brown. Remove from the oven and set on a wire rack to cool.

When completely cool, use the foil to pull the entire cake from the pan and set it on a cutting board. Gently peel the foil from the sides of the cake and cut the bars, carefully lifting them from the foil with a metal spatula.

Store the cooled bars in an airtight container for up to 6 days, or wrap tightly and freeze for up to 2 months. (See freezing instructions on page 12.)

The pretty colors in Pecan-Apricot Dreams make them a nice touch for a buffet table or for the holidays. Enjoy them with coffee or liqueurs.

Macadamia and
White Chocolate Dreams

This is truly a dreamy combination. It is sweet, gooey, and flavorful. Be sure not to chop the macadamias too much, as larger pieces will give the texture more character and appeal. The quality of this cookie depends greatly on the quality of white chocolate you use to make it. Buy the best you can find, and look for cocoa butter, not vegetable shortening, as the main ingredient.

Makes 2 dozen 2¼ × 2-inch bars.

Crust:

½   **cup granulated sugar**
½   **cup unsalted butter, softened**
1½ **cups all-purpose flour, preferably unbleached**

Filling:

1   **cup brown sugar, firmly packed**
¼   **cup granulated sugar**
½   **teaspoon baking powder**
3   **large eggs**
1   **teaspoon pure vanilla extract**
2   **tablespoons unsalted butter, melted**
¼   **cup all-purpose flour, preferably unbleached**
2   **cups coarsely chopped macadamia nuts (unsalted)**
9   **ounces chopped white chocolate *or* good-quality white chocolate chips, such as Ghirardelli**

Preheat a conventional oven to 350 degrees Fahrenheit. Line a 9 × 13-inch baking pan with foil and brush it with softened butter.

Using an electric mixer on medium speed, beat the ½ cup sugar and the ½ cup butter for about 2 minutes, until light in color and fluffy. Add the 1½ cups flour and beat on low speed for 20 to 30 seconds, until blended. Pat into the prepared pan, being careful to spread it evenly, and bake in the preheated oven for 15 minutes. Remove the pan from the oven and set it aside on a wire rack.

On medium speed, blend the brown sugar, the ¼ cup sugar, and the baking powder for 20 seconds. Add the eggs, vanilla, and melted butter and beat on medium speed for 2 minutes, until smooth. Sprinkle the flour over and beat on low speed for 20 seconds. Stir in the macadamias and the white chocolate. Pour the filling over the crust, spreading gently into an even layer. Bake for 25 minutes, reversing the pan halfway through. The top will feel firm when touched gently, and will be slightly brown. Remove from the oven and place on a wire rack to cool. When cool, cut into bars.

Store cooled bars in an airtight container for up to 5 days, or wrap tightly and freeze for up to 2 months. (See freezing instructions on page 12.)

Enjoy Macadamia and White Chocolate Dreams as part of a tea table, or for dessert after a light, but special, dinner. They are a delight with espresso.

Pecan-Honey Dream Bars

The filling in these bars is a honey variation of a pecan pie, in a large format. Pecans in the crust add a toasted nut flavor that enhances the filling. Make these for a fancy dessert, served with fresh whipped cream. They are rich, so cut them small.

Makes 28 1¾ × 1½-inch bars.

Crust:
- ⅓   cup unsalted butter, softened
- ⅓   cup granulated sugar
- 1   cup all-purpose flour, preferably unbleached
- ¼   cup finely chopped pecans

Filling:
- 1¼   cup brown sugar, firmly packed
- ½   teaspoon baking powder
- 3   large eggs
- ¼   cup mild-flavored honey, such as orange blossom
- ½   cup butter, melted
- 1   teaspoon pure vanilla extract
- 1   tablespoon all-purpose flour, preferably unbleached
- 1½   cups chopped pecans

Preheat a conventional oven to 350 degrees Fahrenheit. Line a 7 × 11-inch baking pan with foil and brush it with softened butter.

Using an electric mixer on medium speed, beat the ⅓ cup butter and sugar for 2 minutes, until light in color and fluffy. Add the flour and the pecans and beat on low speed for 20 to 30 seconds, until evenly blended. Pat into the bottom of the prepared pan and bake in the preheated oven for 15 minutes. Remove from the oven and set aside. Do not turn the oven off.

Beat the brown sugar and baking powder on medium speed to combine for 20 seconds. Add the eggs, honey, the melted butter, and the vanilla. Beat on medium speed for 30 seconds to mix. The mixture should be smooth. Sprinkle the flour over and blend on low speed for 10 to 15 seconds. Add the pecans and stir to combine. Pour over the baked crust in the pan. Smooth with a rubber spatula and bake in the oven for 25 to 30 more minutes, reversing the pan halfway through. The surface will be dull and firm. Do not overbake. Remove from the oven and set on a wire rack to cool. When completely cool, cut into bars.

Store the cooled bars in an airtight container with wax paper between the layers, for up to 6 days, or wrap tightly and freeze for up to 2 months. (See freezing instructions on page 12.)

Pecan-Honey Dream Bars make a sweet ending to a special dinner. Serve them with coffee or espresso.

Coconut-Pecan Dreams

Toasting the coconut and pecans for this recipe heightens their flavors. This is a rich and satisfying dream bar that is moist, densely chewy, and ambrosial. It is easy to make and keeps very well. If you bring a tray of these bars to a potluck supper, you will likely be the hit of the party.

Makes 32 bars, 2¼ × 1½-inches.

¾   **cup chopped pecans**
1½   **cups sweetened coconut, flaked or shredded, firmly packed**

Crust:

⅓   **cup unsalted butter**
⅓   **cup brown sugar, firmly packed**
1   **cup all-purpose flour, preferably unbleached**

Filling:

2   **cups brown sugar, firmly packed**
½   **teaspoon baking powder**
2   **large eggs**
¼   **cup pure maple syrup (not maple-flavored pancake syrup)**
2   **teaspoons pure vanilla extract**
1   **tablespoon all-purpose flour, preferably unbleached**

Preheat a conventional oven to 350 degrees Fahrenheit. Line a 9 × 13-inch baking pan with foil and brush it with softened butter.

Place the pecans on a baking sheet in a single layer and bake for about 8 minutes, until they start to brown. Do the same with the coconut, stirring it once halfway through so it will brown evenly. Remove both pans from the oven and set aside to cool while you make the crust and filling.

Using an electric mixer on medium speed, beat the butter and ⅓ cup brown sugar for 2 minutes, until light in color and fluffy. Add the flour and beat on low speed for 20 seconds, until evenly blended. Pat into the bottom of the prepared pan and bake in the preheated oven for 15 minutes. Remove from the oven and set aside. Do not turn the oven off.

While the crust is baking, make the filling. Beat the 2 cups brown sugar and the baking powder on medium speed to combine for 20 seconds. Add the eggs, maple syrup, and vanilla. Beat on medium speed for 30 seconds to mix. The mixture should be smooth. Sprinkle the flour in and blend on low speed for 10 to 15 seconds. Add the pecans and coconut and stir to combine. Pour over the baked crust in the pan. Smooth with a rubber spatula and bake in the oven for 25 minutes, reversing the pan halfway through. The surface will be dull and firm. Do not overbake. Remove from the oven and set on a wire rack to cool. When completely cool, cut into bars.

Store the cooled bars in an airtight container with wax paper between the layers for up to 1 week, or wrap tightly and freeze for up to 2 months. (See freezing instructions on page 12.)

You can enjoy Coconut-Pecan Dreams with coffee or tea, or just about any beverage.

Chocolate-Walnut Dreams

Rich and gooey, these are sure to satisfy even the most intense sweet tooth. The walnuts add a crunch to the texture, and the combination of nuts and chocolate is a pleasant flavor. Cut these bars small; they are sweet.

Makes 48 1½ × 1½-inch bars.

Crust:

⅓ **cup unsalted butter**
⅓ **cup granulated sugar**
1 **cup all-purpose flour, preferably unbleached**

Filling:

3 large eggs
1 cup brown sugar, firmly packed
¾ **cup granulated sugar**
2 **teaspoons pure vanilla extract**
¼ **cup all-purpose flour, preferably unbleached**
10 **ounces real semisweet chocolate chips *or* 10 ounces chopped semisweet chocolate**
1 **cup walnuts, coarsely chopped**

Topping:

⅔ **cup chopped walnuts**

Preheat a conventional oven to 350 degrees Fahrenheit. Line a 9 × 13 inch baking pan with foil and brush it with softened butter. Set the oven racks so they divide the oven in half.

Using an electric mixer on medium speed, beat ⅓ cup butter and ⅓ cup sugar until fluffy and light in color, about 2 minutes. Scrape the bowl with a rubber spatula and add 1 cup flour, beating on low speed just until blended, about 20 seconds. Press the dough evenly into the prepared pan and bake in the preheated oven for about 10 to 12 minutes, until the crust just starts to brown slightly. Remove from the oven and set aside.

Using a mixer on medium speed, beat the eggs, sugars, and vanilla for 2½ minutes, or until the mixture is light in color and smooth. Scrape the bowl with a rubber spatula and add the flour. Beat on low speed for about 15 seconds, just until the mixture is blended evenly. Scrape the bowl again and add the chocolate chips or chunks and 1 cup of walnuts. Beat on low speed just until mixed in, about 15 seconds. Pour the mixture onto the baked crust, smoothing and distributing evenly with a rubber spatula. Sprinkle the top with ⅔ cup chopped walnuts and bake on the middle rack in a preheated oven for 25 minutes, reversing the pan halfway through. The top will be just firm. Remove from the oven and cool in the pan on a wire rack.

When completely cool, use the foil to pull the entire cake from the pan and set it on a cutting board. Gently peel the foil from the sides of the cake and cut the bars, carefully lifting them from the foil with a metal spatula.

Store the completely cooled bars in an airtight container for up to 6 days or freeze, tightly wrapped, for up to 2 months. (See freezing instructions on page 12.)

Chocolate-Walnut Dream Bars go well with coffee or milk.

Raspberry Dream Bars

Sweet and gooey, with the agreeable flavor combination of walnuts and raspberries, these bars are truly a dream. They are homey enough to go to a picnic and sophisticated enough to conclude a fine dinner. The raspberry jam that you use should be top quality, because the raspberry flavor is a prominent one in these bars.

Makes 32 2¼ × 1½-inch bars.

Crust:

½   **cup unsalted butter**
⅓   **cup granulated sugar**
1   **cup all-purpose flour, preferably unbleached**
1   **cup good-quality seedless raspberry jam**

Filling:

1   **cup brown sugar, firmly packed**
½   **teaspoon baking powder**
2   **large eggs**
½   **teaspoon pure vanilla extract**
1½   **cups chopped walnuts**
¾   **cup sweetened coconut, flaked or shredded, firmly packed**
2   **tablespoons all-purpose flour, preferably unbleached**

Preheat a conventional oven to 350 degrees Fahrenheit. Line a 9 × 13-inch baking pan with foil and brush it with softened butter.

Using an electric mixer on medium speed, beat the butter and sugar for 2 minutes, until light in color and fluffy. Add the flour and beat on low speed for 20 seconds, until evenly blended. Pat into the bottom of the prepared pan and bake in the preheated oven for 15 minutes. Remove from the oven and set aside. After the crust cools, spread the raspberry jam on it. Do not turn the oven off.

While the crust is baking, make the filling. Beat the brown sugar and the baking powder on medium speed to combine for 20 seconds. Add the eggs and vanilla, beating on medium speed for 30 seconds to mix. The mixture should be smooth. Add the walnuts and coconut and mix on low speed for 20 seconds to combine. Sprinkle the flour in and blend on low speed for 15 seconds. Pour over the baked crust in the pan. Smooth with a rubber spatula and bake for about 30 minutes, reversing the pan halfway through. The center will feel slightly firm when gently touched and the top will be lightly browned. Remove the pan from the oven and set on a wire rack to cool.

When completely cool, use the foil to pull the entire cake from the pan and set it on a cutting board. Gently peel the foil from the sides of the cake and cut the bars, carefully lifting them from the foil with a metal spatula.

Store the cooled bars in an airtight container for up to 5 days or wrap tightly and freeze for up to 2 months. (See freezing instructions on page 12.)

Raspberry Dream Bars are sublime with hot tea or coffee.

Cookie Jar and Lunch-Box Treats

The cookies and bars in this chapter are unpretentious. No outrageous chocolate extravaganzas or sophisticated fantasies here. These cookies are down-home and delicious with the familiar flavors of maple, honey, granola, and spice. Many contain oats, dried fruits, nuts, or whole wheat to lend a healthful aspect to these snacks. Cookies with fruits and nuts offer a pleasant way to get a nutritious snack. The natural moisture of the fruit adds texture and extends the life of the cookie. These cookies are the essence of comfort food. A great way to say "I love you" in a lunch box.

Honey Oatmeal Cookies

When I was developing this recipe, I just couldn't find the right combination of flavors to make this a standout. Then Marti Bowditch suggested I add sunflower seeds. She was absolutely right. The result is a healthful, chewy, almost creamy texture that is not sweet but is satisfying and delicious. You can use quick rolled oats if you want less chewiness.

Makes 5 dozen 2-inch cookies.

1   cup all-purpose flour, preferably unbleached
1   cup whole wheat flour, preferably stone-ground
2   cups old-fashioned rolled oats (uncooked)
1½   teaspoons baking soda
½   teaspoon baking powder
½   teaspoon salt
½   cup unsalted butter
¾   cup brown sugar, firmly packed
2   large eggs
2   teaspoons pure vanilla extract
½   cup mild-flavored honey, such as orange blossom
3   teaspoons ground cinnamon
½   cup milk
1½   cups raisins, dates, or apricots (or a combination of them)
1½   cups raw sunflower seeds

Preheat convection ovens to 310 degrees Fahrenheit or conventional ovens to 325 degrees Fahrenheit. Set the racks in the conventional oven so they divide the oven into thirds. Line the cookie sheets with parchment paper or use non-stick pans. If you are baking in a conventional oven, put one baking sheet inside another of the same size to make a double pan, or use insulated pans to protect the bottoms of the cookies.

In a medium-size bowl with a wire whisk, stir together the flours, oats, baking soda, baking powder, and salt. Set aside.

Using an electric mixer on medium speed, beat the butter, brown sugar, eggs, and vanilla until smooth and light in color, about 3 minutes. Add the honey and cinnamon and beat 1½ minutes more. Scrape the bowl with a rubber spatula and add half of the dry ingredients. Beat on low speed just until the dry ingredients are mixed in. Add the milk, and beat on low speed again just until smooth. Scrape the bowl with a rubber spatula and add the remaining dry ingredients, beating on low just until the mixture is thoroughly combined, about 30 seconds. Scrape the bowl again and stir in the raisins and sunflower seeds.

Drop by rounded tablespoonfuls onto the prepared baking sheets and bake in the preheated oven for 11 to 13 minutes, reversing the baking sheets and switching them top to bottom halfway through the baking time. The cookies will be just firm to the touch. Do not overbake. Let the cookies cool on the baking sheet on a wire rack for 5 to 7 minutes. Carefully remove the cookies from the sheets and let them finish cooling on wire racks. They will be crumbly when warm, but will firm up somewhat when cool.

Store the completely cooled cookies in an airtight container with wax paper between layers for up to 10 days, or freeze, wrapped tightly, for up to 2 months. (See freezing instructions on page 12.)

Honey Oatmeal Cookies taste good with milk or juice and go well with coffee or tea.

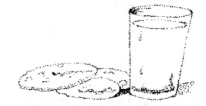

Maple Oatmeal Chews

Thin, soft-chewy, and mildly flavored, this is a cookie for eating while sitting in front of a fire, sipping tea, or hot cider. Pure maple syrup and pecans produce a nutty cookie with a wonderful, subtle flavor that is not too sweet.

Makes about 4 dozen 2½-inch cookies.

1	**cup brown sugar, firmly packed**
½	**cup granulated sugar**
½	**teaspoon baking powder**
1	**teaspoon baking soda**
¾	**cup unsalted butter**
2	**large eggs**
⅔	**cup pure maple syrup**
1	**cup all-purpose flour, preferably unbleached**
1	**cup whole wheat flour, preferably stone-ground**
1¼	**cups quick or old-fashioned rolled oats, uncooked (not instant)**
2	**cups coarsely chopped pecans (8 ounces)**

Preheat convection ovens to 310 degrees Fahrenheit or conventional ovens to 325 degrees Fahrenheit. Set the racks in the conventional oven so they divide the oven into thirds. Line the cookie sheets with parchment paper. If you are baking in a conventional oven, put one baking sheet inside another of the same size to make a double pan, or use insulated pans to protect the bottoms of the cookies.

With a mixer on low speed, blend the sugars, baking powder, and baking soda. Add the butter, eggs, and syrup, beating on medium speed for about 2 minutes, until the mixture is smooth and fluffy. It may look curdled, but that is all right. Scrape the bowl with a rubber spatula and add the flours, oats, and pecans. Mix on low speed for about 30 seconds, until the flour is thoroughly combined. Using a wooden spoon or rubber spatula, stir the mixture, scraping down to the bottom of the bowl, to be sure it is evenly mixed.

Drop the dough by rounded tablespoonfuls onto prepared sheets, leaving about 3 inches between cookies to allow for them to spread. Bake in the preheated oven for 13 to 15 minutes, reversing the baking sheets and switching them top to bottom halfway through the baking time. The cookies will be lightly browned and just start to feel firm when touched gently. When the cookies are done, let them cool on the sheets for 5 minutes and then remove them with a metal spatula to wire racks to finish cooling.

Store the completely cooled cookies in an airtight container for up to 6 days, or freeze, wrapped tightly, for up to 2 months. (See freezing instructions on page 12.)

Maple Oatmeal Chews are a great flavor combination with a cup of hot coffee or a glass of milk.

Raisin Spice Jumbles

Just the right amount of spices and packed full of raisins, this is a comforting cookie that will remind you of your grandmother. It is a soft-chewy cookie with a bit of whole wheat flour in the wholesome combination of ingredients.

Makes about 5 dozen 2-inch cookies.

¾	cup brown sugar, firmly packed
¾	cup granulated sugar
2	teaspoons cinnamon
1	teaspoon ground allspice
1	teaspoon ground nutmeg
1	teaspoon baking soda
1	teaspoon baking powder
¾	cup unsalted butter
¼	cup molasses
2	large eggs
2	teaspoons pure vanilla extract
2	cups whole wheat flour, preferably stone-ground
½	cup milk
2	cups all-purpose flour, preferably unbleached
1½	cups seedless raisins, light or dark

Preheat convection ovens to 325 degrees Fahrenheit or conventional ovens to 350 degrees Fahrenheit. Set the racks in the conventional oven so they divide the oven into thirds. Line the cookie sheets with parchment paper. If you are baking in a conventional oven, put one baking sheet inside another of the same size to make a double pan, or use insulated pans to protect the bottoms of the cookies.

Using an electric mixer on low speed, combine the sugars, spices, baking soda, and baking powder until evenly mixed. Add the butter, molasses, eggs, and vanilla and beat on medium speed for about 2 minutes, until the mixture is fluffy and light in color. Scrape the bowl with a rubber spatula and add the whole wheat flour, beating on low speed just until mixed in, about 20 seconds. Add the milk and beat on low for about 30 seconds. Scrape the bowl again and add the remaining flour, beating on low speed only until the flour is blended in. Stir in the raisins.

Drop the dough by rounded teaspoonfuls onto the prepared sheets and bake in the preheated oven for about 13 to 15 minutes, reversing the sheets and switching them top to bottom halfway through the baking time. When the cookies are done, let them cool on the sheets for 5 minutes and then remove them with a metal spatula to wire racks to finish cooling.

Store the completely cooled cookies in an airtight container for up to 6 days, or freeze, wrapped tightly, for up to 2 months. (See freezing instructions on page 12.)

Raisin Spice Jumbles are made for milk.

Brazilian Chews

The earthy flavor and unusual texture of Brazil nuts make them one of my favorites. These cookies are mildly spiced and crunchy-chewy with Brazil nuts and coconut. Don't overbake them, or they will be very crunchy.

Makes about 4 dozen 2½-inch cookies.

2	cups all-purpose flour, preferably unbleached
½	teaspoon baking soda
1	teaspoon baking powder
½	cup unsalted butter
1½	cups brown sugar, firmly packed
2	large eggs
1	teaspoon pure vanilla extract
1	teaspoon ground cinnamon
½	teaspoon ground nutmeg
½	teaspoon ground allspice
1	cup coarsely chopped Brazil nuts (4½ ounces)
1½	cups sweetened coconut (7½ ounces), lightly packed

Preheat convection ovens to 325 degrees Fahrenheit or conventional ovens to 350 degrees Fahrenheit. Set the racks in the conventional oven so they divide the oven into thirds. Line the cookie sheets with parchment paper or use nonstick pans. If you are baking in a conventional oven, put one baking sheet inside another of the same size to make a double pan, or use insulated pans to protect the bottoms of the cookies.

In a medium-size bowl using a wire whisk, stir together the flour, baking soda, and baking powder. Set aside.

Using an electric mixer, beat the butter, brown sugar, eggs, vanilla, and spices until light colored and fluffy, about 2½ minutes. Scrape the bowl with a rubber spatula and add the flour mixture, beating on low until well blended, about 30 seconds. Scrape the bowl again and add the nuts and coconut, stirring to mix thoroughly.

Drop the dough by heaping tablespoonfuls onto the prepared baking sheets. Bake in the preheated oven for 10 to 12 minutes, reversing the sheets and switching them top to bottom halfway through the baking time. The cookies will be done when they just feel slightly firm to the touch. Remove the pans from the oven and cool the cookies for 5 minutes on the pans on wire racks. Then remove the cookies with a metal spatula to wire racks to finish cooling.

Store the completely cooled cookies in an airtight container for up to 10 days or freeze, wrapped tightly, for up to 2 months. (See freezing instructions on page 12.)

Brazilian Chews go well with coffee or milk.

Hermits

There are some cookies that transcend time. This is just that kind of cookie. It has been made for generations, with as many variations to the ingredients as there are people making them. Hermits usually contain nuts, raisins, and spices, and they keep very well. This is a soft, chewy, comforting cookie with a great flavor of spice.

Makes 5 dozen 2½-inch cookies.

1½	**cups brown sugar, firmly packed**
1	**teaspoon ground cinnamon**
½	**teaspoon ground cloves**
1	**teaspoon ground nutmeg**
½	**teaspoon allspice**
½	**teaspoon baking soda**
1	**teaspoon baking powder**
¾	**cup unsalted butter**
2	**large eggs**
1	**teaspoon pure vanilla extract**
2½	**cups all-purpose flour, preferably unbleached**
2	**cups coarsely chopped walnuts (8 ounces)**
2	**cups raisins *or* currants *or* dates, *or* a combination**

Preheat convection ovens to 310 degrees Fahrenheit or conventional ovens to 325 degrees Fahrenheit. Set the racks in the conventional oven so they divide the oven into thirds. Line the cookie sheets with parchment paper or use non-stick pans. If you are baking in a conventional oven, put one baking sheet inside another of the same size to make a double pan, or use insulated pans to protect the bottoms of the cookies.

Using an electric mixer on medium speed, combine the brown sugar, spices, baking soda, and baking powder for about 20 seconds. Add the butter, eggs, and vanilla, and beat on medium speed for about 2 minutes, until light in color and fluffy. Scrape the bowl with a rubber spatula and add the flour, nuts, and raisins, beating on low speed until thoroughly combined, about 30 to 40 seconds.

Drop the dough by heaping teaspoonfuls onto the prepared pans and bake in the preheated oven for 11 to 13 minutes, turning the pans around and switching them from top to bottom halfway through the baking time. Remove the baked cookies from the oven and cool on the baking sheets for about 5 minutes. Using a metal spatula, move the cookies to wire racks to finish cooling.

Store the cooled cookies in an airtight container for up to 1 week, or wrap tightly and freeze for up to 2 months. (See freezing instructions on page 12.)

Hermits are wonderful with milk or hot cider.

Oatmeal Gems

Big, soft, and thick, these cookies are a pleasant alternative to the crisp oatmeal cookies baked by many cooks. Don't overlook the kids for these. In fact, you can substitute chocolate or butterscotch chips for the raisins and this will become a great school bake-sale cookie.

Makes 3 dozen 3-inch cookies.

¼	cup granulated sugar
1	cup brown sugar, firmly packed
1	teaspoon baking soda
½	teaspoon baking powder
1	teaspoon ground cinnamon
½	cup unsalted butter
2	large eggs
2	teaspoon pure vanilla extract
⅓	cup milk
⅓	cup molasses
1½	cups all-purpose flour, preferable unbleached
3	cups quick or old-fashioned rolled oats, uncooked (not instant)
¾	cup finely chopped pecans
1	cup raisins

Preheat convection ovens to 310 degrees Fahrenheit or conventional ovens to 325 degrees Fahrenheit. Set the racks in the conventional oven so they divide the oven into thirds. You will *not* need to line the pans with parchment for this recipe. If you are baking in a conventional oven, put one baking sheet inside another of the same size to make a double pan, or use insulated pans to protect the bottoms of the cookies.

Using an electric mixer on medium speed, combine the sugar, brown sugar, baking soda, baking powder, and cinnamon for about 20 seconds, or until mixed evenly. Add the butter, eggs, and vanilla, and beat on medium speed for about 2 minutes, or until light in color and fluffy. Add the milk and molasses and beat on low speed just until blended. The mixture may look curdled at this point. Scrape the bowl with a rubber spatula and add the flour, oats, nuts, and raisins. Beat on low speed for about 30 seconds, or until thoroughly combined. Using a rubber spatula, scrape the sides and bottom of the bowl, stirring the dough to be sure it is evenly mixed.

Drop the dough by heaping tablespoonfuls onto the baking sheets and bake in the preheated oven for 13 to 15 minutes, reversing the sheets and switching them top to bottom halfway through. Cookies are done when they just begin to turn brown. They will still be soft to the touch, but will firm up as they cool. Let them cool on the sheets for 5 minutes, then move them to wire racks to finish cooling.

Store the cooled cookies in an airtight container for up to 1 week, or wrap tightly and freeze for up to 2 months. (See freezing instructions on page 12.)

Oatmeal Gems taste great with just about any beverage.

Oatmeal Doodles

Thin, chewy, and flavored with spice, this variation on the traditional doodle is made even chewier with the addition of dried currants and oats. You can substitute any dried fruits for the currants. Dried blueberries are an interesting addition, but they are expensive. Try Oatmeal Doodles with your favorite dried fruit. These cookies spread quite a bit while baking, so allow 2 inches between cookies when placing the dough on the baking sheets.

Makes 4 dozen 2½-inch cookies.

2   cups granulated sugar
1½   teaspoons baking soda
¼   teaspoon salt
1   cup unsalted butter
2   large eggs
1½   teaspoons pure vanilla extract
2½   cups all-purpose flour, preferably unbleached
1   cup quick-cooking rolled oats, uncooked (not instant)
1   cup dried currants or blueberries

Coating:
½   cup granulated sugar
½   teaspoon ground cinnamon

Preheat convection ovens to 310 degrees Fahrenheit or conventional ovens to 325 degrees Fahrenheit. Set the racks in the conventional oven so they divide the oven into thirds. You will *not* need to line the pans with parchment for this recipe. If you are baking in a conventional oven, put one baking sheet inside another of the same size to make a double pan, or use insulated pans to protect the bottoms of the cookies.

Using an electric mixer set on medium speed, combine the 2 cups sugar, baking soda, and salt for 15 seconds. Add the butter, eggs, and vanilla and beat on medium speed for 2 minutes, until the mixture is light in color and smooth. Scrape the bowl with a rubber spatula and add the flour, oats, and currants. Beat on low speed for about 30 seconds, just until evenly combined.

Using a rubber spatula, scrape the sides and bottom of the bowl, stirring the dough to be sure it is evenly mixed. In a small, shallow bowl stir together the ½ cup granulated sugar and the cinnamon with a wire whisk or fork until evenly combined. Using heaping teaspoonfuls of dough, shape them into balls and coat them in the sugar-cinnamon mixture. Place the coated balls on the baking sheets, allowing 2 inches between the balls of dough, and bake in the preheated oven for 10 to 20 minutes, reversing the baking sheets and switching them top to bottom halfway through the baking time. The cookies will puff up and then fall in the oven. They will be light brown when they are done. Do not overbake them. Remove the pans from the oven and set them on wire racks for 5 minutes to cool. Then, using a metal spatula, remove the cookies from the sheets and let the cookies finish cooling on the wire racks.

Store the cooled cookies in an airtight container for up to 2 weeks, or wrap tightly and freeze for up to 2 months. (See freezing instructions on page 12.)

Savor the flavor of Oatmeal Doodles with a glass of milk or a cup of warm tea.

Chewy Orange-Granola Bars

No mixer is required for this easy-to-assemble, dense-chewy bar cookie. Everything is mixed in a saucepan and then baked. The orange juice and zest add a refreshing flavor to a healthful snack. Look for granola that does not contain raisins, because raisins that are mixed in with cereal become too hard for this bar. It is best to add your own soft raisins to get the best flavor and texture. Feel free to substitute any dried fruit, finely chopped if large, for the raisins.

Makes 20 1¾ × 2¼-inch bars.

½	cup unsalted butter
¼	cup brown sugar, firmly packed
¼	cup mild-flavored honey, such as orange blossom or clover
¼	cup orange juice
1	tablespoon freshly grated orange zest
1	teaspoon pure vanilla extract
2½	cups of your favorite granola cereal, without raisins
½	cup sliced almonds, skins on
½	cup soft raisins

Preheat a conventional oven to 350 degrees Fahrenheit. Line a 7 × 11-inch or 9 × 9-inch baking pan with foil and brush lightly with butter.

In a medium-size saucepan, melt the butter over medium-high heat with the brown sugar, honey, orange juice, and zest until the sugar dissolves. This will take 5 to 10 minutes. Remove from heat. Add vanilla stirring until combined. Stir in the granola, almonds, and raisins, mixing completely with a wooden spoon. Spread the mixture into the prepared pan, smoothing the top, and bake in the preheated oven for 15 to 20 minutes, reversing the baking pan halfway through the baking time. The bars will be light brown. Remove from the oven and set the pan on a wire rack to cool.

When completely cool, remove the entire cake from the pan with the foil still on it and carefully remove the foil. Cut into small bars and wrap each bar in plastic wrap.

Store in an airtight container for up to 2 weeks, or wrap tightly and freeze for up to 2 months. (See freezing instructions on page 12.)

Chewy Orange-Granola Bars are a nutritious energy provider when on a bike trip or a hike. Serve with juice.

Almond Granola Bars

Made without a premixed granola, these tasty bars contain coconut and seeds to add to their chewy appeal. You can make your own interesting variation by substituting other types of seeds, nuts, or dried fruits. This is an easy-to-make snack that offers a healthful, quick pick-me-up.

Makes 20 2¼ × 1¾-inch bars.

- ½ **cup unsalted butter**
- ½ **cup brown sugar, firmly packed**
- ¼ **cup mild-flavored honey, such as orange blossom or clover**
- 1 **teaspoon pure vanilla extract**
- 1 **cup quick-cooking rolled oats, uncooked (not instant)**
- ½ **cup chopped almonds**
- ½ **cup sweetened coconut, shredded or flaked, firmly packed**
- ⅓ **cup hulled sesame seeds (the lighter kind)**
- ⅓ **cup shelled sunflower seeds**
- ½ **cup soft raisins or other dried fruit in small pieces**

Preheat a conventional oven to 350 degrees Fahrenheit. Line a 7 × 11-inch or 9 × 9-inch baking pan with foil and brush lightly with butter.

In a medium-size saucepan melt the butter over medium-high heat with the brown sugar, honey, and vanilla until the sugar dissolves. This will take 5 to 10 minutes. Stir in the oats, almonds, coconut, sesame seeds, sunflower seeds, and raisins, mixing completely with a wooden spoon. Spread the mixture into the prepared pan, smoothing the top, and bake in the preheated oven for 15 to 20 minutes, reversing the baking pan halfway through the baking time. The bars will be light brown. Remove from the oven and set the pan on a wire rack to cool.

When completely cool, remove the entire cake from the pan with the foil still on it and carefully remove the foil. Cut into small bars and wrap each bar in plastic wrap. Store in an airtight container for up to 2 weeks, or wrap tightly and freeze for up to 2 months. (See freezing instructions on page 12.)

Almond Granola Bars are a tasty and healthful snack to eat with milk or juice.

Raspberry Nut Chocolate-Chunk Chews

The flavors of raspberry and chocolate are a compatible combination that never seems to become outdated. In this dense, chewy bar you will find a raspberry-flavored dough surrounding dark chocolate chunks. It is delightful. Keep some on hand in the freezer for unexpected guests or to have as an impressive but easy dessert with coffee. It is important to use seedless jam for this recipe, as the seeds will interfere with the texture of the cookies.

Makes 32 2¼ × 1½-inch bars.

¾   cup brown sugar, firmly packed
½   cup granulated sugar
1   teaspoon baking soda
½   cup unsalted butter
1   large egg
1   large egg white
1   teaspoon pure vanilla extract
1   tablespoon freshly grated lemon zest
⅓   cup good-quality seedless raspberry jam
1½   cups all-purpose flour, preferably unbleached
8   ounces coarsely chopped semisweet chocolate (1¼ cups)

Preheat a conventional oven to 350 degrees Fahrenheit. Line a 9 × 13-inch baking pan with foil and lightly butter it. Set the oven rack in the center of the oven.

Using a mixer set on medium speed, combine the brown sugar, sugar, and baking soda for about 15 seconds. Add the butter, egg, egg white, vanilla, and zest and beat on medium speed for about 2 minutes, until smooth and light in color. Scrape the bowl with a rubber spatula and add the jam, beating again on medium speed for about 15 seconds, until it is well combined. Add the flour and the chocolate all at once and beat on low speed for about 20 seconds, just until the flour is mixed in. Using a rubber spatula, scrape the sides and bottom of the bowl, stirring the dough to be sure it is evenly mixed.

Spread the dough into the prepared pan, smoothing the top. Bake in the preheated oven for 20 minutes, reversing the baking pan halfway through the baking time. The top will be just firm to the touch and light brown in color. Remove the pan from the oven and set it on a wire rack to cool. When completely cool, cut into bars.

Store the cooled bars in an airtight container with wax paper between the layers for up to 1 week, or wrap tightly and freeze for up to 2 months. (See freezing instructions on page 12.)

Raspberry Nut Chocolate-Chunk Chews taste spectacular with hot coffee.

Papaya Paradise

When you are reminiscing about a tropical vacation, this cookie will bring back memories of the flavors you might have experienced on your trip. Chewy with dried papaya, macadamia nuts, and coconut, it will deliciously put you back on a sunny beach.

Makes 4 dozen 2-inch cookies.

- ¾ cup brown sugar, firmly packed
- ¾ cup granulated sugar
- 1 teaspoon baking powder
- ¾ cup unsalted butter
- 2 large eggs
- 1 tablespoon freshly grated orange zest
- 2 teaspoons pure vanilla extract
- 2 cups all-purpose flour, preferably unbleached
- 1 cup chopped macadamia nuts (not salted)
- 1 cup sweetened coconut, flaked or shredded, firmly packed
- 1 cup finely chopped dried papaya
- 2 tablespoons orange juice

Preheat convection ovens to 310 degrees Fahrenheit or conventional ovens to 325 degrees Fahrenheit. Set the racks in the conventional oven so they divide the oven into thirds. You will *not* need to line the pans with parchment for this recipe. If you are baking in a conventional oven, put one baking sheet inside another of the same size to make a double pan, or use insulated pans to protect the bottoms of the cookies.

In a small bowl toss the papaya and orange juice. Set aside.

Using an electric mixer on medium speed, combine the brown sugar, sugar, and baking powder for 20 seconds. Add the butter, eggs, zest, and vanilla and beat on medium speed for 2 minutes, until light in color and smooth. Add the flour, macadamias, coconut, and papaya and mix on low speed for about 20 seconds, until evenly combined. Using a rubber spatula, scrape the sides and bottom of the bowl, stirring the dough to be sure it is evenly mixed.

Drop the dough by heaping teaspoonfuls onto the baking sheets and bake in the preheated oven for 10 to 12 minutes, reversing the baking sheets and switching them top to bottom halfway through the baking time. The cookies are done when they just feel firm to the touch and have begun to turn light brown. Do not overbake. Remove the pans from the oven and set them on wire racks to cool for 5 minutes. Carefully remove the cookies from the pans with a metal spatula and place them on the wire racks to finish cooling.

When completely cooled, store the cookies in an airtight container with wax paper between the layers for up to 5 days, or wrap tightly and freeze for up to 2 months. (See freezing instructions on page 12.)

Papaya Paradise cookies are quite tasty with a glass of fresh orange juice.

Banana Oatmeal Pecan Clusters

The toasted pecans perfectly set off the spicy banana dough in these soft-chewy cookies. A touch of oats and dried fruits add extra chewiness to a delicious combination of flavors. The banana makes these cookies moist, and they keep well. They are a great treat to take camping or hiking.

Makes 4 dozen 3-inch cookies.

- 1½ **cups coarsely chopped pecans**
- 1 **cup brown sugar, firmly packed**
- 1 **teaspoon baking powder**
- ½ **teaspoon baking soda**
- 1 **teaspoon ground cinnamon**
- ½ **teaspoon ground nutmeg**
- ½ **cup unsalted butter**
- 2 **large eggs**
- 1½ **cups quick-cooking rolled oats, uncooked (not instant)**
- 1 **cup mashed ripe banana (1 large and 1 medium banana)**
- 1½ **cups all-purpose flour, preferably unbleached**
- 1 **cup chopped dates**
- ½ **cup raisins**

Preheat convection ovens to 325 degrees Fahrenheit or conventional ovens to 350 degrees Fahrenheit. Set the racks in the conventional oven so they divide the oven into thirds. You will *not* need to line the cookie sheets with parchment paper for this recipe. If you are baking in a conventional oven, put one baking sheet inside another of the same size to make a double pan, or use insulated pans to protect the bottoms of the cookies.

Place the pecans in a single layer on a baking sheet and bake in the preheated oven for 8 or 9 minutes, until lightly browned. Remove from the oven and set on a wire rack to cool.

Using an electric mixer on medium speed, combine the brown sugar, baking powder, baking soda, cinnamon, and nutmeg for 20 seconds. Add the butter and eggs and beat on medium speed for 2 minutes, until fluffy and light in color. Scrape the bowl with a rubber spatula and add the oats, beating on low speed for 20 seconds, just until blended in. Scrape the bowl again and add the banana puree, beating on low speed for about 20 seconds. Again scrape the bowl and add the flour, nuts, and fruits. Mix on low speed just until the flour is blended in. Using a wooden spoon or rubber spatula, stir the mixture, scraping down to the bottom of the bowl, to be sure it is evenly mixed.

Drop the dough by rounded tablespoonfuls onto the baking sheets and bake in the preheated oven for 11 to 13 minutes, reversing the baking sheets and switching them top to bottom halfway through the baking time. When done, the tops of the cookies will be lightly browned and just start to feel firm to the touch. Do not overbake. Remove the pans from the oven and set on a wire rack to cool. When completely cool store in an airtight container for up to 1 week, or wrap tightly and freeze for up to 2 months. (See freezing instructions on page 12.)

Banana Oatmeal Pecan Clusters are a great cookie to have with tea or juice.

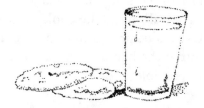

Sesame Banana Cakes

Sesame seeds are flavorful and nutritious. When you buy them, be sure to buy the white (hulled) variety for this recipe, because the darker kind will lend a harsh flavor and texture to the cookies. This is a cookie that is dense-chewy, with a slight crunch from the sesame seeds and a chewiness from the whole wheat. The flavor of the banana takes center stage. Be sure it is ripe: the peel should be deep yellow, flecked with brown spots. If your bananas are not ripe, they will make the cookies taste bitter. Use a food processor or potato masher to puree the banana, and get it as smooth as possible.

Makes 3 dozen 2-inch cookies.

- 1 **cup sesame seeds (hulled)**
- 1 **cup brown sugar, firmly packed**
- ½ **teaspoon ground nutmeg**
- 1 **teaspoon baking powder**
- ¼ **teaspoon salt**
- ⅓ **cup unsalted butter**
- 2 **large eggs**
- 1 **teaspoon pure vanilla extract**
- ½ **cup whole wheat flour, preferably stone-ground**
- 1 **cup all-purpose flour, preferably unbleached**
- 1 **cup pureed ripe banana (3 medium-sized bananas)**

Preheat convection ovens to 310 degrees Fahrenheit or conventional ovens to 325 degrees Fahrenheit. Set the racks in the conventional oven so they divide the oven into thirds. You will *not* need to line the pans with parchment for this recipe. If you are baking in a conventional oven, put one baking sheet inside another of the same size to make a double pan, or use insulated pans to protect the bottoms of the cookies.

Using a heavy medium or large skillet placed over medium-high heat, toast the sesame seeds for about 5 minutes, stirring constantly, until they are lightly browned. Remove the pan from the heat and immediately pour the seeds out into a bowl so they will not continue to cook. Set aside.

Using an electric mixer on medium speed, beat the brown sugar, nutmeg, baking powder, and salt for 20 seconds to blend. Add the butter and beat on medium speed for 2 minutes, until light in color and fluffy. Add the eggs and vanilla and beat on medium speed for 2 minutes, until smooth. Scrape the bowl with a rubber spatula and add the whole wheat and all-purpose flours all at once. Blend on low speed for 20 to 30 seconds, until well combined. Add the banana puree and the sesame seeds, beating on low speed for 20 seconds, just until blended thoroughly.

Drop the dough by heaping teaspoonfuls onto the baking sheets and bake in the preheated oven for 10 to 12 minutes, reversing the baking sheets and switching them top to bottom halfway through the baking time. Do not overbake them. When done, the cookies will feel firm to the touch and will just start to turn brown. Remove them from the oven and cool on the pans on wire racks.

Store the completely cooled cookies in an airtight container with wax paper between the layers for up to 5 days, or wrap tightly and freeze for up to 2 months. (See freezing instructions on page 12.)

Sesame Banana Cakes are a perfect cookie to have with milk.

Apricot-Oatmeal Drops

The sublime flavor and satisfying chewiness of soft, dried apricots make this a delectable snack or lunch-bag dessert. Chewy with oats and whole wheat, this is a truly satisfying cookie. If you love nuts in your cookies, add a cup of chopped walnuts when you blend in the flour.

Makes 3 dozen 2-inch cookies.

1	**cup brown sugar, firmly packed**
1	**teaspoon baking powder**
½	**teaspoon baking soda**
1	**teaspoon ground cinnamon**
½	**cup unsalted butter**
2	**large eggs**
1	**tablespoon freshly grated orange zest**
1½	**cups quick-cooking rolled oats, uncooked (not instant)**
½	**cup whole wheat flour, preferably stone-ground**
½	**cup all-purpose flour, preferably unbleached**
1	**cup finely chopped dried apricots**
2	**tablespoons orange juice**

Preheat convection ovens to 310 degrees Fahrenheit or conventional ovens to 325 degrees Fahrenheit. Set the racks in the conventional oven so they divide the oven into thirds. You will *not* need to line the pans with parchment for this recipe. If you are baking in a conventional oven, put one baking sheet inside another of the same size to make a double pan, or use insulated pans to protect the bottoms of the cookies.

In a small bowl, toss the apricots with the orange juice. Set aside.

Using an electric mixer on medium speed, combine the brown sugar, baking powder, baking soda, and cinnamon for 20 seconds. Add the butter, eggs, and zest and beat on medium speed for 2 minutes. The mixture will be smooth and light in color. Scrape the bowl with a rubber spatula and add the oats, whole wheat flour, and flour, mixing on low speed for about 20 seconds, until well combined. Add the apricots and mix on low speed for another 10 seconds. Using a rubber spatula, scrape the sides and bottom of the bowl, stirring the dough to be sure it is evenly mixed.

Drop the dough by heaping teaspoonfuls onto the baking sheets and bake in the preheated oven for 8 to 10 minutes, reversing the baking sheets and switching them top to bottom halfway through the baking time. The cookies are done when they just feel firm to the touch and have begun to turn light brown. Do not overbake. Remove the pans from the oven and set them on wire racks to cool for 5 minutes. Carefully remove the cookies from the pans with a metal spatula and place them on the wire racks to finish cooling.

When completely cooled, store the cookies in an airtight container with wax paper between the layers for up to 5 days, or wrap tightly and freeze for up to 2 months. (See freezing instructions on page 12.)

Apricot-Oatmeal Drops are a pleasant snack to have with a cup of hot tea or milk.

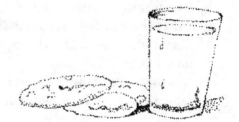

Pineapple-Cashew Squares

The sweet taste of pineapple pairs nicely with the creamy nuttiness of the cashew butter in this flavorful cookie. You can use either fresh pineapple or canned pineapple packed in its own juice for this recipe. Either way, save the juice to use in the recipe. This is an unusual and pleasant bar cookie.

Makes 32 2¼ × 1½-inch bars.

1 **cup brown sugar, firmly packed**
½ **teaspoon baking powder**
½ **teaspoon baking soda**
⅓ **cup unsalted butter, melted**
⅓ **cup cashew butter (available in specialty food and nut shops)**
1 **large egg**
1 **teaspoon pure vanilla extract**
1 **tablespoon freshly grated lemon zest**
2 **cups all purpose flour, preferably unbleached**
⅓ **cup unsweetened pineapple juice**
1 **cup finely chopped pineapple, well drained**
1 **cup sweetened coconut, shredded or flaked, firmly packed**
½ **cup golden raisins**

Preheat a conventional oven to 350 degrees Fahrenheit. Line a 9 × 13-inch baking pan with foil and lightly butter it.

Using an electric mixer on medium speed, combine the brown sugar, sugar, and baking powder and baking soda for 20 seconds. Add the butter, cashew butter, egg, zest, and vanilla, and pineapple juice and beat on medium speed for 2 minutes, until light in color and smooth. Add the flour, macadamias, coconut, and raisins, and mix on low speed for about 20 seconds, until evenly combined. Using a rubber spatula, scrape the sides and bottom of the bowl, stirring the dough to be sure it is evenly mixed.

Spread the batter evenly in the prepared pan and bake in the preheated oven for 25 to 30 minutes, reversing the baking pan halfway through the baking time. The top should be lightly browned and feel firm when touched gently with your fingertip. Remove the pan from the oven and set it on a wire rack to cool.

When completely cool, remove the bar from the pan with the foil and gently remove the foil from the bar. Cut into squares and store in an airtight container with wax paper between the layers for up to 5 days, or wrap tightly and freeze for up to 2 months. (See freezing instructions on page 12.)

Enjoy Pineapple-Cashew Squares with milk or juice for a pleasant afternoon lift.

Whole Wheat Fig Bars

Reminiscent of the fig-filled cookies we all grew up with, these bars are dense, chewy, and packed with delicious fruits and nuts. This is an especially pleasing flavor combination, with a moist texture. They are not too sweet and totally satisfying.

Makes 20 1¾ × 2¼-inch bars.

- ⅔ **cup brown sugar, firmly packed**
- ½ **teaspoon baking powder**
- ½ **teaspoon salt**
- 2 **large eggs**
- 1 **teaspoon pure vanilla extract**
- ¼ **cup all-purpose flour, preferably unbleached**
- ½ **cup whole wheat flour, preferably stone-ground**
- ½ **cup quick-cooking rolled oats, uncooked (not instant)**
- 14 **ounces dried figs, stems removed and coarsely chopped**
- 2 **cups coarsely chopped walnuts**

Preheat a conventional oven to 350 degrees Fahrenheit. Line a 7 × 11-inch or 9 × 9-inch baking pan with foil and lightly butter it.

Using an electric mixer on medium speed, combine the brown sugar, baking powder, and salt for 15 seconds. Add the eggs and vanilla, and beat on medium speed for about 2 minutes, until the mixture is smooth. Scrape the bowl with a rubber spatula and add the flour, whole wheat flour, oats, figs, and walnuts and mix on low speed for about 20 seconds, just until the flour is blended in. Using a rubber spatula, scrape the sides and bottom of the bowl, stirring the dough to be sure it is evenly mixed.

Spread the batter evenly in the prepared pan and bake in the preheated oven for 25 minutes, reversing the baking pan, halfway through the baking time. The top should be lightly browned and feel firm when touched gently with your fingertip. Remove the pan from the oven and set it on a wire rack to cool.

When completely cool, remove the bar from the pan with the foil and gently remove the foil from the bar. Cut into squares and store in an airtight container with wax paper between the layers for up to 5 days, or wrap tightly and freeze for up to 2 months. (See freezing instructions on page 12.)

Whole Wheat Fig Bars are heavenly with milk or coffee.

Sour Cream–Date Drops

Slightly spicy and chewy with chopped dates, this moist cookie will ease its way onto your list of favorites. Sour cream keeps this cookie moist and whole wheat flour lends it some dense chewiness. It is sweet and a little gooey, with a wonderful homey flavor.

Makes about 6 dozen 2-inch cookies.

1   **cup brown sugar, firmly packed**
½   **cup granulated sugar**
½   **teaspoon baking soda**
1   **teaspoon baking powder**
1   **teaspoon ground nutmeg**
⅓   **cup unsalted butter**
2   **large eggs**
2   **teaspoons pure vanilla extract**
1   **cup all-purpose flour, preferably unbleached**
1   **cup sour cream (not low fat)**
2   **cups whole wheat flour, preferably stone-ground**
2   **cups chopped dates**

Preheat convection ovens to 310 degrees Fahrenheit or conventional ovens to 325 degrees Fahrenheit. Set the racks in the conventional oven so they divide the oven into thirds. You will *not* need to line the pans with parchment for this recipe. If you are baking in a conventional oven, put one baking sheet inside another of the same size to make a double pan, or use insulated pans to protect the bottoms of the cookies.

Using an electric mixer on medium speed, combine the brown sugar, sugar, baking soda, baking powder, and nutmeg for 20 seconds. Add the butter, eggs, and vanilla and beat on medium speed for 2 minutes, until light in color and smooth. Scrape the bowl with a rubber spatula. Add the all-purpose flour, beating on low speed for 20 seconds. Scrape the bowl and add the sour cream, beating on low speed for 20 seconds. Again scrape the bowl and add the whole wheat flour and dates, beating on low speed for about 30 seconds, until the flour is evenly blended into the dough. Using a rubber spatula, scrape the sides and bottom of the bowl, stirring the dough to be sure it is evenly mixed.

Drop the dough by heaping teaspoonfuls onto baking sheets and bake in the preheated oven for 15 to 18 minutes, reversing the baking sheets and switching them top to bottom halfway through the baking time. The cookies are done when they are light brown. Do not overbake. Remove the pans from the oven and set them on wire racks to cool.

When the cookies are completely cool, use a metal spatula to remove them from the baking sheets. Store the cooled cookies in an airtight container for up to 4 days, or wrap tightly and freeze for up to 2 months. (See freezing instructions on page 12.)

Have Sour Cream–Date Drops on hand to serve to friends with coffee or tea.

Chewy Date-Walnut Squares

I have been making these bars for many years. They were my dad's favorite cookies. Rich with dates and walnuts and not too sweet, they are a heavenly treat. They are soft-chewy with the inviting gooeyness of chopped dates. Be sure to use soft dried dates for this recipe, because dates that are too dry will not give the same good results. When you chop the dates, it's easiest to use a good pair of kitchen scissors that have been wiped lightly with a vegetable oil-coated paper towel.

Makes 16 2 × 2-inch squares.

- ½ **cup all-purpose flour, preferably unbleached**
- ½ **teaspoon baking soda**
- ½ **teaspoon salt**
- 1 **cup walnuts, coarsely chopped (4 ounces)**
- 2 **cups chopped dates, lightly packed (12 ounces)**
- 2 **large eggs**
- ½ **cup granulated sugar**
- ½ **teaspoon pure vanilla extract**
- ½ **cup confectioners' sugar for coating**

Preheat a conventional oven to 350 degrees Fahrenheit. Line an 8 × 8-inch baking pan with foil and brush it with softened butter.

In a medium-size bowl using a wire whisk, stir together the flour, baking soda, salt, walnuts, and dates. Set aside.

Using an electric mixer on medium speed, combine the eggs, sugar, and vanilla just until smooth, about 1 minute. Add the flour mixture and beat on low speed until thoroughly blended, about 30 seconds. Using a wooden spoon or rubber spatula, stir the mixture, scraping down to the bottom of the bowl, to be sure it is evenly mixed.

Pour into the prepared baking pan and smooth the top with a rubber spatula. Bake in the preheated oven about 30 to 35 minutes, reversing the baking pan halfway through the baking time. The squares are done when the top is nicely browned. Remove the pan from the oven and set on a wire rack to cool completely. When cool, cut into 16 squares. Put the confectioners' sugar on a piece of wax paper and coat the squares on all sides with it.

Store the coated squares in an airtight container with wax paper between the layers for up to 1 week.

Chewy Date-Walnut Squares go well with milk, juice, tea, or coffee.

Chewy Whole Wheat Spice Drops

If you are looking for a thick, sink-your-teeth-into-it cookie, this is it. Packed with nuts, coconut, and spices, these cookies are given extra chewiness from the whole wheat flour. This is a homey, wonderful cookie to eat while snuggling on the sofa watching an old movie. The recipe makes a lot of cookies, but fear not—they will disappear quickly.

Makes 40 3-inch cookies.

1¼   **cup brown sugar, firmly packed**
¾   **cup granulated sugar**
2   **teaspoons baking soda**
¼   **teaspoon baking powder**
1   **teaspoon ground cinnamon**
½   **teaspoon ground allspice**
1   **teaspoon ground nutmeg**
¼   **teaspoon ground cloves**
¼   **teaspoon ground ginger**
1   **cup unsalted butter**
3   **large eggs**
2   **teaspoons pure vanilla extract**
1½   **cups all-purpose flour, preferably unbleached**
2½   **cups whole wheat flour, preferably stone-ground**
1½   **cups coarsely chopped pecans**
1½   **cups sweetened coconut, shredded or flaked, firmly packed**

Preheat convection ovens to 310 degrees Fahrenheit or conventional ovens to 325 degrees Fahrenheit. Set the racks in the conventional oven so they divide the oven into thirds. You will *not* need to line the pans with parchment for this recipe. If you are baking in a conventional oven, put one baking sheet inside another of the same size to make a double pan, or use insulated pans to protect the bottoms of the cookies.

Using an electric mixer set on medium speed, combine the brown sugar, sugar, baking soda, baking powder, cinnamon, allspice, nutmeg, cloves, and ginger for about 20 seconds. Add the butter, eggs, and vanilla and beat on medium speed for about 2 minutes, until the mixture is light in color and smooth. Scrape the bowl with a rubber spatula and add the flours, pecans, and coconut. Mix on low speed for about 30 seconds, until the flour is blended in. Using a rubber spatula, scrape the sides and bottom of the bowl, stirring the dough to be sure it is evenly mixed.

Drop the dough by heaping tablespoonfuls onto the baking sheets and bake in the preheated oven for 13 to 15 minutes, reversing the sheets and switching them top to bottom halfway through. Cookies are done when they just begin to turn brown. They will still be soft to the touch, but will firm up as they cool. Let them cool on the sheets for 5 minutes, then move them to wire racks to finish cooling.

Store the cooled cookies in an airtight container for up to 1 week, or wrap tightly and freeze for up to 2 months. (See freezing instructions on page 12.)

Chewy Whole Wheat Spice Drops and milk can make you feel like a well-loved child.

Chunky Apple Spice Jumbles

Apple season holds such great memories for me: picking tart, crisp apples in a chilly breeze; smelling hot apple pie cooking; and baking these moist, chunky cookies. The spices in this recipe will fill your home with an intoxicating fragrance, beckoning your family to gather in the kitchen, waiting for the cookies to cool just enough to be eaten.

Makes 4 dozen 2½-inch cookies.

1½ cups brown sugar, firmly packed
1 teaspoon ground cinnamon
½ teaspoon ground cloves
½ teaspoon ground nutmeg
1 teaspoon baking soda
½ teaspoon baking powder
½ cup unsalted butter
2 large eggs
1 teaspoon pure vanilla extract
1 cup whole wheat flour,
    preferably stone-ground
½ cup applesauce
1½ cups all-purpose flour, preferably
    unbleached
1 cup diced, peeled tart, firm apple,
    like Granny Smith
1 cup coarsely chopped pecans
1 cup golden raisins

Preheat convection ovens to 350 degrees Fahrenheit or conventional ovens to 375 degrees Fahrenheit. Set the racks in the conventional oven so they divide the oven into thirds. You will *not* need to line the pans with parchment for this recipe. If you are baking in a conventional oven, put one baking sheet inside another of the same size to make a double pan, or use insulated pans to protect the bottoms of the cookies.

Using an electric mixer on medium speed, combine the brown sugar, cinnamon, cloves, nutmeg, baking soda, and baking powder for 20 seconds. Add the butter, eggs, and vanilla and beat on medium speed for 2 minutes, until light in color and smooth. Scrape the bowl with a rubber spatula. Add the whole wheat flour, beating on low speed for 20 seconds. Add the applesauce and beat on low speed for 20 seconds, scraping the bowl again. Add the all-purpose flour, apple, pecans, and raisins and beat on low speed for about 30 seconds, or until evenly blended. Using a rubber spatula, scrape the sides and bottom of the bowl, stirring the dough to be sure it is evenly mixed.

Drop the dough by heaping tablespoonfuls onto baking sheets and bake in the preheated oven for 10 to 12 minutes, reversing the baking sheets and switching them top to bottom halfway through the baking time. The cookies are done when they are light brown. Do not over-bake. Remove the pans from the oven and set them on wire racks to cool.

When the cookies are completely cool, use a metal spatula to remove them from the baking sheets. Store the cooled cookies in an airtight container for up to 4 days, or wrap tightly and freeze for up to 2 months. (See freezing instructions on page 12.)

Chunky Apple Spice Jumbles are a wonderful treat with hot cider, milk, or juice.

Eat Your Veggies

There isn't any more enjoyable way to eat vegetables than as dessert. This chapter contains cookies and bars made with carrots, white and sweet potatoes, winter squash, pumpkin, and zucchini. All of these vegetables lend moisture and texture to cookies while adding nutritional value. If you have trouble getting your kids to eat vegetables, try one of these recipes and see if they'll reconsider.

Chunky Carrot Oatmeal Cookies

Healthful and delicious, homey and not too sweet, this is a cookie with a crunchy, soft-chewy texture that has good keeping qualities. The grated carrots add a pretty fleck of color.

Makes about 50 2-inch cookies.

¾	cup unsalted butter
1½	cups brown sugar, firmly packed
2	large eggs
1	teaspoon pure vanilla extract
2	teaspoons ground cinnamon
½	teaspoon salt
1	teaspoon baking soda
1	teaspoon baking powder
1½	cups all-purpose flour, preferably unbleached
½	cup whole wheat flour, preferably stone-ground
2	cups quick-cooking rolled oats, uncooked (not instant)
1	cup grated fresh carrots, lightly packed
1	cup golden raisins

Preheat convection ovens or conventional ovens to 325 degrees Fahrenheit. Set the racks in the conventional oven so they divide the oven into thirds. It is *not* necessary to line the cookie sheets with parchment paper. If you are baking in a conventional oven, put one baking sheet inside another of the same size to make a double pan, or use insulated pans to protect the bottoms of the cookies.

Using an electric mixer on medium speed, beat together the butter, brown sugar, eggs, vanilla, salt, cinnamon, baking soda, and baking powder until the mixture is fluffy and light in color, about 2 minutes. Scrape the bowl with a rubber spatula and add the flours and oats. Beat on low speed until thoroughly combined, about 30 to 40 seconds. Scrape the bowl again and add the carrots and raisins on low speed, beating only until blended, about 20 seconds. Using a rubber spatula or wooden spoon, scrape the sides and bottom of the bowl and stir to be sure the dough is completely mixed.

Drop the dough by heaping teaspoonfuls onto the baking sheets and bake in a preheated oven for 14 to 16 minutes, reversing the baking sheets and switching them top to bottom halfway through the baking time. When done, the cookies will just start to brown and begin to feel firm when lightly touched. Remove them from the oven and cool on the baking sheets. The cookies will break easily when warm, but will become more firm as they cool. Use a metal spatula to transfer the cooled cookies from the baking sheets to an airtight container for storage.

Store the cookies for up to 7 days in an airtight container, or freeze, tightly wrapped, for up to 2 months. (See freezing instructions on page 12.)

Chunky Carrot Oatmeal Cookies are great with tea, milk, or cider.

Cranberry Zucchini Nut Jumbles

The zucchini in these cookies adds a pleasant moistness and flecks of green color. The combination of cranberries and zucchini makes a colorful cookie that is soft-chewy and moist, with a delicious spicy flavor.

Makes about 4 dozen 2-inch cookies.

- 1   cup brown sugar, firmly packed
- 1   teaspoon baking powder
- ½   teaspoon baking soda
- 1½   teaspoons ground cinnamon
- ½   teaspoon ground nutmeg
- 1   large egg
- ⅔   cup unsalted butter
- 1   teaspoon pure vanilla extract
- 1   cup grated raw zucchini
- 1¼   cups all-purpose flour, preferably unbleached
- 1   cup whole wheat flour, preferably stone-ground
- 1   cup dried cranberries
- 1   cup coarsely chopped pecans
- ½   cup coconut, lightly packed

Preheat convection ovens to 310 degrees Fahrenheit or conventional ovens to 325 degrees Fahrenheit. Set the racks in the conventional oven so they divide the oven into thirds. You will *not* need to line the pans with parchment for this recipe. If you are baking in a conventional oven, put one baking sheet inside another of the same size to make a double pan, or use insulated pans to protect the bottoms of the cookies.

Using an electric mixer on medium speed, beat the brown sugar, baking powder, baking soda, cinnamon, and nutmeg on low speed for 30 seconds to combine evenly. Add the egg, butter, and vanilla. Beat on medium speed for about 2 minutes, until light in color and fluffy. Scrape the bowl with a rubber spatula and add the zucchini. Mix on low speed just until evenly distributed, about 20 seconds. Add the flour, cranberries, nuts, and coconut, and beat on low for 15 to 20 seconds, just until well combined. Using a rubber spatula or wooden spoon, scrape the sides and bottom of the bowl and stir to be sure the dough is completely mixed.

Drop by heaping teaspoonfuls onto the baking sheets and bake in the preheated oven for 12 to 14 minutes, reversing the sheets and switching them top to bottom halfway through the baking time. The cookie will be just firm to the touch. No imprint should be made when you touch the cookie gently with your fingertip. When they are done, cool the cookies on the baking sheets for 5 minutes and then move them to wire racks to finish cooling.

Store the cooled cookies in an airtight container for up to 7 days, or wrap tightly and freeze for up to 2 months. (See freezing instructions on page 12.)

Cranberry Zucchini Nut Jumbles are a nutritious after-school snack and add the perfect color combination to a holiday cookie tray.

Orange Carrot Squares

The flavor of orange is a refreshing addition to these healthful bars, and the nuts add just the right texture. This moist and soft-chewy bar is iced with an orange cream cheese glaze. Scrumptious.

Makes 2 dozen 2½ × 2½-inch bars.

1	cup brown sugar, firmly packed
1	cup granulated sugar
1½	teaspoons ground cinnamon
2	teaspoons baking powder
½	teaspoon salt
1	cup unsalted butter
4	large eggs
1	teaspoon pure vanilla extract
1	tablespoon freshly grated orange zest
2	tablespoons orange juice
2	cups all-purpose flour, preferably unbleached
1	pound fresh carrots, peeled and finely shredded
1	cup chopped pecans
¾	cup golden raisins

Glaze:

6	ounces cream cheese, softened
½	cup confectioners' sugar, stirred to eliminate any lumps
2	teaspoons freshly grated orange zest

Preheat a conventional oven to 350 degrees Fahrenheit. Line a 10 × 15-inch baking pan (with ¾-inch sides) with foil and brush it with softened butter. Dust it with flour.

Using an electric mixer on medium speed, blend the brown sugar, sugar, cinnamon, baking powder, and salt for 20 seconds. Add the butter, eggs, vanilla, orange zest, and orange juice, beating on medium speed for 2 minutes. Add the flour and beat on low speed for 20 seconds. Scrape the bowl with the rubber spatula and add the carrots, nuts, and raisins. Blend on low speed for about 30 to 40 seconds, until evenly combined. Using a rubber spatula or wooden spoon, scrape the sides and bottom of the bowl and stir to be sure the dough is completely mixed.

Pour into the prepared pan, smoothing the top, and bake in the preheated oven for 25 minutes, reversing the baking pan halfway through the baking time. The surface will be firm to the touch and lightly brown. Remove from the oven and set on a wire rack to cool.

Meanwhile, make the glaze. Beat the cream cheese and confectioners' sugar on medium speed until smooth. Add the zest and beat for 20 seconds to blend.

When the cake is cool, glaze the top. Cut into bars.

Store the cooled bars in a single layer in an airtight container in the refrigerator for up to 1 week, or wrap tightly and freeze for up to 2 months. (See freezing instructions on page 12.)

Serve tea and Orange Carrot Squares for a delightful lift.

Potato Spice Pillows

Moist, soft, and chewy, these spicy cookies have a rich maple flavor that just says "more." When you make mashed potatoes, cook extra potatoes and reserve some for this use. Do not add butter or milk to the potatoes you will be using in this recipe, or the dough will be too soft.

Makes 4 dozen 2-inch cookies.

½	**cup unsalted butter**
1	**cup pure maple syrup**
1	**teaspoon pure vanilla extract**
2	**cups all-purpose flour, preferably unbleached**
2	**teaspoons baking powder**
½	**teaspoon baking soda**
½	**teaspoon salt**
1	**teaspoon ground cinnamon**
½	**teaspoon ground allspice**
½	**teaspoon ground nutmeg**
1	**cup cold mashed potatoes**
1	**cup raisins**
1	**cup chopped pecans**

Preheat convection ovens to 325 degrees Fahrenheit or conventional ovens to 350 degrees Fahrenheit. Set the racks in the conventional oven so they divide the oven into thirds. You will *not* need to line the pans with parchment for this recipe. If you are baking in a conventional oven, put one baking sheet inside another of the same size to make a double pan, or use insulated pans to protect the bottoms of the cookies.

In a heavy saucepan, heat the butter and maple syrup over medium heat, stirring occasionally, until the butter melts. Meanwhile, in a mixer bowl, blend together on low speed the flour, baking powder, baking soda, salt, cinnamon, allspice, and nutmeg. When the butter is melted, stir the potatoes and vanilla into the butter mixture with a wooden spoon, until smooth. Add the potato mixture to the flour mixture in a bowl. Using an electric mixer, beat the dough on low speed for about 1 minute, until well blended. Stir in the raisins and the pecans. Using a rubber spatula or wooden spoon, scrape the sides and bottom of the bowl and stir to be sure the dough is completely mixed.

Drop by heaping teaspoonfuls onto the baking sheets and bake in the preheated oven for 10 minutes or until just starting to turn light brown. Reverse the baking sheets and switch them top to bottom halfway through the baking time. The cookies will feel soft, but will become firmer as they cool. Cool the cookies on the baking sheets for 5 minutes, then remove thecookies to a wire rack to finish cooling.

Store the cooled cookies in an airtight container for up to 5 days, or wrap tightly and freeze for up to 2 months. (See freezing instructions on page 12.)

Potato Spice Pillows are a splendid addition to an afternoon tea.

Pumpkin Oatmeal Cookies

Simple to make and flavorful, this is a cookie that is wonderfully versatile. It is a natural for a holiday buffet table or a lunch box. The pumpkin gives it the moist texture and the oatmeal, walnuts, and dates add a satisfying chewiness. The coconut is a nice surprise.

Makes 4 dozen 2-inch cookies.

1¼ **cups brown sugar, firmly packed**
1 **teaspoon baking power**
½ **teaspoon baking soda**
1 **teaspoon ground cinnamon**
½ **teaspoon ground nutmeg**
½ **teaspoon ground cloves**
½ **cup unsalted butter**
2 **large eggs**
2 **teaspoons pure vanilla extract**
1 **cup cooked or canned pumpkin puree**
2 **cups all-purpose flour, preferably unbleached**
2 **cups rolled oats, old-fashioned, or quick, uncooked (not instant)**
1¼ **cups chopped walnuts**
1 **cup chopped dates**
¾ **cup sweetened coconut, flaked or shredded (3¾ ounces), firmly packed**

Preheat convection ovens to 325 degrees Fahrenheit or conventional ovens to 350 degrees Fahrenheit. Set the racks in the conventional oven so they divide the oven into thirds. You will *not* need to line the pans with parchment for this recipe. If you are baking in a conventional oven, put one baking sheet inside another of the same size to make a double pan, or use insulated pans to protect the bottoms of the cookies.

Using an electric mixer on medium speed, blend the brown sugar, baking powder, baking soda, cinnamon, nutmeg, and cloves for 20 seconds. Add the butter and eggs, and beat on medium speed for 2 minutes. The mixture will be smooth and light in color. Scrape the bowl with a rubber spatula and add the pumpkin, beating on low speed for 30 to 40 seconds. Scrape the bowl again and add the flour, oats, walnuts, dates, and coconut. Blend on low speed for 20 to 30 seconds. Using a rubber spatula or wooden spoon, scrape the sides and bottom of the bowl and stir to be sure the dough is completely mixed.

Drop by heaping teaspoonfuls onto the baking sheets and bake in the preheated oven for 12 to 14 minutes, reversing the baking sheets and switching them top to bottom halfway through the baking time. When done, the cookies will just start to turn light brown. They will feel a little soft, but will firm up as they cool. Let the cookies cool on the baking sheets for 5 minutes, then move them to wire racks to finish cooling.

Store the cooled cookies in an airtight container for up to 5 days or wrap tightly and freeze for up to 2 months. (See freezing instructions on page 12.)

Warm spiced cider is the perfect accompaniment to Pumpkin Oatmeal Cookies.

Squash Gems

The addition of squash in this recipe creates a moist cookie with the pleasant chewiness of raisins and candied ginger. Lemon zest and spices makes this an intriguing flavor combination.

Makes 4 dozen 2-inch cookies.

¾   **cup brown sugar, firmly packed**
½   **cup granulated sugar**
2   **teaspoons baking power**
1   **teaspoon baking soda**
½   **teaspoon ground cinnamon**
½   **teaspoon ground nutmeg**
½   **cup unsalted butter**
2   **large eggs**
1   **tablespoon fresh grated lemon zest**
1½   **cups pureed cooked squash, fresh or frozen**
2½   **cups all-purpose flour, preferably unbleached**
1   **cup raisins**
1   **cup walnuts or pecans**
2   **teaspoons very finely diced candied ginger**

Preheat convection ovens to 325 degrees Fahrenheit or conventional ovens to 350 degrees Fahrenheit. Set the racks in the conventional oven so they divide the oven into thirds. You will *not* need to line the pans with parchment for this recipe. If you are baking in a conventional oven, put one baking sheet inside another of the same size to make a double pan, or use insulated pans to protect the bottoms of the cookies.

Using an electric mixer on medium speed, mix together the brown sugar, sugar, baking powder, baking soda, cinnamon, and nutmeg for about 30 seconds, or until evenly blended. Add the butter, eggs, and zest and beat on medium speed for about 2 minutes, until fluffy and light in color. Scrape the bowl with a rubber spatula and add the squash, blending in on low speed for about 1 minute. Scrape the bowl again and add the flour all at once, mixing on low speed for about 30 seconds, until the mixture is thoroughly combined. Scrape the bowl and add the raisins, nuts, and ginger, mixing on low speed just until evenly combined. Using a rubber spatula or wooden spoon, scrape the sides and bottom of the bowl and stir to be sure the dough is completely mixed.

Drop by rounded teaspoonfuls onto the baking sheets and bake in the pre-heated oven for 12 to 14 minutes, reversing the baking sheets and switching them top to bottom halfway through the baking time. The cookies will be done when they are light brown and just barely firm when you touch them with your fingertip. Remove the pans from the oven and let the cookies cool on the sheets for 5 minutes. Use a metal spatula to move the cookies to a wire rack to finish cooling. They will firm up as they cool.

Store the completely cooled cookies in an airtight container for up to 6 days, or wrap tightly and freeze for up to 2 months. (See freezing instructions on page 12.)

The spices in Squash Gems make them an appealing cookie to have with tea or a great partner for milk.

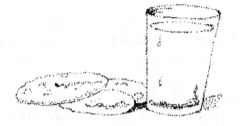

Honey Sweet-Potato Gems

If you like the flavor of candied yams, you will be quite fond of this cookie. This is a soft, flavorful combination of sweet potatoes and spices. Add some toasted pecans if you want an interesting crunch.

Makes 4 dozen 2-inch cookies.

½	cup granulated sugar
½	cup brown sugar, firmly packed
½	teaspoon ground cinnamon
¼	teaspoon ground ginger
¼	teaspoon ground cloves
2	teaspoons baking powder
⅔	cup unsalted butter
2	large eggs
½	cup mild-flavored honey
1	teaspoon pure vanilla extract
2¾	cups all-purpose flour, preferably unbleached
¾	cup finely grated raw yams

Preheat convection ovens to 325 degrees Fahrenheit or conventional ovens to 350 degrees Fahrenheit. Set the racks in the conventional oven so they divide the oven into thirds. You will *not* need to line the pans with parchment for this recipe. If you are baking in a conventional oven, put one baking sheet inside another of the same size to make a double pan, or use insulated pans to protect the bottoms of the cookies.

Using an electric mixer on medium speed, mix the sugar, brown sugar, cinnamon, ginger, cloves, and baking power for about 30 seconds, until evenly blended. Add the butter, eggs, honey, and vanilla and beat on medium speed for about 2 minutes. The mixture will be fluffy and light in color. Using a rubber spatula, scrape the bowl and add the flour all at once. Beat on low speed just until evenly combined, about 20 to 30 seconds. Scrape the bowl again and add the shredded yams. Beat on low again just until combined, about 20 seconds. Using a rubber spatula or wooden spoon, scrape the sides and bottom of the bowl and stir to be sure the dough is completely mixed.

Drop by heaping teaspoonfuls onto the baking sheets and bake in the preheated oven for 15 minutes, reversing the baking sheets and switching them top to bottom halfway through the baking time. The cookies will be done when they begin to brown lightly and just feel firm to the touch. Remove the pan from the oven and let the cookies cool on the pan for 5 minutes. Use a metal spatula to move the cookies to a wire rack to finish cooling.

Store the completely cooled cookies in an airtight container for up to 5 days, or wrap tightly and freeze for up to 2 months. (See freezing instructions on page 12.)

Honey Sweet-Potato Gems taste terrific with a cup of warm apple cider.

Chocolate Carrot Bars

The deep orange color of the carrots in these bars contrasts beautifully with the dark brown chocolate. Orange zest adds a lush and appealing flavor. They are dense and moist and crunchy with nuts.

Makes 32 2¼ × 1½-inch bars.

- **10 ounces coarsely chopped semisweet chocolate**
- **1 ounce unsweetened chocolate**
- **¾ cup unsalted butter**
- **1 cup granulated sugar**
- **1 teaspoon salt**
- **5 large eggs**
- **1 large egg yolk**
- **3 tablespoons freshly grated orange zest**
- **2 teaspoons pure vanilla extract**
- **1⅓ cups all-purpose flour, preferably unbleached**
- **1⅓ cups chopped pecans**
- **½ cup dried currants, raisins, *or* chopped dates (or a combination of them)**
- **2 cups finely grated peeled carrots**

Preheat a conventional oven to 350 degrees Fahrenheit. Line a 9 × 13-inch baking pan with foil and brush it with softened butter.

Melt the butter and the chocolate together in a covered microwavable dish for 2 minutes in the microwave oven, or place in a heavy pan on the stove top over low heat, until the chocolate is almost melted. Remove the mixture from the heat and stir with a whisk until smooth. Let the chocolate mixture cool for about 5 minutes.

Using an electric mixer on medium speed, beat together the sugar, salt, eggs, and egg yolk for about 2 minutes, until smooth. Add the melted chocolate mixture, zest, and vanilla and beat on low speed just until thoroughly mixed, about 30 to 40 seconds. Scrape the bowl with a rubber spatula and add the flour, pecans, and currants, mixing again on low speed until the mixture is evenly combined, about 30 seconds. Scrape the bowl again and add the carrots. Beat on low speed just until the carrots are mixed in evenly, about 20 seconds. Using a rubber spatula or wooden spoon, scrape the sides and bottom of the bowl and stir to be sure the dough is completely mixed.

Pour the batter into the prepared pan and smooth the top. Bake in the preheated oven for 25 to 30 minutes, reversing the baking pan halfway through the baking time. The bars will be done when the top springs back when touched very lightly with your fingertip. Remove the pan from the oven and cool the bars in the pan on a wire rack. When completely cool, cut into bars.

Store the cooled bars in an airtight container with wax paper between the layers for up to 6 days, or wrap tightly and freeze for up to 2 months. (See freezing instructions on page 12.)

Luxuriate on Chocolate Carrot Bars with a steaming hot mug of coffee or a cold glass of milk.

Whole Wheat Zucchini Nut Bars

Whole wheat flour, zucchini, and yogurt combine to form a delicious bar with a healthy twist. Don't be fooled by the healthful sounding ingredients—this is a rich-tasting, yummy bar that is soft-chewy and satisfying. The lemon glaze adds a distinctive touch.

Makes 32 2¼ × 1½-inch bars.

1½	cups brown sugar, firmly packed
1	teaspoon baking powder
1	teaspoon baking soda
1	teaspoon ground cinnamon
½	teaspoon ground nutmeg
½	teaspoon ground cardamom
½	cup unsalted butter
2	large eggs
1	tablespoon freshly grated lemon zest
2	cups whole wheat flour, preferably stone-ground
½	cup plain yogurt
¾	cup all-purpose flour, preferably unbleached
2	cups grated raw zucchini
¾	cup currants or raisins
¾	cup chopped dates
¾	cup sweetened coconut, shredded or flaked, firmly packed
1½	cups coarsely chopped walnuts (about 6½ ounces)

Lemon Glaze:

3	tablespoons unsalted butter
2	tablespoons strained fresh-squeezed lemon juice (1 or 2 lemons)
2	cups confectioners' sugar, stirred with a fork to eliminate any lumps
¼	teaspoon ground cinnamon

Preheat a conventional oven to 350 degrees Fahrenheit. Line a 9 × 13-inch baking pan with foil and brush it with softened butter.

Using an electric mixer on medium speed, mix together the brown sugar, baking powder, baking soda, cinnamon, nutmeg, and cardamon for about 30 seconds, or until evenly combined. Add the butter, eggs, zest, and vanilla and beat on medium speed until light in color and smooth, about 2 minutes. Scrape the bowl with a rubber spatula and add the whole wheat flour all at once, mixing on low speed for about 20 to 30 seconds, until it is combined. Scrape the bowl again and add the yogurt, mixing on low speed for 20 seconds. Add the all-purpose flour and beat on low speed just until blended, about 20 seconds. Scrape the bowl again and add the zucchini, currants, dates, coconut, and walnuts. Mix briefly on low speed just to combine, about 20 seconds. Using a rubber spatula or wooden spoon, scrape the sides and bottom of the bowl and stir to be sure the dough is completely mixed.

Pour into the prepared pan and bake in the preheated oven for 25 to 30 minutes, reversing the baking pan halfway through the baking time. When done, the bars will be lightly browned and the surface will spring back when gently touched with your fingertip.

While the bars are baking, make the glaze. Melt the butter in a small saucepan over medium heat. Remove from the heat and stir in the lemon juice, confectioners' sugar, and cinnamon. Stir until smooth. Cover with a wet towel and set aside.

When the bars are done, remove the pan from the oven and set it on a wire rack. Let the bars cool for about 10 minutes, and pour the glaze over the warm bars, spreading with a spatula. Cool the bars in the pan on a wire rack.

Store the completely cooled bars in an airtight container with wax paper between the layers for up to 5 days, or wrap tightly and freeze for up to 2 months. (See freezing instructions on page 12.)

You will find many beverages to complement the rich mix of flavors in Whole Wheat Zucchini Nut Bars. My favorite is a warm mug of lemon tea.

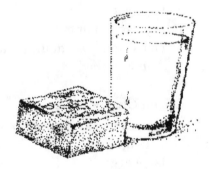

Pumpkin Cheese Praline Bars

The cream cheese that is marbled through these bars gives them a rich texture while the crunchy topping of sugar and pecans adds just the right touch of chewiness. They are spicy and not too sweet. Enjoy them as an afternoon snack or pack them in your kids' lunch bags.

Makes 32 1 × 3¼-inch bars.

1 **cup brown sugar, firmly packed**
2 **teaspoons ground cinnamon**
1 **teaspoon ground ginger**
½ **teaspoon ground cloves**
½ **teaspoon baking powder**
½ **teaspoon baking soda**
½ **cup unsalted butter**
2 **large eggs**
1 **cup canned or cooked pumpkin**
1 **cup all-purpose flour, preferably unbleached**

Cream Cheese Batter:
8 **ounces cream cheese, room temperature**
1 **large egg**
1 **teaspoon pure vanilla extract**
⅓ **cup granulated sugar**

Topping:
¼ **cup unsalted butter**
½ **cup brown sugar, firmly packed**
¾ **cup all-purpose flour, preferably unbleached**
¾ **cup chopped pecans**

Preheat a conventional oven to 350 degrees Fahrenheit. Line a 9 × 13-inch baking pan with foil and brush it with softened butter.

Using an electric mixer on medium speed, mix together the brown sugar, cinnamon, ginger, cloves, baking powder, and baking soda for about 30 seconds, or until evenly combined. Add the butter, eggs, and pumpkin, beating on medium speed for 2 minutes, until smooth. Scrape the bowl with a rubber spatula and add the flour all at once, beating on low speed for 30 seconds, until the flour is evenly blended in. Pour half of the pumpkin batter into the prepared pan and reserve the other half in a small bowl, scraping the mixing bowl well.

Using the same mixing bowl, beat the cream cheese, egg, and vanilla on medium speed for about 2 minutes, until fluffy and smooth. Add the sugar and beat on medium speed again for about 1 minute. Spread the cream cheese batter over the pumpkin batter in the pan, and then pour the reserved pumpkin batter over the cream cheese layer. Using a rubber spatula, cut through the batter several times through the length of the pan and then through the width of the pan, to create a marbled effect.

Make the topping. Using an electric mixer on medium speed, beat the ¼ cup butter and the ½ cup brown sugar for 2 minutes, until fluffy and light in color. Add the flour and pecans and beat on low speed for about 1 minute. The mixture will be crumbly. Sprinkle the crumbs evenly over the marbled batter in the pan and bake in the preheated oven for 30 to 35 minutes, reversing the baking pan halfway through the baking time. The topping will begin to brown and the top will feel slightly firm when touched gently with your fingertip. Remove the pan from the oven and set it on a wire rack to cool. When completely cool, cut it into bars.

Store the cooled bars in an airtight container for up to 1 week in the refrigerator, or wrap tightly and freeze for up to 2 months. (See freezing instructions on page 12.)

You will enjoy serving Pumpkin Cheese Praline Bars as an afternoon snack with milk or coffee.

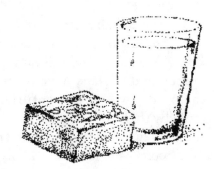

Macaroons: Real Cookies That Are Butter-Free

*L*ight and airy little bites of heaven, macaroons are a chewy cookie eater's delight. It is no wonder the French and Italians have been making them for over four centuries. Their crunchy shells contrast so perfectly with their chewy, soft interiors. The early macaroons were made with only almond paste, sugar, and egg whites. They are still made with very few ingredients. No butter here. The only fat in these cookies comes from the addition of nuts, coconut, or chocolate. The flavors are subtle yet striking. And as an added bonus, they are easy to make. While classic French macaroons are smooth and shiny on the surface, a result of piping the batter, you can get the same wonderful flavor results with less effort by dropping the dough with a spoon. The recipes in this chapter are also designed to appeal to the palates of Americans and sometimes contain other types of nuts than almonds, or even no nuts at all. You will find that most of the recipes contain a small amount of flour (not found in French macaroons), which provides a less mushy texture than macaroons made in France and appeals more to the American palate. Macaroons demand some courtesies: never make them on a rainy day, and *always* line the cookie sheets with parchment paper. If you follow the directions here, you will be rewarded with a bounty of sublime ecstasy.

Coconut Macaroons

To my palate (and to those of my tasters, also) this is just about the perfect cookie: chewy on the inside, crunchy on the outside, sweet, but not too much so, and full of good coconut flavor. Be sure the coconut you use is moist and has not dried out, or your cookies will be dry instead of chewy.

Makes 3 dozen macaroons.

- 3 large egg whites at room temperature
- ¾ cup granulated sugar
- 2¼ cups coconut, firmly packed (11½ ounces), sweetened or flaked
- 2 tablespoons all-purpose flour, preferably unbleached

Preheat convection ovens to 310 degrees Fahrenheit or conventional ovens to 325 degrees Fahrenheit. Set the racks in the conventional oven so they divide the oven into thirds. Line the cookie sheets with parchment paper. If you are baking in a conventional oven, put one baking sheet inside another of the same size to make a double pan, or use insulated pans to protect the bottoms of the cookies.

Using an electric mixer fitted with the whisk attachment if possible, beat the egg whites on medium speed until thick and foamy, about 2 minutes. Slowly add the sugar with the mixer running, and continue to mix for 1 minute after the sugar has all been added. Beat in the coconut on low speed until thoroughly combined, about 30 seconds. Sprinkle the flour over the dough and stir it in, using a rubber spatula to scrape the sides and bottom of the bowl to be sure the dough is well mixed.

Drop the dough by rounded tablespoonfuls onto the prepared baking sheets and bake in a preheated oven, until lightly browned and set, about 24 to 26 minutes. Reverse the baking sheets and switch them top to bottom halfway through the baking time. Remove the macaroons from the oven and let them cool on the baking sheets. When cool, transfer with a metal spatula to a storage container or serving tray.

Store the completely cooled macaroons in an airtight container for up to 1 week, or freeze, wrapped tightly, for up to 2 months. (See freezing instructions on page 12.)

Coconut Macaroons go well with just about any beverage, but especially well with tea or coffee.

Almond-Hazelnut Mounds

Here is a cookie that is ever-so-subtle in flavor. It has a wonderful chewy texture and the perfect taste combination of almonds and hazelnuts—a marriage made in heaven. The chocolate filling completes the picture, making this a cookie you will serve again and again.

Makes 3 dozen macaroons.

1	cup (heaping) hazelnuts with the skins on, finely ground (5 ounces)
1¼	cups almonds with the skins on, finely ground (5½ oz.)
3	large egg whites at room temperature
⅔	cup granulated sugar
2½	tablespoons all-purpose flour, preferably unbleached
8	ounces good-quality dark chocolate, for filling

Preheat convection ovens to 310 degrees Fahrenheit or conventional ovens to 325 degrees Fahrenheit. Set the racks in the conventional oven so they divide the oven into thirds. Line the cookie sheets with parchment paper. If you are baking in a conventional oven, put one baking sheet inside another of the same size to make a double pan, or use insulated pans to protect the bottoms of the cookies.

Combine the nuts in a small bowl, stirring to mix, and set aside.

Using an electric mixer, beat the egg whites and sugar on medium speed until thick and foamy, about 3 minutes. Add the nuts all at once and beat on low to mix, about 1 minute. Scrape the bowl with a rubber spatula and add the flour, mixing on low speed just until thoroughly combined. The dough will not be firm.

Drop the dough onto the prepared baking sheets in heaping teaspoonfuls and bake in a preheated oven for about 12 minutes, reversing the baking sheets and switching them top to bottom halfway through the baking time. Bake until the macaroons are not shiny and they are firm but your finger still leaves an imprint when you touch one gently. These cookies should not brown. Remove the trays from the oven and slide the parchment, with the macaroons still on it, onto a cooling rack. While the macaroons are cooling, melt the chocolate according to the directions on page 10. When the macaroons are completely cool, dip the bottoms in the melted chocolate and set the dipped macaroons on a wax paper-lined baking sheet, chocolate side down. When you have dipped all the macaroons, place them in the refrigerator for about 10 minutes to set the chocolate.

Store the macaroons in an airtight container with wax paper between layers, for about 2 weeks. Keep them away from heat. The macaroons can also be frozen, tightly wrapped, for up to 2 months. (See freezing instructions on page 12.)

Serve Almond-Hazelnut Mounds with tea or coffee for an after-dinner delight.

Chocolate-Almond Macaroons

A milk chocolate flavor in a subtle, chewy cookie that is not too sweet. The grated chocolate enriches the chocolate flavor without adding any bitterness.

Makes 3½ dozen 2-inch cookies.

- **3   large egg whites, at room temperature**
- **1½ cups granulated sugar**
- **4   tablespoons unsweetened cocoa powder**
- **2   cups ground almonds**
- **2¾ ounces grated semisweet chocolate**

Beat the egg whites with an electric mixer on medium speed using the whisk attachment if possible, until thick and foamy, about 3 minutes. Add the sugar slowly while the mixer is on and continue to beat for 1 minute after the sugar is added. Scrape the bowl with a rubber spatula and add the almonds and grated chocolate, beating on low speed until the mixture is blended. Using the rubber scraper, stir the dough, scraping down to the bottom of the bowl to be sure the dough is evenly mixed.

Drop the dough in heaping teaspoonfuls onto the prepared pans and bake in the preheated oven for about 15 minutes, turning the sheets around and switching them top to bottom halfway through the baking time. Bake until the macaroons feel firm when touched gently. Remove the pans from the oven and let the cookies cool on the sheets. When cool, use a metal spatula to transfer the cookies to a container or serving dish.

Store the completely cooled macaroons in an airtight container with wax paper between the layers for up to 1 week, or freeze them, tightly wrapped, for up to 2 months. (See freezing instructions on page 12.)

Chocolate-Almond Macaroons are especially good with a cup of hot coffee.

Almond Macaroons

An incredible almond taste and a light, airy texture are your rewards for making this delicious treat. This is a cookie that just about everyone likes. Serve it at a tea or luncheon, for dessert at a special meal, or just tuck some into your child's lunch box.

Makes 4 dozen 2-inch cookies

- **3   large egg whites, at room temperature**
- **1   cup granulated sugar**
- **12   ounces natural almonds (skins on), finely ground**
- **1   teaspoon pure almond extract**
- **4   tablespoons all-purpose flour, preferably unbleached**
- **1½   tablespoons sliced natural almonds *or* chocolate chips, for garnish**

Preheat convection ovens to 310 degrees Fahrenheit or conventional ovens to 325 degrees Fahrenheit. Set the racks in the conventional oven so they divide the oven into thirds. Line the cookie sheets with parchment paper. If you are baking in a conventional oven, put one baking sheet inside another of the same size to make a double pan, or use insulated pans to protect the bottoms of the cookies.

Using an electric mixer fitted with the whisk attachment if possible, beat the egg whites on medium speed until foamy, about 1 minute. Add the sugar slowly with the mixer running and continue to beat on medium speed for 1 minute after all the sugar has been added. The mixture will be thick and glossy but there will be no peaks. Add the nuts and the extract and beat on low speed until thoroughly blended. Scrape the bowl with a rubber spatula and sprinkle the flour over the dough, beating on low for about 30 seconds, until the flour is mixed into the dough. With the rubber spatula scrape the bottom and sides of the bowl, to be sure the dough is evenly mixed.

Drop the dough by rounded teaspoonfuls onto the prepared sheets. Put one almond slice or chocolate chip in the center of each and bake in a preheated oven about 13 to 15 minutes, reversing the baking sheets and switching them top to bottom halfway through the baking time. Bake just until firm. Do not overbake. Remove the trays from the oven and slide the parchment, with the macaroons still on it, onto a cooling rack.

Store the completely cool macaroons in an airtight container for up to 2 weeks, or freeze, wrapped tightly, for up to 2 months. (See freezing instructions on page 12.)

Almond Macaroons go nicely with tea or coffee.

Walnut Chews

This might just be my all-time favorite cookie. To me a cookie is simply not a cookie unless it has nuts in it. The walnuts in these chewy morsels take on a delicious toasted flavor that is nicely enhanced by the cinnamon. They are a melt-in-your-mouth delight.

Makes 3 dozen 1½-inch cookies.

1   **cup brown sugar firmly packed**
½   **teaspoon ground cinnamon**
2   **large egg whites, room temperature**
3   **cups finely chopped walnuts**
1   **teaspoon pure vanilla extract**
2   **tablespoons all-purpose flour, preferably unbleached**

Preheat convection ovens to 310 degrees Fahrenheit or conventional ovens to 325 degrees Fahrenheit. Set the racks in the conventional oven so they divide the oven into thirds. You will need to line the pans with parchment for this recipe, or the cookies will stick to the cookie sheets. If you are baking in a conventional oven, put one baking sheet inside another of the same size to make a double pan, or use insulated pans to protect the bottoms of the cookies.

In a small bowl, mix the brown sugar and cinnamon with a wire whisk. Set aside. Using an electric mixer on medium speed with the wire whisk attachment if one is available, beat the egg whites for 2 minutes, or until foamy, but not stiff. Add the brown sugar and cinnamon mixture and beat about 2 minutes on medium speed, until thick. Scrape the bowl with a rubber spatula and add the nuts and vanilla. Beat on low speed for 30 seconds, scrape the bowl again, and add the flour. Beat on low speed for about 15 seconds, or until thoroughly mixed. Using a rubber spatula, scrape the sides of the bowl and stir the dough to be sure it is completely mixed.

Drop by rounded teaspoonfuls onto the prepared baking sheets. Bake in the preheated oven about 11 to 13 minutes, reversing the baking sheets and switching them top to bottom halfway through the baking time. The surface of the cookies will be dull and cracks will form. Do not overbake. Cool the cookies on the baking sheets.

Store the completely cooled cookies in an airtight container for up to 1 week, or wrap tightly and freeze for up to 2 months. (See freezing instructions on page 12.)

Walnut Chews are wonderful with coffee, tea, milk, juice, or just by themselves.

Spicy Pecan Macaroons

Akin to Walnut Chews, this delightful cookie offers a pleasant marriage of pecans and spices. The extra step of adding a cinnamon-sugar coating to this cookie creates an interesting crust to contrast with the chewy center.

Makes 3 dozen 1½-inch cookies.

Coating:
½ cup granulated sugar
½ teaspoon ground cinnamon

Macaroons:
1 cup brown sugar, firmly packed
½ teaspoon ground nutmeg
2 large egg whites
2 cups finely ground pecans
1 teaspoon pure vanilla extract
3 tablespoons all-purpose flour, preferably unbleached

Preheat convection ovens to 310 degrees Fahrenheit or conventional ovens to 325 degrees Fahrenheit. Set the racks in the conventional oven so they divide the oven into thirds. You will need to line the pans with parchment for this recipe, or the cookies will stick to the cookie sheets. If you are baking in a conventional oven, put one baking sheet inside another of the same size to make a double pan, or use insulated pans to protect the bottoms of the cookies.

Make the coating by combining the granulated sugar and cinnamon in a shallow bowl and set aside.

In a small bowl, mix the brown sugar and nutmeg with a wire whisk. Set aside.

Using an electric mixer on medium speed with the wire whisk attachment if one is available, beat the egg whites for 1 minute, or until foamy, but not stiff. Add the brown sugar and nutmeg and beat about 2 minutes on medium speed, until thick. Scrape the bowl with a rubber spatula and add the nuts and vanilla. Beat on low speed for 30 seconds, scrape the bowl again, and add the flour. Beat on low speed for about 20 to 30 seconds, or until thoroughly mixed. Using a wooden spoon or rubber spatula, scrape the sides of the bowl and stir the dough to be sure it is completely mixed.

Drop by rounded tablespoonfuls into the cinnamon-sugar mixture, rolling to completely coat the macaroon. Place onto the prepared baking sheets. Bake in the preheated oven for about 12 minutes, reversing the baking sheets and switching them top to bottom halfway through the baking time. The surface of the cookies will be dull and cracks will form. Do not overbake. Cool the cookies on the baking sheets.

Store the completely cooled cookies in an airtight container for up to 1 week, or wrap tightly and freeze for up to 2 months. (See freezing instructions on page 12.)

Spicy Pecan Macaroons go extremely well with hot tea or coffee.

Orange-Flower Macaroons

Delicately flavored with orange-flower water and fresh orange zest, these luscious treats are a wonderful Sunday brunch dessert to have with tea. They are crisp on the outside and dense-chewy on the inside. Orange-flower water is available at specialty food stores and most spice stores.

Makes 4 dozen 2-inch cookies.

3	large egg whites
1¼	cups granulated sugar
1	tablespoon orange-flower water
1	tablespoon freshly grated orange zest
3	cups sweetened coconut, flaked or shredded, tightly packed
3	tablespoons all-purpose flour, preferably unbleached

Preheat convection ovens to 310 degrees Fahrenheit or conventional ovens to 325 degrees Fahrenheit. Set the racks in the conventional oven so they divide the oven into thirds. You will need to line the pans with parchment for this recipe, or the cookies will stick to the cookie sheets. If you are baking in a conventional oven, put one baking sheet inside another of the same size to make a double pan, or use insulated pans to protect the bottoms of the cookies.

Using an electric mixer on medium speed with the wire whisk attachment if one is available, beat the egg whites for 2 minutes, or until foamy, but not stiff. Add the sugar and beat about 2 minutes on medium speed, until thick. Scrape the bowl with a rubber spatula and add the coconut, zest, and orange-flower water. Beat on low speed for 30 seconds, scrape the bowl again, and add the flour. Beat on low speed for about 15 seconds, or until thoroughly mixed. Using a rubber spatula or wooden spoon, scrape the sides of the bowl and stir the dough to be sure it is completely mixed.

Drop by rounded teaspoonfuls onto the prepared baking sheets. Bake in the preheated oven for about 11 to 13 minutes, reversing the baking sheets and switching them top to bottom halfway through the baking time. The surface of the cookies will be slightly firm. Do not overbake. Cool the cookies on the baking sheets.

Store the completely cooled cookies in an airtight container for up to 1 week, or wrap tightly and freeze for up to 2 months. (See freezing instructions on page 12.)

Peanut Butter Macaroons

I just couldn't forget all of you peanut butter devotees. This recipe is for you. Intense with the taste of peanut butter, it will transport you to peanut butter heaven. There are only three ingredients in this recipe, so you can indulge your cravings almost instantly. Use a good-quality peanut butter, to get the best flavor from these cookies.

Makes 3 dozen 2½-inch cookies.

1   cup smooth peanut butter
1⅓ cups confectioners' sugar, stirred with a fork to remove any lumps and divided in two parts
4   large egg whites at room temperature

Preheat convection ovens to 310 degrees Fahrenheit or conventional ovens to 325 degrees Fahrenheit. Set the racks in the conventional oven so they divide the oven into thirds. You will need to line the pans with parchment for this recipe, or the cookies will stick to the cookie sheets. If you are baking in a conventional oven, put one baking sheet inside another of the same size to make a double pan, or use insulated pans to protect the bottoms of the cookies.

In a medium-size bowl, stir the peanut butter with ⅔ cup of the confectioners' sugar until smooth, using a wooden spoon. Set aside.

Using an electric mixer on medium speed with the wire whisk attachment if one is available, beat the egg whites for 2 or 3 minutes, or until soft peaks form. Add the remaining ⅔ cup confectioners' sugar slowly with the mixer running, and beat about 2 minutes on medium speed, until thick and glossy and stiff peaks form. Stir about ⅓ of the egg white mixture into the peanut butter mixture to lighten it, then gently fold in the remaining egg white mixture in two parts, using a wire whisk or rubber spatula.

When all of the egg whites are folded in, drop the mixture by rounded tablespoonfuls onto the prepared sheets and bake in the preheated oven for 10 to 12 minutes, reversing the baking sheets and switching them top to bottom halfway through the baking time. When the macaroons are done, the surface will start to become dull and crack. Do not overbake. Remove the pans from the oven and set them on wire racks to cool.

When the macaroons are completely cool, remove them from the parchment with a metal spatula and store them in an airtight container for up to 1 week, or wrap them tightly and freeze them for up to 2 months. (See freezing instructions on page 12.)

Peanut Butter Macaroons and hot chocolate are a match made in heaven.

Cookies Kids Love

This chapter could also be called The Peanut Gallery for all the peanut butter that's in it. These are kid-style cookies that were rigorously taste-tested on elementary age children. It was the hard work of the kindergarten and fourth grade classes at the Springside School and the third grade at Chestnut Hill Academy that makes this collection what it is. What follows is a compilation of chocolate, candy-filled, peanut butter, and soft sugar and spice cookies that appeal to the very young (and not so very young) among us. Of course you shouldn't rule out the many other cookies throughout the book that are appealing to the younger generations, but the cookies in this chapter are especially designed to fulfill their cookie fantasies.

Peanut Butter Candy Cookies

This was a hands-down favorite with the tasters. It is a thick, soft, and densely chewy peanut butter cookie with the crunch of chocolate and peanut butter candies. A definite winner.

Makes about 50 2½-inch cookies.

1   cup brown sugar, firmly packed
½   cup granulated sugar
1   teaspoon baking soda
½   cup butter
2   large eggs
¾   cup smooth peanut butter (not the natural kind)
2   cups all-purpose flour, preferably unbleached
1   cup candy-coated peanut butter candies
1   cup candy-coated chocolate candies

Preheat convection ovens to 330 degrees Fahrenheit or conventional ovens to 350 degrees Fahrenheit. Set the racks in the conventional oven so they divide the oven into thirds. It is not necessary to line the cookie sheets with parchment paper. If you are baking in a conventional oven, put one baking sheet inside another of the same size to make a double pan, or use insulated pans to protect the bottoms of the cookies.

Using an electric mixer on medium speed, combine the sugars and baking soda for about 15 seconds. Add the butter and eggs and beat on medium speed until light in color and fluffy, about 2 minutes. Scrape the bowl with a rubber spatula and add the peanut butter. Beat on low speed about 30 seconds to thoroughly combine. Scrape the bowl again and add the flour all at once, beating again on low speed for about 30 seconds. Using the rubber spatula, stir in the candy pieces, scraping the bottom and sides of the bowl to be sure the dough is mixed well.

Drop the dough by rounded tablespoonfuls onto the baking sheets and bake in a preheated oven for 10 to 12 minutes, or until the cookies just start to feel firm to the touch. Turn the sheets around and switch them top to bottom halfway through the baking time. When the cookies are done, remove the baking sheets from the oven, and cool the cookies on the sheets for about 5 minutes before removing them with a metal spatula to wire racks to finish cooling.

Store the cooled cookies in an airtight container for up to 6 days, or freeze, wrapped tightly, for up to 2 months. (See freezing instructions on page 12.)

Serve Peanut Butter Candy Cookies with glasses of milk, chocolate milk, or milk shakes.

Fudgy Peanut Butter Sandwiches

A soft-chewy chocolate cookie sandwiches a sweet, creamy peanut butter filling. This is a great lunch-box surprise or after-school treat.

Makes about 20 2½-inch sandwiches.

1¼ **cups all-purpose flour, preferably unbleached**
½   **cup unsweetened cocoa**
1   **teaspoon baking soda**
½   **teaspoon baking powder**
½   **cup unsalted butter**
1   **cup brown sugar, firmly packed**
2   **large eggs**
1   **teaspoon pure vanilla extract**
½   **cup heavy cream**

Filling:

6   **tablespoons confectioners' sugar**
¾   **cup creamy peanut butter**
1½ **tablespoons heavy or light cream**

Preheat convection ovens to 310 degrees Fahrenheit or conventional ovens to 325 degrees Fahrenheit. Set the racks in the conventional oven so they divide the oven into thirds. Line the cookie sheets with parchment paper. If you are baking in a conventional oven, put one baking sheet inside another of the same size to make a double pan, or use insulated pans to protect the bottoms of the cookies.

In a medium-size bowl, stir together the flour, cocoa, baking soda, and baking powder with a wire whisk. Set aside.

Using an electric mixer on medium speed, beat the butter, brown sugar, eggs, and vanilla until fluffy and light in color, about 2 minutes. Scrape the bowl with a rubber spatula and add about half of the dry ingredients, beating on low speed for about 30 seconds. Scrape the bowl again and add ½ cup heavy cream, mixing on low speed until blended, about 20 seconds. Scrape the bowl and add the remaining dry ingredients, mixing on low speed for about 30 seconds, until

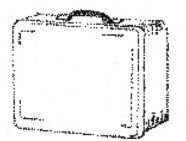

thoroughly blended. With a rubber spatula, stir and scrape the bottom and sides of the bowl to be sure the dough is evenly mixed.

Drop by heaping teaspoonfuls onto the baking sheets and bake in a preheated oven for about 11 to 13 minutes, reversing the baking sheets and switching them top to bottom halfway through the baking time. Remove the cookies from the oven and cool on the baking sheets. The cookies will firm up as they cool.

While the cookies are cooling, make the filling. Place the confectioners' sugar in a small bowl and stir with a wire whisk to remove any lumps. Add the peanut butter and cream and stir until smooth. When the cookies are completely cool, spread half of them with the filling and sandwich them with the remaining cookies.

Store the filled, cooled cookies in an airtight container for up to 5 days or freeze, wrapped tightly, for up to 2 months. (See freezing instructions on page 12.)

Fudgy Peanut Butter Sandwiches are definitely made for milk.

Caramel Drops

This is definitely a kids-only cookie. The caramel is sticky and many adults will find that annoying, but kids sure love it. It is a thin, soft-chewy cookie made extra chewy by the caramel candy inside. It is a great birthday party treat.

Makes 5 dozen 2-inch cookies.

- 1½ **cups brown sugar, firmly packed**
- 1 **teaspoon baking soda**
- ½ **cup unsalted butter**
- 2 **large eggs**
- 1½ **teaspoons pure vanilla extract**
- 3½ **cups all-purpose flour, preferably unbleached**
- ½ **cup milk at room temperature**
- 6 **ounces semisweet real chocolate chips or 6 ounces semisweet chocolate, coarsely chopped**
- 1½ **cups diced vanilla caramels (9 ounces)**

Preheat convection ovens to 330 degrees Fahrenheit or conventional ovens to 350 degrees Fahrenheit. Set the racks in the conventional oven so they divide the oven into thirds. Line the cookie sheets with parchment paper. If you are baking in a conventional oven, put one baking sheet inside another of the same size to make a double pan, or use insulated pans to protect the bottoms of the cookies.

Using an electric mixer on medium speed, combine the brown sugar and baking soda for about 15 seconds, until well blended. Add the butter, eggs, and vanilla and beat on medium speed for about 2½ minutes, until fluffy and light in color. Scrape the bowl with a rubber spatula and add half of the flour, beating on low speed for about 15 seconds. Scrape the bowl again and add the milk, beating on low for 20 seconds, or until evenly mixed. The mixture may look curdled, but that is all right. Add the remaining flour and beat again on low speed for about 15 seconds, until the flour is evenly mixed in. With the rubber scraper, stir the chocolate and caramels into the dough, scraping the bottom and sides to be sure the dough is evenly mixed.

Drop the dough by heaping teaspoonfuls onto the prepared baking pans and bake in a preheated oven for 12 to 14 minutes, or until the cookies just begin to brown. Reverse the baking sheets and switch them top to bottom halfway through the baking time. Remove the cookies from the oven and cool completely on the pans. Be careful—the caramel is very hot when the cookies come out of the oven.

Store the cooled cookies in an airtight container with wax paper between the layers for up to 5 days, or freeze them, tightly wrapped, for up to 2 months. (See freezing instructions on page 12.)

Caramel Drops go well with milk and hot chocolate.

Peanut Butter Cup Jumbles

Thick, chocolaty soft-chewy cookies envelope cut-up peanut butter cup candy. A true child's fantasy. These were one of the most popular among the tasters, and the cookie my son, Benjamin, yearns for most.

Makes about 4 dozen 2½-inch cookies.

2½ **cups all-purpose flour, preferably unbleached**
½   **cup unsweetened cocoa**
1   **teaspoon baking soda**
¼   **teaspoon salt**
¾   **cup unsalted butter**
2   **cups granulated sugar**
2   **large eggs**
2   **teaspoons pure vanilla extract**
2   **cups quartered miniature peanut butter cups (38 miniature cups)**

Preheat convection ovens to 310 degrees Fahrenheit or conventional ovens to 325 degrees Fahrenheit. Set the racks in the conventional oven so they divide the oven into thirds. You do *not* need to line the cookie sheets with parchment paper. If you are baking in a conventional oven, put one baking sheet inside another of the same size to make a double pan, or use insulated pans to protect the bottoms of the cookies.

In a medium-size bowl using a wire whisk, mix together the flour, cocoa, baking soda, and salt. Set aside.

Using an electric mixer on medium speed, beat the butter, sugar, eggs, and vanilla for about 2 minutes, until the mixture is fluffy and light in color. Scrape the bowl with a rubber spatula and add the dry ingredients, beating on low speed until the flour is evenly mixed in, about 30 seconds. With a rubber spatula stir in the chopped peanut butter cups, scraping the sides and bottom of the bowl to be sure the dough is thoroughly mixed.

Drop by rounded tablespoonfuls onto the baking pans and bake in the preheated oven for 11 to 13 minutes, reversing the baking sheets and switching them top to bottom halfway through the baking time. The cookies will seem soft but will firm up as they cool. Remove the sheets from the oven and cool the cookies on the sheets for 5 minutes. Use a metal spatula to move the cookies from the baking sheets to wire racks to finish cooling.

Store the completely cooled cookies in an airtight container for up to 6 days, or freeze, tightly wrapped, for up to 2 months. (See freezing instructions on page 12.)

Peanut Butter Cup Jumbles are a treat with a glass of cold milk.

Snickerdoodles

I haven't encountered a child or adult who doesn't like Snickerdoodles. Variations of this recipe have been around for decades, maybe even generations. It is crunchy on the outside and chewy in the center, and coated with a mixture of cinnamon-sugar before it is baked. Doodles are cookies that rise and fall when baked, so they are thin and chewy inside. There are other good doodle flavor variations in this book, but this is the original recipe. If you have never tasted them, make some and you will see what all the fuss is about. They are easy and delicious.

Makes 5 dozen 2½-inch doodles.

- 1½ **cups granulated sugar**
- 2 **teaspoons cream of tartar**
- 1 **teaspoon baking soda**
- ½ **teaspoon salt**
- ¾ **cup unsalted butter**
- 2 **large eggs**
- 1 **teaspoon pure vanilla extract**
- 2¾ **cups all-purpose flour, preferably unbleached**

Coating:
- ½ **teaspoon ground cinnamon**
- ½ **cup granulated sugar**

Preheat convection ovens to 325 degrees Fahrenheit or conventional ovens to 350 degrees Fahrenheit. Set the racks in the conventional oven so they divide the oven into thirds. It is *not* necessary to line the cookie sheets with parchment paper. If you are baking in a conventional oven, put one baking sheet inside another of the same size to make a double pan, or use insulated pans to protect the bottoms of the cookies.

Using an electric mixer on medium speed, combine the 1½ cups of sugar, cream of tartar, baking soda, and salt. Add the butter, eggs, and vanilla and beat on medium speed for about 2 minutes, until fluffy and light in color. Scrape the bowl with a rubber spatula and add the flour, beating on low speed for about 30 seconds, or until the flour is blended in. With a rubber spatula stir the dough and scrape the sides and bottom to be sure the dough is evenly mixed.

Mix together the cinnamon and ½ cup of sugar in a small bowl. Drop rounded teaspoonfuls of the dough into the cinnamon-sugar mixture and roll each so that it is covered. Place the doodles on the baking sheets and bake in the preheated oven for about 11 to 13 minutes, reversing the baking sheets and switching them top to bottom halfway through the baking time. When done, the doodles are puffed and just starting to brown. They will still be soft to the touch and will fall and become flat as they cool. Let the doodles cool on the sheets for 5 minutes, then with a metal spatula move them to wire racks to finish cooling.

Store the cooled doodles in an airtight container for up to 10 days, or wrap tightly and freeze for up to 2 months. (See freezing instructions on page 12.)

Snickerdoodles are the perfect after-school treat to have with milk or apple juice.

Peanut Butter Doodles

Another doodle that is popular with kids is peanut butter. If your kids like peanut butter, they will love these doodles. Just sweet enough to please a child, and peanut enough to be a good after-school snack.

Makes about 4½ dozen 2½-inch cookies.

- ½ **cup brown sugar, firmly packed**
- ½ **cup granulated sugar**
- ½ **teaspoon baking soda**
- ½ **cup unsalted butter**
- 1 **large egg**
- ½ **teaspoon pure vanilla extract**
- ½ **cup smooth peanut butter (not the natural kind)**
- 1 **cup all-purpose flour, preferably unbleached**

Coating:
- ½ **cup granulated sugar**

Preheat convection ovens to 310 degrees Fahrenheit or conventional ovens to 325 degrees Fahrenheit. Set the racks in the conventional oven so they divide the oven into thirds. It is not necessary to line the cookie sheets with parchment paper. If you are baking in a conventional oven, put one baking sheet inside another of the same size to make a double pan, or use insulated pans to protect the bottoms of the cookies.

Using an electric mixer on medium speed, combine the brown sugar, ½ cup of granulated sugar, and baking soda. Add the butter, egg, and vanilla and beat on medium speed for about 2 minutes, or until the mixture is fluffy and light in color. Scrape the bowl with a rubber spatula and add the peanut butter, beating on medium speed about 30 seconds, until well blended. Scrape the bowl again and add the flour, beating on low speed just until the mixture is combined, about 20 seconds. With a rubber spatula, stir the dough and scrape the sides and bottom of the bowl to be sure the dough is evenly mixed. Cover the bowl and refrigerate the dough for 30 to 45 minutes, or until it is firm enough to work with.

When the dough is firm, form it into 1-inch balls and roll them in the ½ cup granulated sugar. Place them on baking sheets and bake in a preheated oven for 12 to 13 minutes, reversing the baking sheets and switching them top to bottom halfway through the baking time. The cookies are done when they are puffed and just beginning to turn light brown. They will still feel soft to the touch. Remove them from the oven and cool the doodles on the baking sheets for 5 minutes. Using a metal spatula, move them to wire racks to finish cooling.

Store the cooled doodles in an airtight container for up to 10 days, or wrap tightly and freeze for up to 2 months. (See freezing instructions on page 12.)

Peanut Butter Doodles and chocolate milk taste like peanut butter cups.

Double Chocolate-Chunk Peanut Butter Jumbles

Two kinds of chocolate chunks make these thin, soft-chewy peanut butter cookies special. Adults like them as much as kids do. Be sure the white chocolate chunks or chips you use are good quality.

Makes 4 dozen 2½-inch cookies.

- ¾   **cup brown sugar, firmly packed**
- ½   **cup granulated sugar**
- 1   **teaspoon baking powder**
- ¼   **teaspoon baking soda**
- ⅓   **cup unsalted butter**
- ½   **cup smooth peanut butter (not the natural kind)**
- 2   **large eggs**
- 1   **teaspoon pure vanilla extract**
- 1½   **cups all-purpose flour, preferably unbleached**
- 6   **ounces good quality white chocolate chunks, or good-quality white chocolate chips, such as Ghirardelli**
- 6   **ounces chopped milk chocolate or real milk chocolate chips**

Preheat convection ovens to 310 degrees Fahrenheit or conventional ovens to 325 degrees Fahrenheit. Set the racks in the conventional oven so they divide the oven into thirds. You do *not* need to line the cookie sheets with parchment paper. If you are baking in a conventional oven, put one baking sheet inside another of the same size to make a double pan, or use insulated pans to protect the bottoms of the cookies.

Using an electric mixer on medium speed, combine the sugars, baking powder, and baking soda. Add the butter, peanut butter, eggs, and vanilla and beat on medium speed for about 3 minutes, or until fluffy and light in color. Scrape the bowl with a rubber spatula and add the flour and chocolate chunks, beating on low speed until the mixture is well blended.

Drop by rounded tablespoonfuls onto the baking sheets and bake in a preheated oven for 12 to 14 minutes, reversing the baking sheets and switching them top to bottom halfway through the baking time. The cookies will just start to brown. They will be soft when warm, but will firm up as they cool. Cool the cookies on the sheets for 5 minutes, and then move them to wire racks with a metal spatula.

Store the cooled cookies in an airtight container for up to 5 days, or wrap tightly and freeze for up to 2 months. (See freezing instructions on page 12.)

Double Chocolate-Chunk Peanut Butter Jumbles are great with milk, but some of you older kids may like them with a cup of hot coffee.

Scotch Chewies

Thin, sweet, and soft-chewy, this is definitely a cookie for kids. The brown sugar gives it a butterscotch flavor that kids love. How nice to come home from school to a cookie jar full of these!

Makes about 5 dozen 2-inch cookies

2	**cups brown sugar, firmly packed**
1	**teaspoon baking powder**
½	**teaspoon baking soda**
⅔	**cup unsalted butter**
2	**large eggs**
1½	**teaspoons pure vanilla extract**
3	**cups all-purpose flour, preferably unbleached**
½	**cup milk at room temperature**
60	**real chocolate chips or raisins for garnish**

Preheat convection ovens to 310 degrees Fahrenheit or conventional ovens to 325 degrees Fahrenheit. Set the racks in the conventional oven so they divide the oven into thirds. Line the cookie sheets with parchment paper. If you are baking in a conventional oven, put one baking sheet inside another of the same size to make a double pan, or use insulated pans to protect the bottoms of the cookies.

Using an electric mixer on medium speed, combine the sugar, baking powder, and baking soda. Add the butter, eggs, and vanilla and beat on medium speed for about 3 minutes, until the mixture is fluffy and light in color. Add half of the flour and beat on low speed for about 20 seconds, or until blended. Scrape the bowl with a rubber spatula and add the milk, beating on low speed for about 20 seconds. Pour in the remaining flour and beat on low speed until the mixture is well blended, about 30 to 40 seconds.

Drop the dough by rounded teaspoonfuls onto the prepared baking sheets. Place one chocolate chip on each cookie and bake in a preheated oven for 12 to 14 minutes, reversing the baking sheets and switching them top to bottom halfway through the baking time. When done, the cookies will just start to turn light brown. The cookies will be soft when warm, but will firm up as they cool. Remove the baking sheets from the oven and let the cookies cool on the sheets for 5 minutes. Use a metal spatula to move the cookies to wire racks to finish cooling.

Store the cooled cookies in an airtight container for up to 6 days, or freeze, wrapped tightly, for up to 2 months. (See freezing instructions on page 12.)

Scotch Chewies taste great with milk.

Mary's Sour Cream Sugar Cookies

When my good friend, Susan Dyson, found out I was writing this book she gave me this recipe. It is for her mother, Mary DeBusk's, great Pennsylvania Dutch sugar cookies. They are thick and soft, not too sweet, and mildly flavored. Betcha can't eat just one.

Makes 3½ dozen 3-inch cookies.

3	cups all-purpose flour, preferably unbleached
½	teaspoon baking powder
1	teaspoon baking soda
¼	teaspoon salt
⅓	cup unsalted butter
1½	cups granulated sugar
2	large eggs
1	tablespoon pure vanilla extract
1	cup sour cream at room temperature
½	cup raisins, for garnish

Preheat convection ovens to 350 degrees Fahrenheit or conventional ovens to 375 degrees Fahrenheit. Set the racks in the conventional oven so they divide the oven into thirds. Line the cookie sheets with parchment paper or use non-stick baking sheets. If you are baking in a conventional oven, put one baking sheet inside another of the same size to make a double pan, or use insulated pans to protect the bottoms of the cookies.

In a medium-size bowl with a wire whisk, stir the flour, baking powder, baking soda, and salt. Set aside.

Using an electric mixer on medium speed, beat the butter and sugar for about 2 minutes. The mixture will be crumbly. Add the eggs and vanilla and beat on medium speed for 2 minutes. The mixture will become light in color and thick. Scrape the bowl with a rubber spatula and add half of the dry ingredients, beating on low speed for about 20 seconds, until blended. Scrape the bowl again and add the sour cream. Beat just until the mixture is evenly mixed. Add the remaining dry ingredients and beat on low just until mixed in, about 30 seconds. With a rubber spatula, stir the dough, scraping the sides and bottom of the bowl, to be sure the dough is evenly mixed. Cover the bowl and chill the dough in the refrigerator at least 2 hours or overnight.

When chilled, drop the dough by rounded tablespoonfuls onto the prepared pans, garnish with a single raisin, and bake in a preheated oven for 10 to 12 minutes, reversing the baking sheets and switching them top to bottom halfway through the baking time. When done, the cookies will begin to turn light brown and feel slightly firm to the touch. Do not overbake. Remove the baked cookies and let them cool on the baking sheets for 5 minutes. Use a metal spatula to move the cookies to wire racks to finish cooling.

Store the cooled cookies in an airtight container with wax paper between the layers for up to 4 days, or wrap tightly and freeze for up to 2 months. (See freezing instructions on page 12.)

Enjoy Mary's Sour Cream Sugar Cookies with a tall glass of milk or a cup of hot tea.

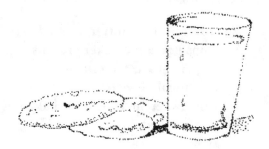

Hello Dolly Cookies

I can still remember when my husband, who is a fairly tall and burly man, first asked me if I could make him some Hello Dolly Cookies. I had never heard of them and the thought of this big guy asking for such a silly-sounding cookie struck me so funny that I laughed until tears rolled down my cheeks. I soon found a recipe and have been making them ever since. I wasn't happy about using the sweetened condensed milk, but I must say these are a big hit with both kids and adults. They are thick, gooey, and very chewy. They are also a snap to make, so they are perfect for a bake sale. Cut them into small squares, because they are rich.

Makes 5 dozen 1⅓ × 1⅓-inch bars.

½	**cup unsalted butter, melted**
1½	**cups graham cracker crumbs (13 squares) or crushed chocolate wafers**
1	**cup sweetened coconut, flaked or shredded, firmly packed**
12	**ounces (large bag) real semisweet chocolate chips**
1	**can (14 ounces) sweetened condensed milk**
1	**cup chopped walnuts (4½ ounces)**

Preheat a conventional oven to 350 degrees Fahrenheit. Set the racks so they divide the oven in half. Line a 9 × 13-inch baking pan with foil.

Pour the melted butter into the foil-lined pan and tilt the pan to coat it. Sprinkle the crumbs over the butter evenly and then layer the rest of the ingredients in the order listed above. Do not stir. Pat the nuts down gently. Bake in a preheated oven for 35 to 40 minutes, reversing the baking pan halfway through the baking time. When done, the nuts are lightly toasted. Cool completely before cutting.

Store the cooled bars in an airtight container for up to 2 weeks.

Eat Hello Dolly Cookies with milk or coffee.

S'More Bars

One of my daughter's favorites, these bars are truly a kids' cookie, easy to make, sweet, and gooey-chewy. When your child tells you at the last minute that you are supposed to send a treat into school, they can be mixed up in a flash.

Makes 20 $1\frac{3}{4} \times 2\frac{1}{4}$-inch bars.

- $\frac{1}{4}$ cup unsalted butter
- 6 milk chocolate candy bars (about 1.55 ounces each)
- 2 cups graham cracker crumbs (26 squares)
- 1 large egg
- 2 cups miniature marshmallows

Preheat a conventional oven to 350 degrees Fahrenheit. Set the racks so they divide the oven into half. Line a 7 × 11-inch baking pan with foil. Put one baking pan inside another of the same size to make a double pan, or use an insulated pan to protect the bottoms of the bars.

Melt the butter and chocolate together in a microwave oven or on a stove top in a small saucepan over low heat. Stir until smooth. Using an electric mixer on medium speed, combine the melted chocolate mixture with the crumbs on low speed for about 30 to 40 seconds. Mixture will be crumbly. Add the egg and beat on medium speed until blended, about 30 seconds. Spread evenly in the prepared baking pan, smoothing with a rubber spatula. Sprinkle the marshmallows over the batter and bake in a preheated oven for about 15 minutes, reversing the baking pan halfway through the baking time. The marshmallows will be lightly browned. Remove from the oven and cool in the pan. When cool, cut into bars.

Store the cooled bars in a single layer in an airtight container for up to 1 week.

S'More Bars can be eaten with milk, juice, or chocolate milk.

1-2-3-4-5 Bars

I developed this recipe for my six-year-old daughter, Emily Mae. She thinks it is so cool to name a cookie with numbers. They are soft-chewy chocolate chip blondie bars that kids love. There are just five ingredients, and they couldn't be easier to mix. Kids can make them without effort (with an adult's supervision) and they can be mixed and baked in about 30 minutes. The hardest part about making these is getting your kids to wait for them to cool. If you use cinnamon-coated graham crackers in this recipe, be sure to reduce the amount of cinnamon in the recipe to ¼ teaspoon.

Makes 20 1¾ × 2¼-inch bars.

2½ **cups graham cracker crumbs
      (32 squares)**
1   **can (14 ounces) sweetened
      condensed milk**
1   **teaspoon pure vanilla extract**
9   **ounces real semisweet chocolate
      chips**
½   **teaspoon ground cinnamon**

Preheat a conventional oven to 350 degrees Fahrenheit. Set the racks in the oven so they divide the oven into half. Line a 7 × 11-inch baking pan with foil.

Place all of the ingredients in a bowl and beat with an electric mixer on medium speed until thoroughly mixed, about 1 minute, scraping the bowl once after 30 seconds. The batter will be stiff. Spread it into the prepared pan, smoothing it with a rubber spatula, and bake it in a preheated oven for 20 minutes, reversing the baking pan halfway through the baking time. Remove the pan from the oven. Cool in the pan. When cool, cut into bars.

Store the cooled bars in an airtight container for up to 1 week.

1-2-3-4-5 Bars are a nice companion to a glass of milk.

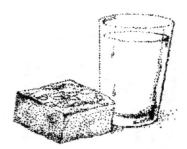

Soft and Chewy Molasses Cookies

The combination of spices and molasses in these thin, chewy cookies is reminiscent of gingerbread people. This is a great cookie to have in the house for snacking whether you are a big kid or a little one.

Makes about 4 dozen 3-inch cookies.

1   **cup granulated sugar**
2   **teaspoons baking soda**
1   **teaspoon ground cinnamon**
½   **teaspoon ground ginger**
¼   **teaspoon ground cloves**
½   **cup unsalted butter**
1   **large egg**
½   **cup molasses**
2¼ **cups all-purpose flour, preferably unbleached**

Preheat convection ovens to 310 degrees Fahrenheit or conventional ovens to 325 degrees Fahrenheit. Set the racks in the conventional oven so they divide the oven into thirds. Line the cookie sheets with parchment paper. If you are baking in a conventional oven, put one baking sheet inside another of the same size to make a double pan, or use insulated pans to protect the bottoms of the cookies.

Using an electric mixer on medium speed, combine the sugar, baking soda, and spices until blended, about 20 seconds. Add the butter, egg, and molasses and beat on medium speed for about 2 minutes. The mixture will be light in color and fluffy. Scrape the bowl with a rubber spatula and add the flour, beating on low speed until evenly mixed, about 30 seconds. Using a rubber spatula, stir the dough, scraping the bottom and sides of the bowl to be sure the dough is evenly mixed.

Drop the dough by heaping teaspoonfuls onto the prepared sheets and bake in a preheated oven for 10 to 12 minutes, reversing the baking sheets and switching them top to bottom halfway through the baking time. The cookies will just begin to brown lightly. Do not overbake; the cookies will become firmer as they cool. The cookies will also puff up and then flatten. Remove the pans from the oven and cool the cookies on the sheets.

Store the completely cooled cookies in an airtight container with wax paper between the layers for up to 5 days, or wrap tightly and freeze for up to 2 months. (See freezing instructions on page 12.)

Soft and Chewy Molasses Cookies are a classic after-school snack with a glass of milk.

Tin Roof Caramel Bars

Chocolate, marshmallows, caramel, and peanuts combine here to produce a bar cookie that is sweet and gooey.

Makes 32 2¼ × 1½-inch bars.

- 5 ounces vanilla caramel candies
- 3 tablespoons milk
- 2 cups brown sugar, firmly packed
- 1 teaspoon baking powder
- 1 teaspoon baking soda
- ¾ cup unsalted butter
- 1 large egg
- 2 cups all-purpose flour, preferably unbleached
- 6 ounces real semisweet chocolate chips
- 1 cup miniature marshmallows
- 1 cup salted peanuts, no skins

Preheat a conventional oven to 350 degrees Fahrenheit. Set the racks in the oven so they divide the oven into half. Line a 9 × 13-inch baking pan with foil.

In a small, heavy saucepan melt together the caramels and milk. Stir until smooth and set aside.

Using an electric mixer on medium speed, mix together the brown sugar, baking powder, and baking soda for about 20 seconds, until evenly blended. Add the butter and egg, and mix on medium speed for about 2 minutes, until the mixture is light in color and smooth. Scrape the bowl with a rubber spatula and add the flour all at once. Mix on low speed just until the flour is blended in, about 20 seconds. Scrape the bowl again and add the chips and marshmallows. Using a wooden spoon or rubber spatula, stir the mixture, scraping down to the bottom of the bowl, to be sure it is evenly mixed. Pour the batter into the prepared pan, spreading evenly and pour the melted caramel mixture on top. Sprinkle with the peanuts.

Bake in the preheated oven for about 25 to 30 minutes, reversing the baking pan halfway through the baking time. When done, the caramel will be bubbly. Remove the pan from the oven and set on a wire rack to cool. When completely cool, cut into bars.

Store the cooled bars in an airtight container for up to 6 days, or wrap tightly and freeze for up to 2 months. (See freezing instructions on page 12.)

Your kids will enjoy Tin Roof Caramel Bars with big glasses of cold milk.

Ginger Pillows

There is something about kids and the flavor of ginger that goes hand in hand. These cookies have a kid-appealing spicy flavor and a sink-your-teeth-into-them texture that tastes so good you want more. If I were a kid, I would love to come home to a cookie jar full of these. The nicest thing about them is how easy they are to make.

Makes 2½ dozen 3-inch cookies.

- 1 **cup granulated sugar**
- 1 **tablespoon ground ginger**
- 1½ **teaspoons ground cinnamon**
- ½ **teaspoon ground cloves**
- 2 **teaspoons baking soda**
- ¼ **teaspoon salt**
- ⅔ **cup unsalted butter**
- 1 **large egg**
- ¼ **molasses**
- 2 **cups all-purpose flour, preferably unbleached**
  granulated sugar for coating

Preheat convection ovens to 310 degrees Fahrenheit or conventional ovens to 325 degrees Fahrenheit. Set the racks in the conventional oven so they divide the oven into thirds. You will *not* need to line the cookie sheets with parchment paper for this recipe. If you are baking in a conventional oven, put one baking sheet inside another of the same size to make a double pan, or use insulated pans to protect the bottoms of the cookies.

Using an electric mixer set on medium speed, combine the sugar, ginger, cinnamon, cloves, baking soda, and salt for 20 seconds. Add the butter, egg, and molasses and beat on medium speed for 2 minutes, until smooth and light in color. Scrape the bowl with a rubber spatula and add the flour, beating on low speed for 20 seconds, until the flour is blended in. Scrape the bottom and sides of the bowl with a rubber spatula or wooden spoon to be sure the dough is completely mixed.

Place some granulated sugar in a shallow bowl. Drop the dough by heaping tablespoonfuls into the sugar, tossing them so that they are completely coated with sugar. Place the dough on the baking sheets and bake in the preheated oven for 10 to 12 minutes, reversing the baking sheets and switching them top to bottom halfway through the baking time. The cookies are done when they are puffed and the tops crack. Remove from the oven. With a metal spatula remove the cookies and place them on wire racks to cool.

When completely cool store the cookies in an airtight container for up to 1 week or wrap tightly and freeze for up to 2 months. (See freezing instructions on page 12.)

A Ginger Pillow, a glass of milk, and wow.

White Chocolate
Peanut Butter Bars

My son, Ben, loves white chocolate and peanut butter, so he was especially delighted when I made these bars for him. White chocolate pairs perfectly with nuts, and the combination of white chocolate and peanut butter is heavenly. This is a sweet, dense, chewy bar with chunks of white chocolate in every bite. Don't use a natural-style peanut butter for this, or your bars will be dry.

Makes 32 2¼ × 1½-inch bars.

- **4 ounces chopped white chocolate or good-quality white chocolate chips such as Ghirardelli**
- **⅔ cup granulated sugar**
- **⅔ cup brown sugar, firmly packed**
- **1 teaspoon baking soda**
- **½ teaspoon baking powder**
- **⅓ cup unsalted butter**
- **1 large egg**
- **1 large egg white**
- **⅔ cup smooth peanut butter (not the natural kind)**
- **2 cups all-purpose flour, preferably unbleached**

- **4 ounces chopped white chocolate, or good-quality white chocolate chips, such as Ghirardelli**

Preheat a conventional oven to 350 degrees Fahrenheit. Set the racks in the oven so they divide the oven into half. Line a 9 × 13-inch baking pan with foil and brush it lightly with butter.

Melt the 4 ounces of white chocolate in a covered microwavable dish for 2 minutes in the microwave oven, or place in a heavy pan on the stove top over low heat, until the chocolate is almost melted. Remove the mixture from the heat and stir with a whisk until smooth. Let the chocolate cool for about 5 minutes.

Using an electric mixer on medium speed, combine the sugar, brown sugar, baking soda and baking powder for 20 seconds. Add the butter, egg, and egg white and beat on medium speed for about 2 minutes, until fluffy and light in color. Scrape the bowl with a rubber spatula and add the peanut butter, beating on low speed for about 30 seconds, until blended. Pour in the melted white chocolate and mix for 30 seconds on low speed. Scrape the bowl again and add the flour and the chopped chocolate or chocolate chips, beating on low speed for about 20 seconds, just until the flour is blended in.

Spread the dough evenly in the prepared pan and smooth the top. Bake in the preheated oven for 20 minutes, reversing the baking pan halfway through the baking time. When done, the top will be lightly browned. Do not overbake. Remove the pan from the oven and set it on a wire rack to cool. When completely cool remove from the pan with the foil and gently peel the foil away. Cut into bars.

Store the cooled bars in an airtight container for up to 5 days, or wrap tightly and freeze for up to 2 months. (See freezing instructions on page 12.)

White Chocolate Peanut Butter Bars are made to be eaten with chocolate milk.

Chocolate Peanut Butter Tassies

Dense, chocolaty cups are filled with a sweet peanut butter filling and iced with white chocolate, making this a child's delight.

Makes 3 dozen tassies.

- ⅔ **cup unsalted butter**
- ½ **cup brown sugar, firmly packed**
- ¾ **cup granulated sugar**
- 2 **large eggs**
- ½ **teaspoon pure vanilla extract**
- 3 **ounces softened cream cheese**
- ½ **cup unsweetened cocoa powder**
- ½ **cup all-purpose flour, preferably unbleached**

Filling:

- ⅔ **cup peanut butter, creamy or chunky (not natural style)**
- ⅓ **cup confectioners' sugar, stirred with a fork to eliminate any lumps**

Frosting:

- 3 **ounces chopped white chocolate or good-quality white chocolate chips such as Ghirardelli**
- 1 **tablespoon heavy cream**

Preheat convection ovens to 310 degrees Fahrenheit or conventional ovens to 325 degrees Fahrenheit. Set the racks in the conventional oven so they divide the oven into thirds. Line 36 miniature muffin pans with paper muffin liners. Place the muffin pans on baking sheets and set aside.

Using an electric mixer on medium speed, beat the butter, brown sugar, sugar, eggs, vanilla, and cream cheese until fluffy, about 2 minutes. Scrape the bowl with a rubber spatula and add the cocoa, beating on low speed for 20 seconds. Scrape the bowl again and add the flour, mixing on low speed just until it is evenly blended.

Make the filling. Stir together the peanut butter and confectioners' sugar until evenly combined. Divide the dough between the 36 lined muffin cups and make a well in each one. Place one teaspoon of the filling into each tassie. Set the muffin pans on baking sheets. Bake in the preheated oven for about 12 minutes, reversing the baking sheets and switching them top to bottom halfway through the baking time. Remove the pans from the oven and set on wire racks to cool.

Make the frosting. Melt the white chocolate and cream in a covered microwavable dish for 2 minutes in the microwave oven, or place in a heavy pan on the stove top over low heat, until the chocolate is almost melted. Remove the mixture from the heat and stir with a whisk until smooth. Let the chocolate mixture cool for about 5 minutes. Spread about ½ teaspoon of frosting over each tassie, covering the filling.

Let the tassies finish cooling and store the cooled tassies in an airtight container for up to 5 days, or wrap tightly and freeze for up to 2 months. (See freezing instructions on page 12.)

Kids love to eat Chocolate Peanut Butter Tassies with hot or cold chocolate milk.

Chewy Chocolate Pixies

My son, Ben, finds these seductive treats irresistible. A sweet cookie with a charming soft chewiness, they have become a favorite in our house. The confectioners' sugar coating forms white spots on the dark brown cookies as the dough bakes and spreads, giving the cookies the appearance of spotted brown cows. Kids love them. Allow time for the dough to chill before baking.

Makes about 3 dozen 3-inch cookies.

½ cup unsalted butter
4 ounces unsweetened chocolate
2 cups all-purpose flour, preferably unbleached
1 teaspoon baking powder
1 teaspoon baking soda
½ teaspoon salt
2 cups granulated sugar
4 large eggs
2 teaspoons pure vanilla extract
1 cup (approximately) confectioners' sugar, stirred with a whisk to remove lumps

Preheat convection ovens to 310 degrees Fahrenheit or conventional ovens to 325 degrees Fahrenheit. Set the racks in the conventional oven so they divide the oven into thirds. You will need to line the cookie sheets with parchment paper for this recipe, or use nonstick baking sheets. If you are baking in a conventional oven, put one baking sheet inside another of the same size to make a double pan, or use insulated pans to protect the bottoms of the cookies.

Melt the butter and the chocolate together in a covered microwavable dish in the microwave oven, or place in a heavy pan on the stove top over low heat, until the chocolate is almost melted. Remove the mixture from the heat and stir with a whisk until smooth. Let the chocolate mixture cool for about 5 minutes.

Put the remaining ingredients into the mixer bowl and add the chocolate mixture. Beat on low 1 minute, scrape the bowl with a rubber spatula, and increase the mixer speed to medium. Beat for an additional minute. The dough will be light in color. Using a wooden spoon or rubber spatula, stir the mixture, scraping down to the bottom of the bowl, to be sure it is evenly mixed.

Cover the dough with plastic wrap and place in the refrigerator to chill for at least 2 hours, or until firm enough to handle.

Remove from the refrigerator and roll rounded tablespoonfuls of dough into balls. Coat each of the balls completely in confectioners' sugar and place the balls of dough about 3 inches apart on the prepared baking sheets. Using the heel of your hand, flatten the cookies so they are about ½ inch high. Bake them in the preheated oven for about 18 to 20 minutes, reversing the baking sheets and switching them top to bottom halfway through the baking time. The cookies will spread as they bake, and will puff up and then flatten. They are done when they just start to feel firm to the touch. Remove them from the oven and let them cool for 5 minutes on the baking sheets. Using a metal spatula, transfer the slightly cooled cookies to cooling racks.

Store the completely cooled cookies in an airtight container for up to 5 days, or freeze for up to 2 months. (See freezing instructions on page 12.)

Chewy Chocolate Pixies are delightful with a glass of cold milk.

Chewy Peanut Butter Oatmeal Squares

The flavor of peanut butter just screams out to be in a chewy cookie. In these squares oatmeal adds the right amount of chewiness and chocolate chips add that classic flavor combination we all love: peanut butter and chocolate. And just in case there isn't enough chocolate in the bars, they are blanketed with a rich chocolate frosting. This is a treat that is homespun and comforting.

Makes 32 2¼ × 1½-inch bars.

- ¾   **cup granulated sugar**
- ¾   **cup brown sugar, firmly packed**
- ¾   **teaspoon baking soda**
- ½   **cup unsalted butter**
- ½   **cup peanut butter**
- 1   **large egg**
- 1   **large egg white**
- ¼   **cup milk**
- 1   **teaspoon pure vanilla extract**
- 1½   **cups all-purpose flour, preferably unbleached**
- 1½   **cups quick-cooking rolled oats, uncooked (not instant)**
- 7½   **ounces real semisweet chocolate chips**

Frosting:

- ⅓   **cup unsalted butter**
- ½   **teaspoon pure vanilla extract**
- ½   **cup unsweetened cocoa powder**
- 1   **cup confectioners' sugar, stirred with a fork to eliminate any lumps**
- 2   **tablespoons milk**

Preheat a conventional oven to 350 degrees Fahrenheit. Line a 9 × 13-inch baking pan with foil and brush it with softened butter.

Using an electric mixer on medium speed, mix the sugar, brown sugar and baking soda for about 20 seconds, until evenly combined. Add the butter, peanut butter, egg, egg white, milk, and vanilla and beat for about 2 minutes, until the mixture is light in color and smooth. Scrape the bowl with a rubber spatula and add the flour, oats, and chips. Beat on low speed for 20 seconds, until the mixture is evenly blended. Scrape the bottom and sides of the bowl with a rubber spatula or wooden spoon to be sure the dough is completely mixed.

Spread into the prepared pan and bake in the preheated oven for 20 to 25 minutes, reversing the baking pan halfway through the baking time. The squares are done when the top is lightly browned. Remove the pan from the oven and set it on a wire rack to cool.

While you wait for the bars to cool, make the frosting. Melt the butter in a glass measure covered with a paper towel in a microwave oven or in a small pan on the stove over medium heat. Using an electric mixer set on medium speed, mix the melted butter, vanilla, and cocoa for 1 minute. Add the confectioners' sugar and milk and beat on medium speed for 1 minute, until the mixture is smooth.

When the baked dough is completely cool, spread the frosting over it and cut into bars. Store in an airtight container in a single layer for up to 5 days or wrap tightly and freeze for up to 2 months. (See freezing instructions on page 12.)

All you need with Chewy Peanut Butter Oatmeal Squares is a tall glass of cold milk.

Peanut Butter Mallow Bars

Heaven to many kids is a jar of marshmallow fluff. These bars combine that gooey article with peanut butter and chocolate to create the quintessential children's layered bar. When you make this recipe, be sure to use the sweetened peanut butter, because the natural kind will not give you a moist product.

Makes 32 2¼ × 1½-inch bars.

1	cup unsalted butter
1	cup granulated sugar
1	large egg yolk
1	tablespoon pure vanilla extract
2	cups all-purpose flour, preferably unbleached
2	cups real semisweet chocolate chips
¾	cup peanut butter (not the natural kind)
1½	cups marshmallow fluff

Preheat a conventional oven to 350 degrees Fahrenheit. Line a 9 × 13-inch baking pan with foil and brush it with softened butter.

Using an electric mixer on medium speed, mix the butter, sugar, egg yolk, and vanilla and beat for about 2 minutes, until the mixture is light in color and smooth. Scrape the bowl with a rubber spatula and add the flour. Beat on low speed for 20 seconds, until the mixture is evenly blended. Scrape the bottom and sides of the bowl with a rubber spatula or wooden spoon to be sure the dough is completely mixed.

Spread into the prepared pan and bake in the preheated oven for 18 to 20 minutes, reversing the baking pan halfway through the baking time. The top will be lightly browned. Remove the pan from the oven and set it on a wire rack to cool for 15 minutes.

Carefully melt the chocolate chips and peanut butter in a heavy pan over low heat, stirring, until the mixture is smooth. Spread the marshmallow fluff over the baked crust. Spread the chocolate mixture evenly over the fluff and let the whole thing finish cooling on the wire rack.

When cool, cut into bars and store in an airtight container in a single layer for up to 4 days or wrap tightly and freeze for up to 2 months. (See freezing instructions on page 12.)

Milk or orange juice go well with Peanut Butter Mallow Bars.

Rainbow Wheat Bars

Filled with those colorful candy-coated chocolate pieces we all love, these bars are especially appealing to small children. The whole wheat cereal adds a nutty chewiness that is pleasing in combination with the tasty brown-sugar dough. These bars are perfect for bake sales and birthday parties; they keep well and are quick to make. They will put a happy rainbow in any child's day.

Makes 32 2¼ × 1½-inch bars.

- 1½ cups brown sugar, firmly packed
- 1 teaspoon baking soda
- ½ teaspoon baking powder
- ¾ cup unsalted butter
- 2 large eggs
- 1 teaspoon pure vanilla extract
- 2 cups all-purpose flour, preferably unbleached
- 2¼ cups whole wheat cereal flakes
- 1 cup multicolored candy-coated chocolate candies

Preheat a conventional oven to 350 degrees Fahrenheit. Place the oven rack in the center of the oven. Line a 9 × 13-inch baking pan with foil and brush it with softened butter.

Using an electric mixer on medium speed, mix the brown sugar, baking soda, and baking powder for 20 seconds. Add the butter, eggs, and vanilla and beat for about 2 minutes, until the mixture is light in color and smooth. Scrape the bowl with a rubber spatula and add the flour and cereal. Beat on low speed for 20 seconds, until the mixture is evenly blended. Scrape the bottom and sides of the bowl with a rubber spatula or wooden spoon to be sure the dough is completely mixed.

Spread into the prepared pan and bake in the preheated oven for 35 minutes, reversing the baking pan halfway through the baking time. The top will be lightly browned. Remove the pan from the oven and set it on a wire rack to cool.

When cool, carefully invert the cake from the pan onto a wire rack and peel off the foil. Turn the cake right side up and cut it into bars.

Store the cooled bars in an airtight container with wax paper between the layers, for up to 6 days, or wrap tightly and freeze for up to 2 months. (See freezing instructions on page 12.)

Serve Rainbow Wheat Bars with a cold glass of milk or a mug of hot chocolate for a smile-creating snack.

Marbled Peanut Butter Bars

A variation on the peanut butter cup, this bar cookie is made up of a rich peanut-butter dough that is swirled with milk chocolate. It is sweet, dense, and chewy. This is another easy-to-make treat that is great for a bake sale or picnic. It will please all the kids on your list—the young ones and the old ones, too.

Makes 32 2¼ × 1½-inch bars.

- **12 ounces (2 cups) chopped milk chocolate or real milk chocolate chips**
- 2 **tablespoons heavy cream**
- 1 **cup brown sugar firmly packed**
- ½ **cup granulated sugar**
- 1 **teaspoon baking powder**
- ⅓ **cup unsalted butter**
- 2 **large eggs**
- 2 **teaspoons pure vanilla extract**
- ½ **cup creamy peanut butter (not natural style)**
- 1 **cup all-purpose flour, preferably unbleached**

Preheat a conventional oven to 350 degrees Fahrenheit. Line a 9 × 13-inch baking pan with foil and brush it with softened butter.

Melt the chocolate and cream in a microwavable dish for 2 minutes in the microwave oven, or place in a heavy pan on the stove top over low heat, until the chocolate is almost melted. Remove from the heat and stir with a whisk until smooth.

Using an electric mixer on medium speed, mix the brown sugar, sugar, and baking powder for 20 seconds. Add the butter, eggs, peanut butter, and vanilla and beat for about 2 minutes, until the mixture is light in color and smooth. Scrape the bowl with a rubber spatula and add the flour. Beat on low speed for 20 seconds, until the mixture is evenly blended. Scrape the bottom and sides of the bowl with a rubber spatula or wooden spoon to be sure the dough is completely mixed. Spread into the prepared pan. Drop the melted chocolate mixture on the batter by spoonfuls. Using a table knife, cut through the batter and chocolate several times, creating a marbled effect. Bake in the preheated oven for 25 to 30 minutes, reversing the baking pan halfway through the baking time. The top will be lightly browned. Remove the pan from the oven and set it on a wire rack to cool.

When cool, carefully invert the cake from the pan onto a wire rack and peel off the foil. Turn the cake right side up and cut it into bars.

Store the cooled bars in an airtight container with wax paper between the layers, for up to 6 days, or wrap tightly and freeze for up to 2 months. (See freezing instructions on page 12.)

Big kids and little kids enjoy Marbled Peanut Butter Bars with milk or juice.

Elegant Offerings

There are times when you need a special dessert to take as a hostess gift or to have at the end of a special dinner party. This chapter offers several special, elegant cookies for just such occasions. They require a little more time than most of the other cookies in this book and will be impressive enough to reward you for the extra effort. These are shaped and molded cookies. They are pretty and taste wonderful. You may decide to have a small dinner party just to serve one of these cookies!

Pecan Tassies

One of the most pleasing flavors around is that found in pecan pies. These small tartlets are chewy, a little gooey, sweet and nutty, and reminiscent of pecan pies. The pastry is easy to work with, so if you usually shy away from making pies because you aren't adept at working with the dough, you will be amazed at how forgiving this pastry dough is. It is worth the extra expense of buying the small muffin pan liners because the tassies will relentlessly stick to the pan if you don't. You also want the muffin pans to be not less than ¾ inch deep, or you will have trouble shaping the dough, and the filling will bubble over the edges. The tassies are about two bites each, so plan on more than one per guest. These are very popular.

Makes about 4 dozen 1¾-inch tartlets.

1	cup unsalted butter
6	ounces cream cheese, room temperature
2	cups cake flour, stirred with a wire whisk to remove lumps
2	large eggs
2	tablespoons unsalted butter, melted
1½	cups brown sugar, firmly packed
1	teaspoon vanilla
1½	cups pecans, broken into large pieces

Preheat convection ovens to 325 degrees Fahrenheit or conventional ovens to 350 degrees Fahrenheit. Set the racks in the conventional oven so they divide the oven into thirds. Line 48 miniature muffin pans with paper muffin liners. Place the muffin pans on baking sheets and set aside.

Using an electric mixer on medium speed, beat the butter and cream cheese until fluffy, about 2 minutes. Scrape the bowl with a rubber spatula and add the flour, mixing on low speed just until combined, about 30 seconds. Cover the bowl with plastic wrap and chill the dough for about 1 hour.

Meanwhile make the filling. Using a wooden spoon combine the eggs, melted butter, brown sugar, and vanilla until thoroughly mixed. Stir in the pecans.

When the dough is firm, divide it into 48 fairly equal pieces and roll them into balls. Flatten each one with the heel of your hand into a round about 2¼ inches in diameter. Press each piece into the bottom and sides of a lined muffin cup. When you have lined all the cups with pastry, spoon the filling into each one. Be sure to get nuts and liquid from the filling in each cup.

Bake the tassies in the muffin pans on baking sheets in a preheated oven for about 30 to 35 minutes, reversing the baking pans and switching them top to bottom halfway through the baking time. The filling will be bubbly and the pastry will just start to become light brown. Do not overbake them. Remove them from the oven and cool in the pans for about 10 minutes. Carefully remove the tassies *with their paper cups* from the pans and finish cooling on wire racks.

Store the completely cooled tassies in an airtight container away from heat for up to 1 week, or wrap tightly and freeze for up to 2 months. (See freezing instructions on page 12.)

Pecan Tassies are especially delightful with hot tea or cappuccino.

Butterscotch Meringue Squares

This dense-chewy bar is also crunchy with pecans. It is sweet with the flavor of butterscotch. The combination of flavors in the different layers is great. Perfect for a luncheon buffet dessert.

Makes 32 1½ × 2¼-inch bars.

1	cup granulated sugar
1	teaspoon baking powder
½	cup unsalted butter
2	large egg yolks
1½	teaspoons pure vanilla extract
2	cups all-purpose flour, preferably unbleached
2	cups butterscotch chips (12 ounces)
2	large egg whites
1	cup brown sugar, firmly packed
1½	cups coarsely chopped pecans

Preheat a conventional oven to 350 degrees Fahrenheit. Set the racks in the oven so they divide the oven into half. Line a 9 × 13-inch baking pan with foil.

Using an electric mixer on medium speed, mix the granulated sugar with the baking powder until evenly combined, about 30 seconds. Add the butter, yolks, and vanilla and beat on medium speed for about 2 minutes, until light in color and fluffy. Scrape the bowl with a rubber spatula and add the flour all at once, mixing on low speed for about 20 seconds. The dough will be crumbly. Pat the dough evenly into the prepared pan, and spread the butterscotch chips over the dough.

In a clean bowl, using a whisk attachment if possible, beat the egg whites on medium-high speed until they form stiff peaks. Do not overbeat, or they will become dry and grainy-looking. Sprinkle the brown sugar over the beaten egg whites and gently stir it in with a wire whisk. Add the nuts, again gently stirring with a wire whisk, and spread the egg white–nut mixture evenly over the butterscotch chips in the pan.

Bake in a preheated oven for 25 minutes, reversing the baking pan halfway through the baking time. When done, the cookies will be lightly browned. Remove from the oven and cool in the pan. When completely cool, cut into bars.

Store the bars in an airtight container for about 1 week.

Butterscotch Meringue Bars are especially delicious with hot coffee or cold milk.

Linzer Bites

Along the same vein as tassies, these linzer bites combine the wonderfully compatible flavors of hazelnuts, lemon, and raspberry. This dough is easy to work with. You will need to use a pastry bag fitted with a number 10 tip to pipe the lattice onto the tops. This may sound like a lot of work, but it really isn't. And, besides, they are well worth the effort.

Makes 4 dozen miniature tartlets.

1	**cup whole hazelnuts (filberts)**
1½	**cups granulated sugar**
1	**teaspoon baking powder**
1	**teaspoon ground cinnamon**
¼	**teaspoon salt**
1	**cup unsalted butter**
1	**tablespoon freshly grated lemon zest, chopped fine**
1	**teaspoon pure vanilla extract**
2	**large eggs**
1	**large egg white**
2½	**cups all-purpose flour, preferably unbleached**
1½	**cups good-quality seedless raspberry jam**

Preheat convection ovens to 340 degrees Fahrenheit or conventional ovens to 350 degrees Fahrenheit. Set the racks in the conventional oven so they divide the oven into thirds. Line 48 miniature muffin cups with paper liners. Put the muffin pans on baking sheets and set aside.

Put the whole hazelnuts on a baking sheet in a single layer and toast them in the preheated oven for about 7 minutes or until the skins crack and the nutmeats just start to crack. Remove the pan from the oven and cool the nuts for about 10 minutes. Do not remove the skins. Grind the nuts finely and set aside.

Using an electric mixer on medium speed, combine the sugar, baking powder, cinnamon, and salt until evenly mixed, about 30 seconds. Add the butter and beat on medium speed for 2 minutes, until fluffy. Scrape the bowl with a rubber spatula and add the zest and vanilla. Beat on low speed to combine, about 30 seconds. Scrape the bowl again and add the eggs and egg white. Beat on low speed just to combine, and then on medium speed for about 2 minutes, until the mixture is fluffy. Add the flour all at once and beat on low speed until no traces of flour remain, about 30 seconds. Add the ground hazelnuts, mixing in on low speed for 30 seconds. Using a rubber spatula stir the dough, scraping the sides and bottom, to be sure the dough is evenly mixed.

Remove ¼ of the dough and place it in a pastry bag fitted with a number 10 tube. Divide the remaining dough into 48 fairly even pieces. Press one piece into each lined muffin cup, covering the bottom and sides evenly with the dough. When all are filled, spoon about 1½ teaspoons of jam into each one. Then, using the pastry bag, pipe an × across the top of each tartlet.

Bake the tartlets in the muffin pans, on baking sheets, in a preheated oven for about 15 to 17 minutes, reversing the baking pans and switching them top to bottom halfway through the baking time. They will just start to brown lightly and the filling will be bubbly. Remove from the oven and let them cool in the pans for about 10 minutes. Remove them from the pans carefully (the jam can burn you if it is hot) and place the tartlets on wire racks to cool.

Store the completely cooled tartlets in a single layer in airtight containers for up to 1 week, or wrap tightly and freeze for up to 2 months. (See freezing instructions on page 12.)

Linzer Bites are an exquisite dessert when served with liqueurs or coffee.

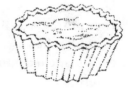

Chocolate-Orange Sandwiches

These thin yet chewy rounds have a sophistication that impresses even the most jaded fancy cookie eaters. They are sandwiched with a chocolate filling, which perfectly complements the fresh orange flavor. Be sure to use fresh orange zest and not the dried kind, which has an unpleasant flavor.

Makes about 3 dozen sandwiched cookies.

3   ounces cream cheese, softened
7   ounces (¾ cup plus 2 table-
        spoons) unsalted butter
1½ cups granulated sugar
½   teaspoon salt
1   tablespoon freshly grated orange
        zest, chopped fine
1   large egg
2   cups all-purpose flour, preferably
        unbleached
1½ cups blanched almonds, ground
        fine
½   cup sugar for flattening the
        cookies

Filling:
8   ounces good-quality dark
        chocolate, coarsely chopped
2   tablespoons heavy cream

Using an electric mixer set on medium speed, beat the softened cream cheese and the butter until fluffy, about 2 or 3 minutes. Add the sugar, salt, and zest and beat about 2 minutes more. Scrape the bowl with a rubber spatula and add the egg. Beat again on medium speed about 2 minutes. The mixture will be light in color and fluffy. Add the flour and beat on low speed just until smooth. Mix in the almonds on low speed until evenly combined. The dough is fairly sticky. Stir the bowl with a rubber spatula, scraping the bottom and sides of the bowl to be sure the dough is evenly mixed. Then scrape the dough out onto a sheet of plastic wrap, patting it into a disk about ½ inch thick. Wrap the disk with the plastic wrap and chill the dough for about 1 hour, or until firm.

Preheat convection ovens to 310 degrees Fahrenheit or conventional ovens to 325 degrees Fahrenheit. Set the racks in the conventional oven so they divide the oven into thirds. Line the cookie sheets with parchment paper. (These cookies will be very difficult to remove from the pans , even nonstick pans, if you don't line them with parchment.) If you are baking in a conventional oven, put one baking sheet inside another of the same size to make a double pan, or use insulated pans to protect the bottoms of the cookies.

Form balls of dough about ¾ inch in diameter and place them 2 inches apart on the prepared baking sheets. Place the ½ cup of granulated sugar in a small bowl. Moisten the bottom of a glass with water and dip it in the sugar. Press the sugar-coated bottom onto a ball of dough with gentle pressure, flattening it to about ¼ to ⅜ inch high. Do not make the cookies any thinner than this, or they will be crisp and not chewy. Dip the glass into the sugar and flatten the next ball of dough, and continue in this manner until all the dough balls have been flattened.

Bake the cookies in the preheated oven for about 12 minutes, reversing the baking sheets and switching them top to bottom halfway through the baking time. The cookies are ready when they are set but your fingertip still leaves an impression when the cookies are gently touched. Remove the baking sheets from the oven and cool the cookies on the sheets.

While they are cooling, make the filling. Melt the chocolate and cream together in a covered microwavable dish in the microwave for 2 minutes, or in a small heavy saucepan on the stove top. Stir until smooth. Set aside to cool slightly. When the cookies are completely cooled, spread a cookie with some of the chocolate mixture and sandwich with another cookie. Continue until all the cookies are used up.

Store the cooled cookies in an airtight container for up to 2 weeks, or wrap tightly and freeze them for up to 2 months. (See freezing instructions on page 12.)

Serve Chocolate-Orange Sandwiches with espresso for a tantalizing ending to a special dinner.

Macadamia Tarts

Elegant and expensive to make, these little gems are rich and delectable. Because the filling is gooey, you need to line the muffin pans with liners or all your efforts will be lost as you find your tarts sticking stubbornly to the pans. The classic combination of white chocolate and macadamia nuts enriched with cream make these truly special.

Makes 4 dozen tarts

Pastry crust:
- 1 **cup unsalted butter, softened**
- ¾ **cup granulated sugar**
- 1 **teaspoon ground cinnamon**
- 1 **tablespoon freshly grated orange zest**
- 2 **cups all-purpose flour, preferably unbleached**

Filling:
- 1 **cup brown sugar, firmly packed**
- 1 **large egg**
- ¾ **cup heavy cream**
- 1 **tablespoon unsalted butter, melted**
- 1 **teaspoon pure vanilla extract**
- 1 **cup chopped unsalted macadamia nuts**
- ½ **cup (3 ounces) finely chopped white chocolate or good-quality white chocolate chips such as Ghirardelli**
- ½ **cup (3 ounces) real semisweet chocolate chips**

Using an electric mixer on medium speed, beat the butter, sugar, zest, and cinnamon until fluffy, about 3 minutes. Scrape the bowl with a rubber spatula and add the flour, mixing on low speed just until combined, about 30 seconds. Cover the bowl with plastic wrap and chill the dough for about 1 hour.

Preheat convection ovens to 325 degrees Fahrenheit or conventional ovens to 350 degrees Fahrenheit. Set the racks in the conventional oven so they divide the oven into thirds. Line 48 miniature muffin pans with paper muffin liners. Place the muffin pans on baking sheets and set aside.

Meanwhile make the filling. In a medium-size bowl using a wooden spoon, combine the brown sugar, egg, cream, melted butter, and vanilla until thoroughly mixed. Stir in the nuts and chocolate. Set aside.

When the dough is firm divide it into 48 fairly equal pieces and roll them into balls. Flatten each one with the heel of your hand into a round about 2¼ inches in diameter. Press each piece into the bottom and sides of a lined muffin cup. When you have lined all the cups with pastry, spoon about 1½ teaspoons of the filling into each one. Be sure to get nuts and liquid from the filling in each cup.

Bake the tarts in the muffin pans on baking sheets in a preheated oven for about 30 to 35 minutes, reversing the baking pans and switching them top to bottom halfway through the baking time. The filling will be bubbly and the pastry will just start to become light brown. Do not overbake them. Remove them from the oven and cool in the pans for about 10 minutes. Carefully remove the tarts *with their paper cups* from the pans and finish cooling on wire racks.

Store the completely cooled tarts in an airtight container away from heat for up to 1 week, or wrap tightly and freeze for up to 2 months. (See freezing instructions on page 12.)

Macadamia Tarts served with an excellent-quality vanilla ice cream and hot coffee are a perfect way to end a fine dinner.

Hazelnut Macaroon Brownies

The consummate flavor combination of hazelnuts and chocolate is paired here in a glazed double layer bar. A dark, sonorous chocolate layer is topped with a blanket of chewy hazelnut macaroon, and then covered with a dark chocolate glaze. An exquisite ending to the finest meal.

Makes 25 2½ × 2½-inch generous bars.

Chocolate Base:

2 **cups granulated sugar**
1 **cup unsalted butter**
3 **large eggs**
1½ **teaspoons pure vanilla extract**
1 **cup unsweetened cocoa powder**
1 **cup all-purpose flour, preferably unbleached**

Macaroon Layer:

3 **large egg whites**
½ **cup granulated sugar**
1½ **cups finely ground hazelnut**
¾ **cup finely ground almonds**
3 **tablespoons all-purpose flour, preferably unbleached**

Glaze:

4 **ounces coarsely chopped semisweet or bittersweet chocolate**
¼ **cup water**

Preheat a conventional oven to 350 degrees Fahrenheit. Set the racks so they divide the oven in half. Line a 15 × 10-inch baking pan (cookie sheet with sides) with foil.

Using an electric mixer on medium speed, mix the sugar, butter, eggs, and vanilla for about 3 minutes, until fluffy and light in color. Scrape the bowl with a rubber spatula and add the cocoa, beating on low speed for about 30 to 40 seconds, just to blend it in. Scrape the bowl again and add the flour all at once, again beating on low speed just until the mixture is well combined. Using a wooden spoon or rubber spatula, stir the mixture, scraping down to the bottom of the bowl, to be sure it is evenly mixed.

Pour the mixture into the prepared pan and smooth it with the rubber spatula. Bake in the preheated oven for 12 minutes. Remove from the oven and set on a wire rack.

While the chocolate base layer is baking, make the macaroon layer. Using an electric mixer on medium speed with a wire whisk attachment if it is available, beat the egg whites and sugar until foamy, about 4 minutes. Add the nuts and beat on low speed for about 30 to 40 seconds, just to blend in the nuts. Beat in the flour on low speed for about 15 seconds, again just until evenly mixed. Using a wooden spoon or rubber spatula, stir the mixture, scraping down to the bottom of the bowl, to be sure it is evenly mixed. Spread the macaroon mixture gently over the chocolate layer, as evenly as possible, and return the pan to the hot oven. Bake for about 15 minutes, reversing the pan halfway through the baking time. The macaroon layer will just feel slightly firm to the touch. Do not overbake this bar, or the cookies will turn out crunchy instead of chewy. The top layer will become firmer as the bar cools. Remove the pan from the oven and set it on a wire rack to cool.

To make the glaze, place the chocolate and water in a covered microwavable dish for 2 minutes in the microwave oven or in a heavy pan over low heat on the stove top until the chocolate is almost melted. Remove the mixture from the heat and stir with a whisk until smooth. Pour and spread the glaze while warm over the hazelnut layer, and let the glaze set. This will take about 45 minutes at room temperature, or about 20 to 25 minutes if you place the pan in the refrigerator. When the glaze is set, cut the bars.

Store the bars in a single layer in an airtight container in the refrigerator for up to 6 days, or wrap tightly and freeze for up to 2 months. (See freezing instructions on page 12.)

Hot espresso or cappuccino and Hazelnut Macaroon Brownies are a memorable ending to an exquisite meal.

Lemon-Almond Tassies

The classic flavor combination of lemon and almond is highlighted in this exquisite tassie. A miniature-size tart shell is filled with an almond filling that is enhanced with an intensely flavored lemon curd. Serve these for your fanciest affair. They are beautiful and delicious.

Makes 2 dozen tassies.

Lemon Filling:
- 1 large egg
- 1 large egg yolk
- ¼ cup granulated sugar
- 3 tablespoons strained fresh lemon juice
- 1 teaspoon freshly grated lemon zest
- ¼ cup unsalted butter

Almond Filling:
- 3 tablespoons unsalted butter
- ¼ cup granulated sugar
- 1 large egg, beaten lightly
- ½ teaspoon ground nutmeg
- ¼ cup ground blanched almonds

Pastry:
- 3 ounces softened cream cheese
- ½ cup unsalted butter
- 1 cup all-purpose flour, preferably unbleached
- ⅔ cup finely ground blanched almonds

Topping:
- ¼ cup sliced almonds, skins on

Make the lemon filling. In a heavy medium-size saucepan over medium-low heat, combine the egg, egg yolk, ¼ cup sugar, lemon juice, and 1 teaspoon zest, beating lightly to break up the eggs. Cook, stirring constantly so the eggs do not curdle, for about 5 to 7 minutes, until the filling is thick. Add the butter, stirring until it is completely melted. Set aside to cool.

Make the almond filling. Using an electric mixer on medium speed, beat the butter and sugar until smooth and fluffy. Add the egg and nutmeg and beat on medium speed for 2 minutes, until well combined. Scrape the bowl and mix in the almonds on low speed for 15 seconds.

Preheat convection ovens to 325 degrees Fahrenheit or conventional ovens to 350 degrees Fahrenheit. Set the racks in the conventional oven so they divide the oven into thirds. Line 24 miniature muffin pans with paper muffin liners. Place the muffin pans on baking sheets and set aside.

Using an electric mixer on medium speed, beat the cream cheese and butter until fluffy, about 2 minutes. Add the flour and beat on low speed for 20 seconds, just to blend. Scrape the bowl with a rubber spatula and add the ground almonds, mixing on low speed for 15 seconds.

Divide the dough into 24 parts, pressing each part into a lined muffin cup and forming a well in each cup for the filling. When all the tassies are shaped, stir the lemon filling into the almond filling,

until completely blended. Fill each of the tassie shells with the filling and sprinkle each with a few sliced almonds.

Bake the tassies in the preheated oven for about 20 minutes, reversing the baking sheets and switching them top to bottom halfway through the baking time. The pastry will be just starting to turn light brown. Remove the pans from the oven and set them on wire racks to cool.

When completely cooled, store in an airtight container in the refrigerator for up to 1 week or wrap tightly and freeze for up to 2 months. (See freezing instructions on page 12.)

Lemon-Almond Tassies are an elegant addition to a formal tea table or fancy dinner buffet. Serve them with hot tea or coffee.

Cherry-Walnut Thumbprints

There are three steps involved in molding and filling these little gems once they are mixed. The process sounds more involved than it actually is. These are soft-chewy bites of dough totally encased in ground nuts and then filled with a bit of cherry preserves. Use good-quality cherry preserves such as those made by Clearbrook Farms. The difference in the final quality of your cookies will be amazing.

Makes 3 dozen 1½-inch cookies.

- ½ **cup unsalted butter**
- ¼ **cup brown sugar, firmly packed**
- 1 **large egg yolk**
- ½ **teaspoon pure vanilla extract**
- 1 **cup all-purpose flour, preferably unbleached**

Nut Coating:
- 1 **large egg white**
- 2 **teaspoons water**
- 1 **cup finely ground walnuts**
- 1 **cup seedless tart red cherry preserves**

Preheat convection ovens to 310 degrees Fahrenheit or conventional ovens to 325 degrees Fahrenheit. Set the racks in the conventional oven so they divide the oven into thirds. Line the cookie sheets with parchment paper. If you are baking in a conventional oven, put one baking sheet inside another of the same size to make a double pan, or use insulated pans to protect the bottoms of the cookies.

With a mixer on medium speed, combine the butter, brown sugar, egg yolk, and vanilla for 2 minutes. The mixture will be fluffy and light in color. Scrape the bowl with a rubber spatula and add the flour. Mix on low speed for about 20 seconds, until the flour is thoroughly combined. Using a wooden spoon or rubber spatula, stir the mixture, scraping down to the bottom of the bowl, to be sure it is evenly mixed.

Divide the dough into 3 equal parts, and then divide each part into 12 pieces. Form each piece into a ball by rolling the dough between the palms of your hands. In a small, shallow bowl, beat the egg white with the water just enough so the egg white is broken down and thin. Set a wire rack next to the egg white bowl and place a piece of wax paper or paper towel under the rack. Place the finely chopped walnuts on a large piece of wax paper next to the wire rack. Take a ball of dough and roll it in the egg white, then place it on the wire rack to drain a bit. Repeat this process for each of the remaining dough balls. Starting with the dough ball you dipped in egg white first, roll it in the chopped nuts so that it is coated on all sides. Place the nut-coated ball on the prepared baking sheet. Repeat with all the remaining balls, placing them about 2 inches apart on the baking sheets. When all of the dough balls have been coated, use a clean thimble or your thumb to make an indentation in the center of the top. Spoon about ½ teaspoon of cherry preserves into the indentation of each cookie.

Bake for 10 to 12 minutes, or until the cookies are lightly browned and just start to feel firm when touched gently. Reverse the sheets and switch them top to bottom halfway through the baking time. When the cookies are done, let them cool on the sheets for 5 minutes and then remove them with a metal spatula to wire racks to finish cooling.

Store the completely cooled cookies in a single layer in an airtight container for up to 6 days, or freeze, wrapped tightly, for up to 2 months. (See freezing instructions on page 12.)

Cherry-Walnut Thumbprint cookies make a wonderful accompaniment to a fine-quality ice cream or sorbet.

Homemade for the Holidays

Winter holidays are always more special with something freshly baked. The aroma of spices and chocolate just seem to go hand in hand with the festivities. The recipes in this chapter are designed to offer an assortment of traditional holiday flavors in a chewy medium. Won't have the time in December? Bake something special over the Thanksgiving holiday and freeze it. I promise it will delight your family or friends and even yourself.

Chewy, Nutty Lebkuchen

Lebkuchen have been around for generations in many different forms. They are chewy and dense with a wonderful spicy flavor. The dough is very sticky, and you need to use a good kitchen parchment to line the baking sheets. Because I love nuts so much, I have developed this recipe with a generous amount of nuts. Your house will smell like Christmas when you bake these cookies.

Makes 3 dozen 3-inch cookies.

1   cup raw almonds (skins on)
1   cup hazelnuts
3   large egg whites
1¼ cups granulated sugar
½   teaspoon baking powder
¾   teaspoon ground cinnamon
½   teaspoon ground cloves
1   teaspoon freshly grated lemon zest
1   teaspoon freshly grated orange zest
⅓   cup mild-flavored honey, such as orange blossom
1   cup all-purpose flour, preferably unbleached
36 whole blanched almonds, or almond slices, for garnish

Glaze:
1   cup granulated sugar
¾   cup water

Preheat a conventional oven to 350 degrees Fahrenheit.

Place the almonds in a single layer on a baking sheet, and the hazelnuts on another sheet. Bake the nuts in the preheated oven for about 8 minutes. Remove from the oven and set the pans on wire racks to cool. After the hazelnuts have cooled for 5 minutes, place them in a clean dish towel and rub them vigorously between your hands. This will loosen most of the skins. Move the hazelnuts from the towel, leaving the skins behind, and grind the hazelnuts finely. When the almonds are cool, grind them finely also.

Using an electric mixer on medium speed with a wire whisk attachment if one is available, beat the eggs with the sugar, baking powder, cinnamon, cloves, and the two zests for about 3 minutes, until foamy. Add the honey and beat on low speed for about 30 seconds to blend evenly, then add the nuts and beat on low to blend them in. Scrape the bowl with a rubber spatula and add the flour, blending on low until evenly distributed.

Using a wooden spoon or rubber spatula, stir the mixture, scraping down to the bottom of the bowl, to be sure it is evenly mixed. The dough will be quite sticky. Wrap the dough in plastic wrap and place it in the refrigerator for overnight or up to a week. When you are ready to bake the cookies, make the glaze. Put the sugar and then the water into a small pan over high heat until it boils. Let it boil for 3 minutes, and remove it from the heat. Set aside.

Preheat convection ovens to 325 degrees Fahrenheit or conventional ovens to 350 degrees Fahrenheit. Set the racks in the conventional oven so they divide the oven into thirds. You *must* line the cookie sheets with parchment paper for this recipe. If you are baking in a conventional oven, put one baking sheet inside another of the same size to make a double pan, or use insulated pans to protect the bottoms of the cookies.

Drop the dough by heaping tablespoonfuls onto the prepared baking sheets and using a flat-bottomed drinking glass that has been *lightly* moistened with water, flatten the cookie so that it is about ¼ inch thick. Do not make them too thin, or they will be hard and crunchy. Bake the cookies in the preheated oven for about 12 to 15 minutes, reversing the baking sheets and switching them top to bottom halfway through the baking time. When done, the cookies will feel firm to the touch. Remove the cookies from the oven and immediately brush them with the glaze. Set the pan on a wire rack and let the cookies cool on the pan. When cool, remove carefully with a metal spatula.

Store the cooled cookies in an airtight container with wax paper between layers for up to 3 weeks.

Chewy, Nutty Lebkuchen are unbeatable with warm cider or milk.

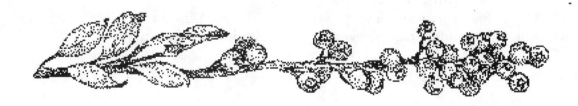

Anise Doodles

One of my favorite Christmas flavors is that of anise. A tin of these subtly flavored cookies are a perfect holiday hostess gift for you to have on hand. When the tin is opened, the aroma of the anise comes drifting up, a sensuous reminder of the holiday season. Be sure to allow several hours for the dough to chill.

Makes 4 dozen 2½-inch cookies.

- 1¼ **cups granulated sugar**
- 1 **teaspoon baking soda**
- 1 **teaspoon cream of tartar**
- ½ **cup unsalted butter**
- 2 **large eggs**
- 2 **tablespoons anise seeds**
- ⅓ **cup milk**
- 3 **cups all purpose flour, preferably unbleached**
-    **additional sugar for coating**

Using an electric mixer on medium speed, combine the sugar, baking soda, and cream of tartar for about 15 seconds. Add the butter and beat for about 2 minutes, until fluffy and light in color. Add the eggs, anise seed, and milk and beat again on medium speed for about 1 minute. The mixture will be smooth. Scrape the bowl with a rubber spatula and add the flour, mixing on low speed for about 20 seconds, or until evenly blended. Using a wooden spoon or rubber spatula, stir the mixture, scraping down to the bottom of the bowl, to be sure it is evenly mixed. Wrap the dough in plastic wrap and chill in the refrigerator for several hours or overnight.

Preheat convection ovens to 310 degrees Fahrenheit or conventional ovens to 325 degrees Fahrenheit. Set the racks in the conventional oven so they divide the oven into thirds. You do *not* need to line the cookie sheets with parchment paper for this recipe. If you are baking in a conventional oven, put one baking sheet inside another of the same size to make a double pan, or use insulated pans to protect the bottoms of the cookies.

Place about ½ cup of granulated sugar in a shallow bowl. Scoop the dough into balls that are 1 inch in diameter. Roll them in the sugar and place them on the baking sheets. Bake in the preheated oven for 8 to 10 minutes, reversing the baking sheets and switching them top to bottom halfway through the baking time. The cookies will puff up and then fall during baking. Cool on the pans on wire racks.

Store the cooled cookies in an airtight container for up to 1 week, or wrap tightly and freeze for up to 2 months. (See freezing instructions on page 12.)

Present Anise Doodles with spicy tea for a pleasant holiday snack.

Spicy Mincemeat Squares

Moist, chewy, and easy to make, these squares use prepared mincemeat to add texture and flavor to a spicy bar. If you make your own mincemeat, or know someone who does, you can use that. But if not, you can buy prepared mincemeat off the shelf in just about any grocery store.

Makes 20 2¼ × 2½-inch bars.

1½	cups brown sugar, firmly packed
¾	teaspoon baking soda
¾	teaspoon baking powder
½	teaspoon ground nutmeg
1½	teaspoons ground cinnamon
¾	cup unsalted butter
1	large egg
1	egg white
1½	teaspoons freshly grated orange zest
1	cup prepared mincemeat
2	cups all-purpose flour, preferably unbleached
¾	cups quick-cooking rolled oats, uncooked (not instant)
1½	cups chopped walnuts confectioners' sugar for coating

Preheat conventional oven to 350 degrees Fahrenheit. Line a 9 × 13-inch baking pan with foil and butter it lightly.

Using an electric mixer set on medium speed, combine the brown sugar, baking soda, baking powder, nutmeg, and cinnamon for 15 seconds. Add the butter, egg, egg white and zest and beat on medium speed for about 2 minutes. The mixture will be light in color and fluffy. Scrape the bowl with a rubber spatula and add the mincemeat, blending on low speed for about 15 seconds to combine evenly. Scrape the bowl again and add the flour, oats, and nuts. Beat on low speed just until the flour is mixed in, about 20 seconds. Using a wooden spoon or rubber spatula, stir the mixture, scraping the sides and down to the bottom of the bowl, to be sure the dough is evenly mixed.

Spread the mixture into the prepared pan and smooth the top. Bake in the preheated oven for 30 to 35 minutes, reversing the baking pan halfway through the baking time. When done, the bars will be lightly browned and barely feel firm when you touch them with your fingertip. Remove the pan from the oven and set it on a wire rack to cool. When cool, cut into bars. Place some confectioners' sugar into a shallow, wide container and dip all sides of each bar into the sugar.

Store in an airtight container for up to 1 week, or wrap tightly and freeze for up to 2 months. (See freezing instructions on page 12.)

Spicy Mincemeat Squares are a great snack to have on hand when sitting by the fire on a snowy holiday night. Enjoy them with spiced punch or hot cider.

Chewy Fruit Bars, Iced and Spiced

Dense with dried fruits and nuts and laced with spices, this bar represents many of the holiday flavors we all love. It is a moist and tasty alternative to fruitcake without the cloying sweetness of candied fruit. You can substitute any combination of dried fruits as long as they aren't candied.

Makes 50 1 × 2-inch bars.

1¼ cups granulated sugar
1½ teaspoons ground cinnamon
½ teaspoon ground nutmeg
½ teaspoon ground cardamom
¼ teaspoon ground allspice
1¼ teaspoons baking powder
2 large eggs
⅓ cup unsalted butter, melted
1 tablespoon orange zest
2 cups all-purpose flour, preferably unbleached
½ cup chopped dates
½ cup chopped dried apricots
½ cup dried sweetened tart cherries
½ cup chopped prunes
1 cup coarsely chopped walnuts

Icing:
1 cup confectioners' sugar
1½ tablespoons strained freshly squeezed lemon juice
½ teaspoon freshly grated lemon zest

Preheat convection ovens to 325 degrees Fahrenheit and conventional ovens to 350 degrees Fahrenheit. Set the racks in the conventional oven so they divide the oven into thirds. You do *not* need to line the cookie sheets with parchment paper for this recipe. If you are baking in a conventional oven, put one baking sheet inside another of the same size to make a double pan, or use insulated pans to protect the bottoms of the cookies.

Using an electric mixer set on medium speed, combine the sugar, cinnamon, nutmeg, cardamom, allspice, and baking powder for about 20 seconds. Add the eggs, melted butter, and orange zest and beat on medium speed for about 2 minutes. The mixture will be smooth and light in color. Scrape the bowl with a rubber spatula and add the flour, dried fruits and nuts. Combine on low speed for 30 to 40 seconds, until evenly blended. Using a wooden spoon or rubber spatula, stir the mixture, scraping the sides and down to the bottom of the bowl, to be sure it is evenly mixed. Divide the dough into 4 equal parts, placing 2 parts on each baking sheet and forming each part into a log that is about 1½ inches wide and about ¾ inches thick.

Bake the logs in the preheated oven for 13 to 15 minutes, reversing the baking sheets and switching them top to bottom halfway through the baking time. They will be just firm to the touch. While the logs are baking, make the icing. Place the confectioners' sugar in a small bowl and stir with a fork or whisk to break up the lumps. Add the juice and zest and stir with a whisk until the icing is smooth. Remove the pans from the oven and let the logs cool on the pans, set on wire racks, for 10 minutes.

Spread the icing on the logs and then slice the logs diagonally into 1-inch bars. Set the bars on wire racks to cool completely.

Store the cooled bars in an airtight container for up to 5 days, or wrap tightly and freeze for up to 2 months. (See freezing instructions on page 12.)

Serve Chewy Fruit Bars with a cup of warm cider as a special holiday treat.

Chocolate-Walnut Rogelach

Soft and densely chewy, rogelach is a special holiday treat. Little rolls of dough, filled with cinnamon, nuts, currants, and chocolate, they will fill your home with wonderful scents of the season. The cream cheese–enriched dough is so forgiving that even the most inexperienced baker will have luck with this recipe. The chocolate-walnut combination is delectable, but you should also try the raspberry variation (page 186). Make some of each and freeze them to have on hand throughout the holiday season. Be sure to allow time for the dough to chill.

Makes 6 dozen 1 × 1½-inch cookies.

1   **cup unsalted butter**
6   **ounces cream cheese, softened**
¼   **teaspoon salt**
2¾   **cups all-purpose flour, preferably unbleached**

Filling:

3   **ounces grated semisweet chocolate**
⅓   **cup granulated sugar**
⅓   **cup dried currants or chopped raisins, finely chopped**
⅓   **cup finely chopped walnuts**
1   **teaspoon ground cinnamon**

Topping:

1   **large egg yolk lightly beaten with 2 teaspoons water**
¼   **cup (approximately) granulated sugar**

Using an electric mixer on medium speed beat the butter, cream cheese, and salt together for about 2 minutes, until fluffy and light in color. Scrape the bowl with a rubber spatula and add the flour, beating on low speed for about 30 seconds, until the flour is mixed in evenly. Divide the dough into 4 equal pieces, wrap the dough in plastic wrap, and chill in the refrigerator for at least 1 hour.

While the dough is chilling, make the filling. Combine the chocolate, sugar, currants, cinnamon, and walnuts in a bowl, stirring until evenly mixed. Set aside.

Preheat convection ovens to 325 degrees Fahrenheit and conventional ovens to 350 degrees Fahrenheit. Set the racks in the conventional oven so they divide the oven into thirds. You need to line the cookie sheets with parchment paper for this recipe, because the filling will leak out of the sides of the cookies and cause the cookies to stick to an unlined pan. If you are baking in a conventional oven, put one baking sheet inside another of the same size to make a double pan, or use insulated pans to protect the bottoms of the cookies.

Work with 1 piece at a time, keeping the unused dough in the refrigerator. On a floured surface, roll out the dough so that it forms a long, narrow rectangle. It is easier to do this if you form the dough piece into a thick, long, and narrow slab before you start rolling it. Roll from the center of the slab out to the ends. You will not need to roll across the short length of the dough, because the dough will widen as you roll it longer. The finished dough should be about 5 inches wide and 15 inches long. Sprinkle ¼ of the filling mixture evenly over the rolled dough, leaving a ½-inch border on all edges. Starting from the long edge farthest from you, roll the dough jelly-roll style, keeping the roll as tight as possible, and ending the roll so that the seam is facing you, near the bottom. Trim about ½ inch from each end, then cut the roll into 18 pieces, each about ¾ inch wide. It is easiest to do this if you first cut the roll into 2 equal pieces, and then cut each of those pieces into 3 equal pieces. You now have 6 short logs. Cut each of the 6 logs into 3 equal pieces. Using a metal spatula, carefully lift the rogelach and place them onto the prepared baking sheets, placing the rogelach within ¼ inch of each other. Repeat the rolling, filling, and cutting process with each of the remaining portions of refrigerated dough.

When you have finished making the rogelach, brush the top of each one with the egg and water mixture, using a pastry brush. Then sprinkle each with a little sugar.

Bake the rogelach in the preheated oven for 18 to 20 minutes, reversing the baking sheets and switching them top to bottom halfway through the baking time. The rogelach will be light brown when they are done. Do not overbake them or they will be dry and hard. Remove the pans from the oven and place the pans on wire racks to cool. Let the rogelach cool completely on the pans.

Remove from the pans and store in an airtight container for up to 1 week, or wrap tightly and freeze for up to 2 months. (See freezing instructions on page 12.)

Chocolate-Walnut Rogelach makes a delightful addition to a holiday dessert table and is especially delicious with warmed cider or tea.

Sour Cream Ginger Jumbles

For those of you who enjoy the sweet, hot taste of candied ginger, this recipe combines that exotic flavor with the homey flavor of molasses. Sour cream adds an appealing moistness and density, while the candied ginger adds an interesting chewiness. They keep well and make a charming hostess gift.

Makes 3 dozen 2-inch cookies.

½ **cup granulated sugar**
¾ **teaspoon baking soda**
½ **teaspoon ground cinnamon**
½ **cup unsalted butter**
1   **large egg**
1   **cup molasses**
½ **cup sour cream**
1   **tablespoon finely chopped candied ginger (available in specialty food stores and many big grocery stores)**
2   **cups all-purpose flour, preferably unbleached**

Coating:
½ **cup (approximately) granulated sugar**

Preheat convection ovens to 310 degrees Fahrenheit and conventional ovens to 325 degrees Fahrenheit. Set the racks in the conventional oven so they divide the oven into thirds. You do *not* need to line the cookie sheets with parchment paper for this recipe. If you are baking in a conventional oven, put one baking sheet inside another of the same size to make a double pan, or use insulated pans to protect the bottoms of the cookies.

Using an electric mixer on medium speed, combine the sugar, baking soda, and cinnamon for 20 seconds. Add the butter and eggs and beat on medium speed for about 2 minutes, until fluffy and light in color. Scrape the bowl with a rubber spatula and add the molasses and sour cream, beating on medium speed for about 1 minute, until smooth. Scrape the bowl again and add the flour all at once with the ginger. Beat on low speed just until the flour is mixed in, about 20 seconds. Using a wooden spoon or rubber spatula, stir the mixture, scraping the sides and down to the bottom of the bowl, to be sure it is evenly mixed.

Place the granulated sugar for the coating into a shallow bowl and drop the dough by heaping teaspoonfuls into the sugar, 1 at a time, tossing each in the sugar so that it is completely coated.

Place the coated balls on the baking sheets and bake in the preheated oven for about 12 minutes, reversing the baking sheets and switching them top to bottom halfway through the baking time. When done, the cookies will just start to feel firm. Remove the pans from the oven and set them on a wire rack to cool. Let the cookies cool on the baking sheets.

Store the cooled cookies in an airtight container for up to 5 days, or wrap them tightly and freeze for up to 2 months. (See freezing instructions on page 12.)

Serve tea or hot cider with Sour Cream Ginger Jumbles, or have them with a spiced punch.

Raspberry-Hazelnut Rogelach

The beautiful red color of raspberry makes this a perfect Christmas treat. Similar to Chocolate-Walnut Rogelach, the flavor combination in this variation offers a sweet, gooey raspberry jam filling in a chewy, cream cheese–enriched dough.

Makes 6 dozen 1 × 1½-inch cookies.

- 1 **cup unsalted butter**
- 6 **ounces cream cheese, softened**
- ½ **teaspoon salt**
- 2¾ **cups all-purpose flour, preferably unbleached**

Filling:
- ½ **cup hazelnuts**
- ¼ **cup granulated sugar**
- ⅓ **cup chopped raisins**
- 1 **teaspoon ground cinnamon**
- 1⅓ **cups good-quality seedless raspberry jam**

Topping:
- 1 **large egg yolk mixed with 2 teaspoons water**
- ½ **cup (approximately) granulated sugar**

Preheat convection ovens to 325 degrees Fahrenheit and conventional ovens to 350 degrees Fahrenheit.

Using an electric mixer on medium speed, beat the butter, cream cheese, and salt together for about 2 minutes, until fluffy and light in color. Scrape the bowl with a rubber spatula and add the flour, beating on low speed for about 30 seconds, until the flour is mixed in evenly. Divide the dough into 4 equal pieces, wrap the dough in plastic wrap, and chill in the refrigerator for at least 1 hour.

While the dough is chilling, make the filling. Spread the hazelnuts in a single layer on a baking sheet and bake in the preheated oven for about 8 minutes, or until the skins have cracked and the nuts are light brown. Remove the pan from the oven and pour the nuts onto a kitchen towel. Rub the skins from the hazelnuts by rubbing through the towel briskly with the palms of your hands together. When you have rubbed off most of the skins, remove the hazelnuts from the towel, leaving the skins behind. Discard the skins and finely chop the toasted hazelnuts. Combine the sugar, raisins, cinnamon, and hazelnuts in a bowl, stirring until evenly combined. Set aside.

Set the racks in the conventional oven so they divide the oven into thirds. You need to line the cookie sheets with parchment paper for this recipe, because the filling will leak out of the sides of the cookies and cause the cookies to stick to an unlined pan. If you are baking in a conventional oven, put one baking sheet inside another of the same size to make a double pan, or use insulated pans to protect the bottoms of the cookies.

Work with 1 piece of dough at a time, keeping the unused portion in the refrigerator. On a floured surface, roll out the dough so that it forms a long, narrow rectangle. It is easier to do this if you form the dough piece into a thick, long, and narrow slab before you start rolling it. Roll from the center of the slab out to the ends. You will not need to roll across the short length of the dough, because the dough will widen as you roll it longer. The finished dough should be about 5 inches wide and 15 inches long. Spread $\frac{1}{3}$ cup of the raspberry jam evenly over the rolled dough, leaving a $\frac{1}{2}$-inch border on all edges. Sprinkle $\frac{1}{4}$ of the filling mixture evenly over the jam. Starting from the long edge farthest from you, roll the dough jelly-roll style, keeping the roll as tight as possible, and ending the roll so that the seam is facing you, near the bottom. Trim about $\frac{1}{2}$ inch from each end, then cut the roll into18 pieces, each about $\frac{3}{4}$ inch wide. It is easiest to do this if you first cut the roll into 2 equal pieces, and then cut each of those pieces into 3 equal pieces. You now have 6 short logs. Cut each of the 6 logs into 3 equal pieces. Using a metal spatula, carefully lift the rogelach and place them onto the prepared baking sheets, placing the rogelach within $\frac{1}{4}$ inch of each other. Repeat the rolling, filling, and cutting process with each of the remaining portions of refrigerated dough.

When you have finished making the rogelach, brush the top of each one with the egg and water mixture, using a pastry brush. Then sprinkle each with a little sugar.

Bake the rogelach in the preheated oven for 18 to 20 minutes, reversing the baking sheets and switching them top to bottom halfway through the baking time. The rogelach will be light brown when they are done. Do not overbake them or they will be dry and hard. Remove the pans from the oven and place the pans on wire racks to cool. Let the rogelach cool completely on the pans.

Remove from the pans and store in an airtight container for up to 1 week, or wrap tightly and freeze for up to 2 months. (See freezing instructions on page 12.)

Raspberry-Hazelnut Rogelach are a nice dessert addition to a holiday table with spiced wine.

Honey Nut Bars

Both chewy and crunchy at the same time, these bars are as easy to make as they are unforgettable. They're not too sweet, yet they will satisfy your sweet tooth while offering an interesting texture combination of a buttery crust, dried fruits, and a light caramel topping.

Makes 40 2 × 2-inch bars.

- ½ cup granulated sugar
- ⅛ teaspoon salt
- 1 cup unsalted butter
- 2 large eggs
- 1 teaspoon freshly grated lemon zest
- 3½ cups all-purpose flour, preferably unbleached

Topping:
- ½ cup unsalted butter
- ½ cup mild-flavored honey, such as orange blossom
- ½ cup granulated sugar
- ¼ cup heavy cream
- 1 teaspoon pure vanilla extract
- ½ teaspoon freshly grated lemon zest
- 1 cup sliced almonds, skins on (4 ounces)
- ¼ cup finely chopped dried apricots
- ¼ cup finely chopped candied orange peel
- ¼ cup chopped golden raisins

Preheat convection ovens to 325 degrees Fahrenheit and conventional ovens to 350 degrees Fahrenheit. Line a 15 × 10-inch jelly roll pan (or cookie sheet with sides) with foil and butter it lightly.

Using an electric mixer set on medium speed, combine the sugar and salt for 10 seconds. Add the ½ cup butter and beat on medium speed for about 2 minutes, or until fluffy and smooth. Add the eggs and zest and beat again on medium speed until smooth and light in color, about 2 minutes. Add the flour and beat on low speed for about 30 seconds, until evenly blended. Press the dough into the prepared pan with your hands, forming a ¼-inch rim at the edges. Bake in the preheated oven about 25 minutes, reversing the pan halfway through the baking time, or until very lightly browned. Remove from the oven.

Ten minutes before the crust is done, melt the ½ cup butter in a medium-size heavy saucepan and add the honey, ½ cup sugar, cream, and vanilla. Heat over moderately high heat until it boils, and boil the mixture for 5 minutes, stirring occasionally. Remove from the heat and stir in the zest, nuts, and fruits. Pour over the hot crust and spread evenly.

Return to the oven for 10 minutes. The topping will be bubbly. Remove the pan from the oven and set it on a wire rack to cool. Cut into 5 long rows, then cut each row into 8 diagonal slices.

Store the cooled bars in an airtight container, with wax paper between the layers, for up to 4 days, or freeze, wrapped tightly, for up to 2 months. (See freezing instructions on page 12.)

Honey Nut Bars make a lovely gift.

Chewy Nut Kipferl

Kipferl are delicious Viennese cookies. There are many variations, but they are almost always filled crescents. Some recipes call for a yeasted dough, while others call for doughs made with cream cheese or sour cream. This recipe is a sour cream dough, which is easier to make than one made with yeast. The overall process is a bit time-consuming, but the end results are luscious. These could easily become a holiday favorite for your family. They are dense and chewy and rich with nuts.

Makes 3 dozen cookies.

Dough:

1	cup unsalted butter
6	large egg yolks
½	cup sour cream (do not use low-fat or nonfat)
3	tablespoons granulated sugar
½	teaspoon salt
½	teaspoon pure vanilla extract
3	cups all-purpose flour, preferably unbleached

Filling:

6	large egg whites
2	cups confectioners' sugar
1½	teaspoons pure vanilla extract
3	cups finely chopped walnuts or almonds (4 ounces)
	additional confectioners' sugar for coating

Using an electric mixer set on low speed, combine the butter, yolks, sour cream, sugar, salt, and the ½ teaspoon vanilla for about 20 seconds. Scrape the bowl with a rubber spatula and increase the speed to medium. Continue beating for 1 minute, until smooth. Add the flour and beat on low speed just until evenly blended, about 30 seconds. Form into a ball, cover with plastic wrap, and refrigerate for at least 1 hour.

While the dough is chilling, make the filling. Using the same mixing bowl, beat the egg whites, confectioners' sugar, and vanilla on medium speed to blend, about 1 minute. Add the nuts and beat on low speed for about 20 seconds, until evenly combined. Set aside.

When the dough has chilled and is firm enough to handle easily, preheat convection ovens to 325 degree Fahrenheit and conventional ovens to 350 degrees Fahrenheit. Set the racks in the conventional oven so they divide the oven into thirds. You need to line the cookie sheets with parchment paper for this recipe. If you are baking in a conventional oven, put one baking sheet inside another of the same size to make a double pan, or use insulated pans to protect the bottoms of the cookies.

Divide the dough into 3 parts, working with 1 part at a time and keeping the unused portion in the refrigerator. Divide the first portion of dough into 12 equal pieces. Roll each one into a ball, then on a floured surface roll each ball into a thin circle. Fill each circle with about 1½ teaspoons of filling. Roll the circle over the filling, rolling it into a crescent shape. Place it on the prepared baking sheet and continue with the remaining circles. When you have completed the 12 crescents, repeat the process for the remaining portions of dough.

Bake the crescents in the preheated oven for 10 to 12 minutes, reversing the baking sheets and switching them top to bottom halfway through the baking time. The crescents will be light brown when they are done. Remove the pans from the oven and place the pans on wire racks to cool.

When the crescents are cool, remove them from the pans. Sprinkle them with confectioners' sugar and store them in an airtight container for up to 5 days, or wrap them tightly and freeze them for up to 2 months. (See freezing instructions on page 12.)

Chewy Nut Kipferl are a wonderful holiday treat to have with coffee or warm cider.

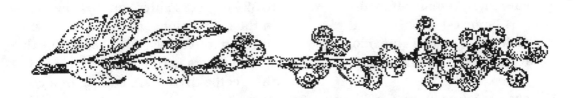

Cinnamon Stars

What would Christmas be without stars? Light and chewy, with a macaroon texture, these stars will definitely put a spark in your holiday cookie tray. Flavored with cinnamon and lemon, they have a refreshing taste, yet are butter-free. You can make them in any shape you wish, but the traditional shape in Germany, where they have been a Christmas tradition for years, is the star. Be careful not to overbake them so they will stay moist inside.

Makes 3 dozen 2½-inch cookies.

2⅔	cups finely ground almonds (13 ounces)
1	tablespoon ground cinnamon
1	teaspoon freshly grated lemon zest
⅓	cup egg white (from 2 or 3 large eggs)
⅛	teaspoon salt
2½	cups confectioners' sugar, sifted after measuring
	extra confectioners' sugar for rolling out the dough
1¾	teaspoons strained fresh squeezed lemon juice

Stir together the almonds, cinnamon, and lemon zest with a wire whisk until evenly combined. Set aside.

Using a mixer set on medium speed with a wire whisk attachment if available, beat the egg whites and the salt until soft peaks form. (When you lift the beater from the egg whites, a peak forms but falls over slightly.) Slowly add the confectioners' sugar, continuing to beat until the mixture is stiff. (The peaks will no longer fall over, and the mixture will be quite opaque and shiny.) Remove ⅓ cup of the egg white mixture and set it aside for the glaze. Fold in the reserved almond mixture.

Preheat convection ovens to 310 degrees Fahrenheit and conventional ovens to 325 degrees Fahrenheit. Set the racks in the conventional oven so they divide the oven into thirds. You need to line the cookie sheets with parchment paper for this recipe. If you are baking in a conventional oven, put one baking sheet inside another of the same size to make a double pan, or use insulated pans to protect the bottoms of the cookies.

Roll the dough ¼ inch thick on a surface that has been dusted with confectioners' sugar. (If the dough is too sticky, sprinkle it with 2 tablespoons of confectioners' sugar and let it sit for about

10 minutes.) Using a 2½-inch star cookie cutter, cut out the cookies and place them on the prepared baking sheets. Reroll the scraps and cut more cookies until the dough is used up.

Make the glaze. Add the lemon juice to the reserved egg white mixture, stirring until smooth. Brush the tops of the stars lightly with the glaze. If the glaze starts to become thick, add a few more drops of lemon juice.

Bake in the preheated oven 20 to 25 minutes, reversing the baking sheets and switching them top to bottom halfway through the baking time. When done, the cookies will be lightly brown and still soft in the center. Remove the pans from the oven and set them on wire racks to cool.

When completely cool, store in an airtight container for up to 2 weeks, or wrap tightly and freeze for up to 2 months. (See freezing instructions on page 12.)

Cinnamon Stars are a perfect adjunct to a cup of tea.

Candied Orange Brownies

When I think of Christmas, the flavor of homemade candied orange peel comes to mind. It is so different from the flavorless kind you will find in grocery stores that most people (who have never tasted the real thing) have no idea just how delightful it is. It is also fairly easy to make and is a superb addition to a holiday coffee table. The recipe for making your own homemade candied orange peel can be doubled or tripled. You can make the candied peel weeks in advance and use it throughout the holiday season. The combination of dark chocolate and sweet, intense, chewy orange peel is absolutely delightful.

Makes 20 1¾ × 2¼-inch bars.

4	tablespoons unsalted butter
3	ounces unsweetened chocolate
2	large eggs
1½	teaspoons pure vanilla extract
1¼	cups granulated sugar
2	tablespoons orange liqueur
⅔	cup all-purpose flour, preferably unbleached
	candied orange peel (see recipe on page 200)

Melt the butter and the chocolate together in a covered microwavable dish for 2 minutes in the microwave oven, or place in a heavy pan on the stove top over low heat, until the chocolate is almost melted. Remove the mixture from the heat and stir with a whisk until smooth. Let the chocolate mixture cool for about 5 minutes.

Preheat a conventional oven to 300 degrees Fahrenheit. Line a 7 × 11-inch or 9 × 9-inch square baking pan with foil and butter it lightly.

Using an electric mixer on medium speed, combine the eggs, vanilla, sugar, and liqueur for about 2 minutes, until smooth, fluffy, and light in color. Scrape the bowl with a rubber spatula and add the melted chocolate and butter. Beat on low speed for about 15 seconds, just to blend. Scrape the bowl again and add the flour and orange peel. Blend on low speed for about 20 seconds, just until the flour is mixed in evenly. Using a wooden spoon or rubber spatula, stir the mixture, scraping the sides and down to the bottom of the bowl, to be sure the dough is evenly mixed.

Spread the mixture into the prepared pan and smooth the top. Bake in the preheated oven for 30 to 35 minutes, reversing the baking pan halfway through the baking time. The brownies are done when a toothpick inserted in the center of the pan comes out clean. Do not overbake. Remove from the oven and set on a rack to cool completely. When cool, place in the refrigerator until cold, then remove the entire bar from the baking pan by pulling it up in the foil. Gently remove the foil from the bar and cut the bar into 20 pieces.

Store in an airtight container with wax paper between the layers for up to 1 week, or wrap tightly and freeze for up to 2 months. (See freezing instructions on page 12.)

Serve these rich bars with espresso or cappuccino for a special treat.

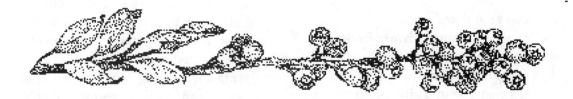

Cranberry Orange Squares

What holiday assortment would be complete without a cranberry-flavored selection? Dense with cranberries and nuts and easy to make, these flavorful bars will add a new favorite to your Thanksgiving dessert table. You may find that your family enjoys them so much you will make extra just to freeze for Christmas.

Makes 32 2¼ × 1½-inch bars.

½   **cup granulated sugar**
½   **cup brown sugar, firmly packed**
½   **teaspoon baking powder**
¼   **teaspoon baking soda**
1   **teaspoon ground cinnamon**
¼   **cup unsalted butter**
1   **large egg**
¼   **cup milk**
¼   **cup orange juice**
1   **teaspoon pure vanilla extract**
1   **tablespoon freshly grated orange zest**
1½   **cups all-purpose flour, preferably unbleached**
2   **cups finely chopped cranberries**
1   **cup coarsely chopped walnuts**

Topping:
¼   **cup granulated sugar**
¼   **teaspoon ground cinnamon**

Preheat conventional oven to 350 degrees Fahrenheit. Line a 9 × 13-inch baking pan with foil and butter it lightly.

Using an electric mixer on medium speed, combine the ½ cup sugar, brown sugar, baking powder, baking soda, and the 1 teaspoon cinnamon for 20 seconds. Add the butter, egg, vanilla, and zest and beat on medium speed for about 2 minutes, until the mixture is smooth and light in color. Add the milk and orange juice and beat on medium for 1 minute. Mixture will look curdled. Scrape the bowl with a rubber spatula and add the flour all at once along with the cranberries and walnuts, mixing on low for 20 seconds, just until the flour is mixed in. Using a wooden spoon or rubber spatula, stir the mixture, scraping the sides and down to the bottom of the bowl, to be sure the dough is evenly mixed.

Spread the mixture into the prepared pan and smooth the top. In a small bowl stir together the ¼ cup sugar with the ¼ teaspoon cinnamon. Sprinkle the topping mixture evenly over the dough and bake in the preheated oven for 20 to 25 minutes, reversing the baking pan halfway through the baking time. The top will be light brown and feel firm when you gently touch it with your fingertip. A toothpick stuck in the center of the pan will come out almost clean. Remove the pan from the oven and set it on a wire rack to cool. When completely cool, cut into bars.

Store the cooled bars in an airtight container for up to 1 week or wrap tightly and freeze for up to 2 months. (See freezing instructions on page 12.)

Serve Cranberry Orange Squares as part of your holiday dessert table with hot coffee or tea.

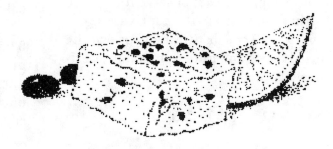

Mixed Fruit Honey Bars

Dense with fruit and nuts and chewy with white chocolate, this bar is as much a confection as it is a cookie. It is easy to make and delicious to eat. Keep some on hand for last-minute guests. You can dress this up as a fancy dessert with whipped cream or serve it by itself. Either way, it will captivate your audience. Try substituting your favorite dried fruits and nuts to make interesting changes.

Makes 32 1 × 3¼-inch bars.

½ **cup heavy cream**
8 **ounces chopped white chocolate, or good-quality white chocolate chips, such as Ghirardelli**
½ **cup orange marmalade or pureed apricot preserves**
½ **cup mild-flavored honey, such as orange blossom**
1 **cup finely chopped dried apricots**
1 **cup dried sweetened tart cherries or dried currants**
1 **cup dried blueberries or raisins**
1½ **cups sweetened coconut, flaked or shredded, firmly packed**
⅓ **cup all-purpose flour, preferably unbleached**

Glaze:
2 **tablespoons heavy cream**
4 **ounces chopped white chocolate, or good-quality white chocolate chips, such as Ghirardelli**

Preheat a conventional oven to 325 degrees Fahrenheit. Line a 9 × 13-inch baking pan with foil and butter it lightly.

Melt the ½ cup cream and the 8 ounces chocolate together in a covered microwavable dish for 2 minutes in the microwave oven, or place in a heavy pan on the stove top over low heat, stirring constantly, until the chocolate is almost melted. Remove the mixture from the heat and stir with a whisk until smooth.

Add the marmalade and honey and stir until smooth. In a large bowl, toss the apricots, cherries, blueberries, coconut, almonds, and hazelnuts with the flour. Add the melted chocolate mixture to the nuts and fruits and stir to blend.

Spread into the prepared pan and smooth the top. Bake in the preheated oven for about 30 minutes, reversing the baking pan halfway through the baking time. Remove from the oven and set the pan on a wire rack to cool.

Make the glaze. Melt the 2 tablespoons cream and the 4 ounces chocolate together in a covered microwavable dish for 2 minutes in the microwave oven, or place in a heavy pan on the stove top over low heat, stirring constantly, until the chocolate is almost melted. Remove the mixture from the heat and stir with a whisk until smooth.

Remove the bar from the pan by lifting it out with the foil. Drizzle the glaze over the top of the cooled bars, and then cut into 32 pieces. Let the glaze set before storing the bars.

Store the cooled bars in an airtight container for up to 10 days, or wrap tightly and freeze for up to 2 months. (See freezing instructions on page 12.)

Coffee is a nice foil for the richness of Mixed Fruit Honey Bars.

Candied Orange Peel

2 oranges, washed
½ cup granulated sugar
½ cup water
2 tablespoons light corn syrup
½ cup granulated sugar, for coating

Remove the peel, including the white pith, from the oranges. Cut the peel into strips about ¼ inch wide.

Place the peel in a saucepan with enough water to cover by an inch and bring to a boil, boiling for one minute. Drain, reserving the peel and rinsing it in fresh water. Repeat this boiling process 2 more times using fresh water each time. Rinse the peel, cover it with water and bring it to a simmer, simmering for 15 minutes. Drain and set aside.

In the same saucepan combine the sugar, water and corn syrup, heating to a boil and boiling for 1½ minutes. Add the orange peel and boil gently, stirring frequently, until the syrup is reduced to about one and one half teaspoons. Drain the syrup from the peel (you can use the syrup for another purpose).

Place the remaining ¼ cup sugar in a saucer and lay the cooked peel on it, tossing the peel with the sugar until the peel is slightly cooled and coated with sugar. Place the peel on a rack to dry, separating the pieces. If making the candied orange peel ahead of time, store it in a tightly covered container or resealable plastic bag.

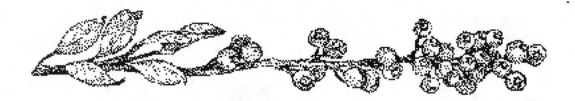

Teatime Treats

Certain cookies are made for tea. The cookies in this section have delicate flavors or contain fruit, making them compatible partners for tea. Of course, don't overlook the other cookies in this book that are good partners for tea, such as macaroons and layered bar cookies.

Glazed Raspberry Hazelnut Slices

When you are looking for a truly impressive pastry to have at a fine tea, this bar cookie will meet your expectations. A crust enriched with hazelnuts sandwiches a filling of seedless raspberry jam. A thin icing is drizzled over the lightly browned top crust, creating a mouthwatering combination of flavors in a pretty bar.

Makes 32 1½ × 2¼-inch bars.

1¼ cups hazelnuts, skins on
⅔ cup unsalted butter
⅔ cup confectioners' sugar, stirred with a fork to remove any lumps
1½ cups all-purpose flour, preferably unbleached
1½ cups fine-quality seedless raspberry jam

Icing:

1 cup confectioners' sugar, stirred with a fork to remove any lumps
2 tablespoons unsalted butter, melted
1 teaspoon strained fresh lemon juice
½ teaspoon freshly grated lemon zest
2 tablespoons heavy cream

Preheat a conventional oven to 350 degrees Fahrenheit. Line a 9 × 13-inch baking pan with foil and brush it with softened butter.

Spread the hazelnuts on a single layer in a shallow baking pan and toast in the preheated oven for about 8 minutes, until the skins are cracked and the nuts are lightly browned. Remove the pan from the oven and set it on a wire rack so the nuts will cool. Do not remove the skins. When the nuts are cool, grind them finely and set them aside. Do not turn the oven off.

Using an electric mixer set on medium speed, beat the butter and the ⅔ cup confectioners' sugar for 2 minutes, until fluffy and smooth. Add the flour and the ground hazelnuts and beat on low speed for 20 seconds to evenly combine the ingredients. Measure 1½ cups of the pastry mixture and pat the remainder evenly into the prepared pan. Spread the raspberry jam over the pastry in the pan and then crumble the reserved 1½ cups pastry mixture over the jam, pressing lightly with your fingertips.

Bake in the oven for 20 to 25 minutes, reversing the baking pan halfway through the baking time. The top will be lightly browned. Remove from the oven and set on a wire rack to cool.

While the cake is baking make the icing. Combine the 1 cup confectioners' sugar with the melted butter, the lemon juice, and the lemon zest in a small bowl with a wire whisk until smooth. Add the cream and continue stirring with the whisk until the cream is mixed in. The icing should be thin enough to drizzle. If not, add another teaspoon of cream and stir until blended.

When the cake has cooled for 15 minutes, drizzle the icing over the top crust. Let the cake cool completely, then use the foil to remove it from the pan. Gently peel the foil from the sides of the cake and cut into bars.

Using a metal spatula, carefully lift the bars from the foil and store them in an airtight container, in a single layer, for up to 3 days. If wrapped tightly, they can be frozen for up to 2 months. (See freezing instructions on page 12.)

Glazed Raspberry Hazelnut Slices can be served with tea or coffee.

Lemon Coconut Spice Drops

When I developed this cookie, I gave one to Ellen Magee and we both thought it was perfect. It is mildly flavored with lemon and nutmeg, and the coconut gives it just the right texture, soft but chewy. These are best the day they are baked, but are also memorable if dunked in tea when they are a day or two old.

Makes 30 1½-inch cookies.

- 1¼ cups all-purpose flour, preferably unbleached
- ½ teaspoon baking powder
- ⅓ cup unsalted butter
- ¾ cup granulated sugar
- 1 large egg
- 1½ ounces (3 tablespoons) cream cheese, at room temperature
- 1 tablespoon freshly grated lemon zest, finely chopped
- ½ teaspoon ground nutmeg
- ½ cup sweetened coconut, shredded or flaked, firmly packed

Preheat convection ovens to 325 degrees Fahrenheit or conventional ovens to 350 degrees Fahrenheit. Set the racks in the conventional oven so they divide the oven into thirds. It is *not* necessary to line the cookie sheets with parchment paper. If you are baking in a conventional oven, put one baking sheet inside another of the same size to make a double pan, or use insulated pans to protect the bottoms of the cookies.

In a medium-size bowl using a wire whisk, stir together the flour and baking powder. Set aside.

Using an electric mixer on medium speed, beat the butter, sugar, egg, cream cheese, zest and nutmeg until fluffy and light in color, about 2 minutes. Scrape the bowl with a rubber spatula and add the flour mixture, beating on low speed just until blended, about 20 seconds. Scrape the bowl again and stir in the coconut.

Drop by rounded teaspoonfuls onto the baking sheets and bake in the preheated oven for 11 to 13 minutes, reversing the baking sheets and switching them top to bottom halfway through the baking time. When done, the cookies will just have begun to brown lightly. Do not overbake. Remove from the oven and remove the cookies with a metal spatula to wire racks to cool.

Store completely cooled cookies in an airtight container up to 2 days or freeze, wrapped tightly, for up to 2 months. (See freezing instructions on page 12.)

Lemon Coconut Spice Drops are a good complement to Darjeeling tea.

Lemon Walnut Gems

Citrus flavors are among my favorites. Here the flavor of lemon is combined with walnuts to provide a fresh taste and cream cheese is mixed into the dough to lend a creamy soft-chewy texture to the cookie.

Makes 5 dozen 2-inch cookies.

3	ounces cream cheese, room temperature
½	cup unsalted butter
1	cup brown sugar, firmly packed
½	cup granulated sugar
2	large eggs
2	tablespoons freshly grated lemon zest, chopped fine
¼	teaspoon salt
2	cups all-purpose flour, preferably unbleached
1½	cups walnuts, coarsely chopped (6 ounces)

Preheat convection ovens to 310 degrees Fahrenheit or conventional ovens to 325 degrees Fahrenheit. Set the racks in the conventional oven so they divide the oven into thirds. It is *not* necessary to line the cookie sheets with parchment paper. If you are baking in a conventional oven, put one baking sheet inside another of the same size to make a double pan, or use insulated pans to protect the bottoms of the cookies.

Using an electric mixer on medium speed, beat together the cream cheese, butter, sugars, eggs, zest, and salt, until the mixture is fluffy and light in color, about 2½ minutes. Scrape the bowl with a rubber spatula and add the flour and nuts. Beat on low speed just until the flour is mixed in. Using a wooden spoon or rubber spatula, stir the mixture, scraping down to the bottom of the bowl, to be sure it is evenly mixed.

Drop the dough by heaping teaspoonfuls onto the baking sheets and bake in the preheated oven for 11 to 13 minutes, reversing the baking sheets and switching them top to bottom halfway through the baking time. When done, the cookies will just begin to feel firm to the touch. Remove the cookies from the sheets with a metal spatula and cool completely on wire racks.

Store the cooled cookies in an airtight container for up to 2 days, or freeze, wrapped tightly, for up to 2 months. (See freezing instructions on page 12.)

Lemon Walnut Gems are great with tea or with liqueur as a light ending to a meal.

Financiers

During my first visit to Paris I fell in love with a financier. Not the human kind, but the small cakelike cookie that is made with ground almonds. They are dense, soft-chewy, buttery, and exquisite. In France they are made in small rectangular-shaped tart pans, so that they look like gold ingots, hence their name. You can use any shape small tart pan, or minimuffin pans, to bake these delicious treasures, but the yield will vary depending on the size of the pans, and you need to watch the timing closely, since any change in pan size will result in a change in baking time.

Makes 2 dozen financiers.

3   **large egg whites at room temperature**
1   **cup confectioners' sugar, stirred with a fork to eliminate any lumps**
⅔   **cup finely ground blanched almonds**
⅓   **cup all-purpose flour, preferably unbleached**
6   **tablespoons unsalted butter, melted**

Preheat a conventional oven to 400 degrees Fahrenheit and brush 24 2-inch rectangular or oval tart pans with melted butter.

Using an electric mixer set on medium speed, beat the egg whites until foamy. Add the sugar and beat on medium speed until thick, about 1 minute. Scrape the bowl with a rubber spatula and add the almonds and the flour, mixing on low speed for 15 seconds, just to blend. By hand, with a wire whisk or rubber spatula, gently fold in the melted butter just until it is mixed in.

Fill the tart pans about ⅔ full and place them on a baking sheet. Put the baking sheet in the preheated oven and bake for 7 or 8 minutes, until the tops are lightly browned. Remove the baking sheet from the oven and set it on a wire rack, letting the financiers cool in their pans for about 5 minutes. Gently invert each pan to remove the financiers and let them cool completely on the wire racks.

Store in an airtight container for up to 3 days or wrap tightly and freeze for up to 2 months. (See freezing instructions on page 12.)

Financiers will add an elegant touch to any tea table.

Apricot Walnut Bars

Cooking apricots in water before adding them to this recipe adds to the moist texture of these bars. They are gooey-chewy with an exceptional apricot flavor. Serve them at an afternoon tea.

Makes 20 1¾ × 2¼-inch bars.

1   cup chopped dried apricots or figs
1¼ cups water

Crust:

⅓   unsalted butter
⅓   cup brown sugar, firmly packed
1   cup all-purpose flour, preferably
      unbleached
½   cup finely ground walnuts

Filling:

1   cup brown sugar, firmly packed
½   teaspoon baking powder
1   teaspoon ground cinnamon
2   large eggs
1   teaspoon pure vanilla extract
1   cup chopped walnuts

Topping:

1   cup sweetened coconut, flaked or
      shredded, firmly packed

Place the chopped apricots and water in a heavy saucepan and bring to a boil. Boil for 10 minutes, drain, and set aside to cool.

Preheat a conventional oven to 350 degrees Fahrenheit. Line a 7 × 11-inch baking pan with foil and brush it with softened butter.

Using an electric mixer on medium speed, beat the butter and the ⅓ cup brown sugar for 2 minutes, until light in color and fluffy. Add the flour and beat on low for 20 to 30 seconds, until evenly blended. Scrape the bowl with a rubber spatula and add the ground nuts, mixing on low speed for 20 seconds. Pat the dough into the prepared pan and bake in the preheated oven for 15 minutes, reversing the pan halfway through baking time. Remove the pan from the oven and set on a wire rack.

Blend the 1 cup brown sugar with the baking powder and cinnamon on low speed for 20 seconds. Add the eggs and vanilla and beat on medium speed for 2 minutes. The mixture will be smooth. Stir in the cooled apricot mixture and then the flour and nuts, scraping the sides and bottom of the bowl with a rubber spatula to be sure the mixture is evenly combined. Gently spread the fruit topping over the baked crust, smoothing with a rubber spatula. Sprinkle the coconut over the fruit layer and bake in the oven for 30 to 35 minutes, reversing the baking pan halfway through the baking time. The coconut will be nicely browned. Remove the pan from the oven and set on a wire rack to cool. When cool, cut into bars.

Store the cooled bars in an airtight container for up to 5 days, or wrap tightly and freeze for up to 2 months. (See freezing instructions on page 12.)

Apricot Walnut Bars taste exceptional with tea or juice.

Cherry Oatmeal Bars

Many types of dried fruits have become widely available over the last few years. One of these is dried tart cherries. The ones I use here are lightly sweetened, but if you prefer a really tart taste, use the unsweetened variety. You can also substitute dried cranberries for the cherries. Use a small food processor, if you have one, to chop the cherries. The dense, chewy consistency of these bars and the tart flavor of the cherries is a great combination.

Makes 36 2¼ × 1½-inch bars.

⅔	**cup brown sugar, firmly packed**
⅔	**cup granulated sugar**
½	**teaspoon baking soda**
½	**teaspoon salt**
¾	**cup unsalted butter**
3	**large eggs**
1	**teaspoon pure vanilla extract**
1½	**teaspoons pure almond extract**
1⅓	**cups all-purpose flour, preferably unbleached**
⅔	**cup whole wheat flour, preferably stone-ground**
1½	**cups rolled oats, uncooked (quick or old-fashioned)**
1	**cup sweetened coconut, shredded or flaked, firmly packed (5 ounces)**
4	**ounces dried tart cherries, finely chopped**

Preheat a conventional oven to 350 degrees Fahrenheit. Line a 9 × 13-inch baking pan with foil and brush it with softened butter.

Using an electric mixer on medium speed, beat together the brown sugar, sugar, baking soda, and salt for 20 seconds. Add the butter, eggs, vanilla, and almond extract and beat on medium speed for 2 minutes, or until light colored and fluffy. Scrape the bowl with a rubber spatula and add the flour, whole wheat flour, and oats on low speed, until thoroughly blended, about 30 seconds. Scrape the bowl again and add the coconut and chopped dried cherries. Blend on low speed for 15 seconds until evenly combined. Using a wooden spoon or rubber spatula, stir the mixture, scraping down to the bottom of the bowl, to be sure it is evenly mixed.

Spread into the prepared pan, using the rubber spatula to smooth the top. Bake in a preheated oven for about 25 to 30 minutes, reversing the baking pan halfway through the baking time. The bars will be firm to the touch. Remove the pan from the oven and cool the bars in the pan on a wire rack. When they are cool, invert the pan onto a wire rack and gently peel off the foil. Turn the cake right side up and cut into bars.

Store the completely cooled bars in an airtight container for up to 5 days, or freeze, wrapped tightly, for up to 2 months. (See freezing instructions on page 12.)

Cherry Oatmeal Bars go well with tea or coffee, and are a great addition to a brunch

Coconut Lemon Chews

Thick and gooey-chewy, the lemon zest in these bars is a perfect foil for the sweetness of the coconut. They are pretty, delicious, and make a nice addition to a tea table.

Makes 32 2¼ × 1½-inch bar cookies.

3½ **cups all-purpose flour, preferably unbleached, divided into 1½ cups and 2 cups**
2   **teaspoons baking powder**
¾   **cup unsalted butter, melted**
1½ **cups granulated sugar**
2   **large eggs**
1   **tablespoon finely chopped lemon zest**
1   **can (15 ounces) sweetened coconut cream**
1   **cup sliced natural (skins on) almonds**
2   **cups (10 ounces) sweetened flaked coconut, firmly packed**

Topping:
1   **cup sliced natural (skins on) almonds**

Preheat a conventional oven to 350 degrees Fahrenheit. Line a 9 × 13-inch baking pan with foil.

In a small bowl stir together 1½ cups of the flour and the baking powder with a wire whisk. Set aside.

With a mixer on medium speed, beat the melted butter, sugar, eggs, and zest for 3 minutes or until light in color and creamy. Add the flour and baking powder mixture and beat on low speed just until thoroughly mixed, about 30 seconds. Scrape the bowl with a rubber spatula and add the coconut cream. Beat on low again just until mixed in, about 30 seconds. Scrape the bowl and add the remaining 2 cups of flour. Beat on low speed until the flour is completely mixed in, about 30 to 40 seconds. Scrape the bowl again and add the coconut and 1 cup of almonds. Mix briefly on low just enough to distribute the nuts and coconut through the batter. Using a wooden spoon or rubber spatula, stir the mixture, scraping down to the bottom of the bowl, to be sure it is evenly mixed.

Spread the batter evenly into the prepared pan and cover with the remaining cup of almonds, gently pressing them into the batter. Bake in the preheated oven for 35 to 40 minutes, reversing the baking pan halfway through the baking time. You will know it's done when the almonds are lightly browned and the cake feels firm when gently touched in the center. Remove from the oven and let cool in the pan on a wire rack. When completely cool, cut into bars.

Store the completely cooled bars in an airtight container for up to 6 days, or freeze for up to 2 months. (See freezing instructions on page 12.)

Coconut Lemon Chews are especially good with a cup of hot tea or iced tea.

Orange Marmalade Crumb Bars

If you can find marmalade made from Seville oranges, use that for these bars. Its not-too-sweet, intensely orange flavor is the perfect touch here. If you cannot find it, you can use any good-quality orange marmalade; just stir an extra tablespoon of grated orange zest into the marmalade before using it in this recipe. The soft, crunchy-chewy texture of this bar is appealing.

Makes 3 dozen 2¼ × 1½-inch bars.

Pastry:
- 1   cup granulated sugar
- ¼   teaspoon salt
- 1   teaspoon baking powder
- 1   tablespoon freshly grated orange zest, chopped fine
- ½   cup unsalted butter
- 2   large egg yolks
- 1½ teaspoons pure vanilla extract
- 2   cups all purpose flour, preferably unbleached

Filling:
- 1   cup Seville orange marmalade (or 1 cup regular orange marmalade mixed with 1 tablespoon freshly grated orange zest, chopped fine)

Topping:
- 1   cup walnuts, chopped
- 1   cup graham cracker crumbs (about 13 squares)
- ¼   cup unsalted butter

Preheat a conventional oven to 350 degrees Fahrenheit. Line a 9 × 13-inch baking pan with foil and brush it with softened butter.

Using an electric mixer on medium speed, combine the sugar, salt, baking powder, and zest until evenly combined, about 20 seconds. Add ½ cup butter, the yolks, and the vanilla and beat on medium speed until smooth, about 2 minutes. Scrape the bowl with a rubber spatula and add the flour. Beat on low just until thoroughly mixed, about 15 to 20 seconds. The mixture will be crumbly. Press into the prepared pan as evenly as you can and spread the marmalade over the pastry.

Place the topping ingredients in the mixer bowl you used for the pastry and mix on low speed, for about 30 to 40 seconds, or until combined. Sprinkle evenly over the marmalade, pressing gently down with your hand. Bake for 30 minutes, reversing the baking pan halfway through the baking time. Remove the pan from the oven and cool the bars in the pan on a wire rack. When completely cool, cut into bars.

Store the cooled bars in an airtight container for up to 1 week, or wrap tightly and freeze for up to 2 months. (See freezing instructions on page 12.)

Orange Marmalade Crumb Bars are a wonderful addition to a tea table and go well with breakfast.

Lemon Poppy Seed Bars

A delicate lemon flavor and chewy poppy seeds make this a wonderful addition to a tea table. This is a soft, cakey bar with a splendid flavor. Serve it dusted with confectioners' sugar or with freshly whipped cream.

Makes 32 2¼ × 1½-inch bars.

1¾	cups granulated sugar
1½	teaspoons baking powder
1	teaspoon baking soda
½	teaspoon salt
1	cup unsalted butter, melted
4	large eggs
2	teaspoons pure vanilla extract
2	tablespoons freshly grated lemon zest
3	cups all-purpose flour, preferably unbleached
1	cup buttermilk
½	cup poppy seeds confectioners' sugar for dusting

Preheat a conventional oven to 350 degrees Fahrenheit. Line a 9 × 13-inch baking pan with foil and brush it with softened butter and dust it with flour.

Using an electric mixer on medium speed, beat together the sugar, baking powder, baking soda, and salt for 20 seconds. Add the butter, eggs, vanilla, and lemon zest and beat on medium speed for 2 minutes, or until light in color and fluffy. Scrape the bowl with a rubber spatula and add 1½ cups of the flour on low speed, mixing for 30 seconds, until thoroughly blended. Scrape the bowl again and add the buttermilk. Blend on low speed for 15 seconds until evenly combined. Add the remaining 1½ cups flour and the poppy seeds and mix on low speed for 30 seconds to combine. Using a wooden spoon or rubber spatula, stir the mixture, scraping down to the bottom of the bowl, to be sure it is evenly mixed.

Spread into the prepared pan, using the rubber spatula to smooth the top. Bake in the preheated oven for about 30 to 35 minutes, reversing the baking pan halfway through the baking time. When done, the bars will feel firm to the touch. Remove the pan from the oven and cool the bars in the pan on a wire rack. When they are cool, invert the pan onto a wire rack and gently peel off the foil. Turn the cake right side up and cut into bars.

Store the completely cooled bars in an airtight container for up to 5 days, or freeze, wrapped tightly, for up to 2 months. (See freezing instructions on page 12.)

Lemon Poppy Seed Bars can be served with a dollop of whipped cream and a spoonful of raspberry preserves at an afternoon tea or a fancy brunch.

Chewy Pear Crumb Bars

In the fall, pears are a heavenly treat that bake into delightful tarts and bars. This recipe calls for a cooked filling of fresh pears with a touch of cinnamon. Use ripe pears. A ripe pear should give slightly when you hold it in your hand and gently squeeze it. It takes a few minutes to peel the pears, but the flavor of this bar cookie is well worth it. If you have any on hand, you can substitute 1 tablespoon chopped crystallized ginger for the cinnamon in the filling.

Makes 24 2¼ × 2-inch bars.

Filling:

- ¼ **cup granulated sugar**
- 2 **teaspoons cornstarch**
- 1 **teaspoon ground cinnamon or 1 tablespoon chopped crystallized ginger**
- 3 **cups chopped peeled raw pears (about 4 or 5 medium-size pears)**
- ⅓ **cup pear nectar**
- 1 **tablespoon strained fresh lemon juice**

Crust and Crumb Topping:

- ⅓ **cup brown sugar, firmly packed**
- ¼ **cup sugar**
- ⅓ **cup butter**
- ⅔ **cup all-purpose flour, preferably unbleached**
- 1 **cup quick-cooking rolled oats, uncooked (not instant)**

Preheat a conventional oven to 350 degrees Fahrenheit. Line a 9 × 13-inch baking pan with foil and brush it with softened butter.

In a small bowl, stir together the ¼ cup sugar, cornstarch, and cinnamon or crystallized ginger. Set aside. In a heavy medium-size saucepan, cook the pears, nectar, and lemon juice at medium-high heat, until the mixture comes to a boil. Add the reserved cornstarch mixture and cook until thickened. Remove from the heat and set aside to cool.

Using an electric mixer on medium speed, beat the brown sugar, ¼ cup sugar, and butter until light in color and fluffy. Add the flour and oats and beat on low speed for about 30 to 40 seconds, until evenly combined. The mixture will be crumbly.

Pat about half of the crumb mixture into the bottom of the prepared pan. Pour the filling over this and spread smoothly with a rubber spatula. Sprinkle the remaining crumbs over the filling and bake in the preheated oven for 30 to 35 minutes, reversing the baking pan halfway through the baking time. When done, the top is lightly browned and the filling is bubbly around the edges. Remove from the oven and cool on a wire rack. When cool, cut into bars.

Store the cooled bars in an airtight container in the refrigerator for up to 1 week, or wrap tightly and freeze for up to 2 months. (See freezing instructions on page 12.)

Offer Chewy Pear Crumb Bars to your guests as an alternative to pie after a casual dinner, or pack them in a pretty container and give them as a hostess gift. They go well with tea.

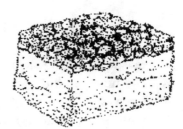

Maple Date Chews

The sweet gooeyness of dates is a great companion to maple syrup in this dense and chewy cookie. Packed with fruit and nuts, this cookie is a virtuous change from chocolate. An easy way to chop dates is to cut them with scissors that have been brushed very lightly with vegetable oil. Do not use maple-flavored pancake syrup when you make these cookies. It just doesn't have the flavor of the real thing.

Makes 4 dozen 2-inch cookies.

¾   **cup brown sugar, firmly packed**
1   **teaspoon baking powder**
½   **teaspoon baking soda**
½   **cup unsalted butter**
2   **large eggs**
1   **tablespoon freshly grated orange zest**
⅓   **cup pure maple syrup**
1½   **cups all-purpose flour, preferably unbleached**
¾   **cup whole wheat flour, preferably stone-ground**
1   **cup finely chopped dates**
1   **cup coarsely chopped pecans**

Preheat convection ovens to 310 degrees Fahrenheit or conventional ovens to 325 degrees Fahrenheit. Set the racks in the conventional oven so they divide the oven into thirds. You will *not* need to line the pans with parchment for this recipe. If you are baking in a conventional oven, put one baking sheet inside another of the same size to make a double pan, or use insulated pans to protect the bottoms of the cookies.

Using an electric mixer on medium speed, combine the brown sugar, baking powder, and baking soda for 20 seconds. Add the butter, eggs, zest, and maple syrup and beat on medium speed for 2 minutes. The mixture will be smooth and light in color. Scrape the bowl with a rubber spatula and add the flour, whole wheat flour, dates, and pecans and beat on low speed for about 30 seconds, just until blended. Using a rubber spatula, scrape the sides and bottom of the bowl, stirring the dough to be sure it is evenly mixed.

Drop the dough by heaping teaspoonfuls onto the baking sheets and bake in the preheated oven for 10 to 12 minutes, reversing the baking sheets and switching them top to bottom halfway through the baking time. When done, the cookie will just feel firm to the touch and have begun to turn light brown. Do not over-bake. Remove the pans from the oven and set them on wire racks to cool for 5 minutes. Carefully remove the cookies from the pans with a metal spatula and place them on the wire racks to finish cooling.

When completely cooled, store the cookies in an airtight container with wax paper between the layers for up to 5 days, or wrap tightly and freeze for up to 2 months. (See freezing instructions on page 12.)

You will enjoy Maple Date Chews with a glass of milk or juice as a nutritious snack.

Index

F

Figs
- Apricot Walnut Bars, 206–207
- Whole Wheat Fig Bars, 101

Flour (unbleached, white)
- guidelines for using, 5–6
- *See also* whole-wheat flour

Foil, guidelines for using, 4

Food processors, 5

Freezing, baked cookies and bars, 12

Fruit. *See* Dried fruits; specific fruits

G

Ginger
- candied, Chewy Pear Crumb Bars, 212–213
- candied, Sour Cream Ginger Jumbles, 184–185
- candied, Squash Gems, 114–115
- Ginger Pillows, 149

Graham cracker crumbs
- 1-2-3-4-5 Bars, 146
- as ingredient, 11
- Hello Dolly Cookies, 144
- Orange Marmalade Crumb Bars, 210
- S'More Bars, 145
- Sweet and Easy Dream Bars, 64–65

Granola cereal
- Almond Granola Bars, 91
- Chewy Orange-Granola Bars, 90

H

Hazelnuts
- Almond-Hazelnut Mounds, 124–125
- Chewy, Nutty Lebkuchen, 176–177
- Hazelnut-Cinnamon Bars, 38–39
- Hazelnut Macaroon Brownies, 170–171
- Linzer Bites, 164–165

Raspberry Hazelnut Slices, 201–202
Raspberry-Hazelnut Rogelach, 186–187

Hermits, 86

Holiday cookies
- Anise Doodles, 178
- Candied Orange Brownies, 194–195
- Candied Orange Peel, 200
- Chewy Fruit Bars, Iced and Spiced, 180–181
- Chewy Nut Kipferl, 190–191
- Chewy, Nutty Lebkuchen, 176–177
- Chocolate-Walnut Rogelach, 182–183
- Cinnamon Stars, 192–193
- Cranberry Orange Squares, 196–197
- Honey Nut Bars, 188–189
- Mixed Fruit Honey Bars, 198–199
- Raspberry-Hazelnut Rogelach, 186–187
- Sour Cream Ginger Jumbles, 184–185
- Spicy Mincemeat Squares, 179

Honey
- Almond Granola Bars, 91
- Chewy Orange-Granola Bars, 72f73
- Chewy, Nutty Lebkuchen, 176–177
- Chocolate Honey Nut Chews, 49
- Honey Oatmeal Cookies, 81–82
- Honey Sweet-Potato Gems, 116
- Honey-Nut Bars, 188–189
- Mixed Fruit Honey Bars, 198–199
- Pecan-Honey Dream Bars, 76

I

Ingredients
- for chewy cookies, 1–2
- selection guidelines, 5f11

J

Jam, cookies with
- Cherry-Walnut Thumbprints, 174–175